Cold War Letters

Cold War Letters

Thomas Merton

Edited by
Christine M. Bochen and William H. Shannon

ORBIS BOOKS
Maryknoll, New York 10545

Founded in 1970, Orbis Books endeavors to publish works that enlighten the mind, nourish the spirit, and challenge the conscience. The publishing arm of the Maryknoll Fathers and Brothers, Orbis seeks to explore the global dimensions of the Christian faith and mission, to invite dialogue with diverse cultures and religious traditions, and to serve the cause of reconciliation and peace. The books published reflect the views of their authors and do not represent the official position of the Maryknoll Society. To learn more about Maryknoll and Orbis Books, please visit our website at www.maryknoll.org.

Published by Orbis Books, Maryknoll, NY 10545-0308.
Previously published letters by Thomas Merton are reprinted with the cooperation of Farrar, Straus, & Giroux.

Manufactured in the United States of America.

Library of Congress Cataloging-in-Publication Data

Merton, Thomas, 1915-1968.
  Cold War letters / Thomas Merton ; edited by Christine M. Bochen and William H. Shannon.
    p. cm.
  Includes index.
  ISBN-13: 978-1-57075-662-7 (pbk.)
  ISBN-10: 1-57075-662-7
  1. Peace—Religious aspects—Christianity. 2. Merton, Thomas, 1915-1968—Correspondence. I. Bochen, Christine M. II. Shannon, William Henry, 1917- III. Title.
  BT736.4.M45 2006
  261.8'709046--dc22

                         2006026274

Contents

Foreword

James W. Douglass

In the summer of 1961, at the Abbey of Gethsemani in the hills of Kentucky, the contemplative, Thomas Merton, was enlightened about the imminent threat of total nuclear war. He saw it as "purely and simply the crucifixion over again."[1] Having realized the necessity that war be abolished, Merton began churning out poems, essays, and letters on war and peace, trying to create a spiritual chain reaction counter to the Bomb.

I learned of Merton's resistance to nuclear war from reading his poem, "Chant to be Used in Processions around a Site with Furnaces," which appeared in *The Catholic Worker*. The poem was really an anti-poem. Merton presented the commandant of a Nazi death camp describing his daily routine overseeing genocide. The war criminal concluded: "Do not think yourself better because you burn up friends and enemies with long-range missiles without ever seeing what you have done."[2]

Merton's "Chant" electrified me when I read it in the fall of 1961 as a graduate theology student at the University of Notre Dame. What it meant was that a silent monk had shattered a larger silence. The greatest spiritual writer of our time had suddenly joined Dorothy Day and the Catholic Worker community in breaking the silence of the American Catholic Church on the threat of nuclear holocaust.

What a gift it is to be able to look back now, through the eyes of Thomas Merton in his "Cold War Letters," into the heart of the Cold War that almost became a nuclear war. And what a responsibility it is to understand his insights today in the context of our terrifying War on Terror.

As he wrote these letters from October 1961 to October 1962, in the year leading up to the Cuban Missile Crisis, Merton saw clearly what was at stake in the Cold War. It was the survival of the human race—survival not only physically, from inconceivably destructive weapons, but also spiritually from the ways in which we made the weapons our gods and obeyed their commands. Merton wrote his "Cold War Letters" with relentless love into the coldness of our collective willingness to kill everyone and everything alive in the world.

In October 1961, when Merton began writing these letters, the United States and the Soviet Union were risking nuclear war in a confrontation at the Berlin Wall. Merton wrote his first Cold War Letter on October 25, 1961, the eve of what one journalist called "the first nuclear-age American-Soviet confrontation: soldiers and weapons eyeball to eyeball."[3] President John F. Kennedy's personal representative, General Lucius Clay, had provoked a confrontation with Soviet troops at Checkpoint Charlie dividing East and West Berlin. For twenty hours, U.S. and Soviet tanks stood facing each other with their motors running, each line of tanks threatening to open fire and spark a nuclear war. Finally, President Kennedy and Soviet Premier Nikita Khrushchev mutually agreed to withdraw their tanks. However, the Cold War conflict continued to escalate toward nuclear war. It would climax in the Cuban Missile Crisis one year later, when Merton would write the last of his Cold War Letters.

In that year between the Berlin Crisis and the Cuban Missile Crisis, Merton wrote the 111 letters found in this volume. Only through an awareness that he was living in what was probably the most dangerous year in history can one understand the passion and compassion of his letters. Without a sense of that supreme crisis of human survival in 1961-62, we cannot fathom what he is saying and praying about so furiously, alternately thundering and whispering into the ears of his correspondents, pleading with us all through these letters to see and act while there is still time.

What most appalled Thomas Merton about the threat of a nuclear holocaust was the way in which Christians, and Catholics in particular, justified preparing for such mass murder.

In his opening letter, he wrote: "Those who think there can be a just cause for measures that gravely risk leading to the destruction of the entire human race are in the most dangerous illusion, and if they are Christian they are purely and simply arming themselves with hammer and nails, without realizing it, to crucify and deny Christ."[4]

What, then, did Merton make of the fact that John F. Kennedy, the commander-in-chief of our nuclear forces, was the first Catholic president? Merton allowed how it was true that "President Kennedy is a shrewd and sometimes adventurous leader. He means well and has the highest motives, and he is, without doubt, in a position sometimes so impossible as to be absurd."[5] Merton was on target. Just how impossible and absurd Kennedy's position was in relation to his own government would emerge gradually in the years after his death.

Merton's letters became increasingly urgent as he recognized that pressures were mounting in the U.S. government for a nuclear first strike against the Soviet Union. In a letter to the editors of *Commonweal,* he asked, "What is our policy shaping up to now if not to preemption? I do not say it has got that far, but can anyone assert that the idea of the preemptive first strike is not taken seriously in America today?"[6]

Certainly John F. Kennedy knew that his military advisers took seriously the idea of a preemptive strike. They were pushing him to do the same, as revealed in a top-secret document declassified in 1993. At a July 20, 1961, meeting of the National Security Council, the Joint Chiefs of Staff and CIA Director Allen Dulles presented a plan for a nuclear surprise attack on the Soviet Union "in late 1963, preceded by a period of heightened tensions."[7] Kennedy resisted them. After raising a series of questions to the plan, the President got up and walked out of the meeting in disgust. He found intolerable the idea of launching a nuclear Pearl Harbor attack on the Soviet Union.

Besides walking out, Kennedy said afterwards what he thought of the proceeding to Secretary of State Dean Rusk. With what Rusk described as "a strange look on his face," Kennedy said, "And we call ourselves the human race."[8]

Yet, faced by constant demands from the Pentagon and the CIA, Kennedy made concessions to his Cold War chiefs that took everyone nearer to the brink. Merton's letters reflect a deteriorating situation, with policies for nuclear war advancing steadily through the country's moral vacuum. In a letter to Archbishop T.

D. Roberts in London, he feared the situation "amounts in reality to a moral collapse, in which the policy of the nation is more or less frankly oriented toward a war of extermination . . . step by step we come closer to it because the country commits itself more and more to policies which, *but for a miracle,* will make it inevitable"[9] (emphasis added).

Merton's analysis was bleak, but he hoped and prayed for a miracle. The Cold War was on the verge of becoming hot. The condition of our survival was our transformation in heart, mind, and soul all across the world that would otherwise become a ball of fire. As 1962, the year of the Cuban Missile Crisis, began, Merton wrote to Catholic peace activist Jim Forest:

"Really we have to pray for a total and profound change in the mentality of the whole world." Critically needed if we were to survive the nuclear age was our "complete change of heart" and a "totally new outlook on the world," so that we could see our duty to humanity as a whole. This was no option but the bottom line, the condition of our surviving a world of nuclear weapons. "The great problem," as Merton saw it, the crisis underlying the nuclear crisis, "is this inner change . . ."[10]

How did one even begin to act toward the goal of "a total and profound change in the mentality of the whole world"—especially when one was a cloistered monk whose greatest way to influence people on the critical subject of war and peace, by writing articles and a book, was about to be squelched by one's superiors?

In early 1962, Merton was in fact silenced on the issue he felt compelled to speak out on. "Now here is the axe," he wrote Jim Forest on April 12, 1962. "The orders are, no more writing about peace."[11]

How was a monk, forbidden to publish his most prophetic thoughts, to seek the impossible goal of changing the mentality of millions of people?

Thomas Merton simply continued to write letters, one by one.

Each of his letters is a prayer. Merton is trying to call forth the saving presence of God in each of his Cold War correspondents, and implicitly in everyone on earth. Writing in what he perceived as total darkness, the monk is praying his way through these individual letters in pursuit of the global miracle needed to save us from our own violence. Maybe that is what his "Cold War Letters" are all about—enabling us to see how a necessary but impossible collective change could happen, through a miraculous process beyond any power but prayer. Writing faith-filled letters to these few dozen correspondents in the spiritual and political darkness leading up to the Cuban Missile Crisis, this monk was praying very consciously at the edge of the abyss.

The two men most responsible for the Cuban Missile Crisis, John F. Kennedy and Nikita Khrushchev, seemed locked in a hopeless ideological conflict that confirmed Merton's dire analysis. The U.S. and Soviet leaders were following policies which, but for a miracle, would make inevitable a war of extermination. Yet, as we have since learned, Kennedy and Khrushchev, like Thomas Merton, had been writing their own desperate but somehow hopeful Cold War letters—secretly, and to each other. Even as they moved step by step toward a Cold War climax that would almost take the world over the edge with them, they were at the same time smuggling confidential letters back and forth that recognized each other's humanity and hoped for a solution.[12] They were enemies who, in the midst of deepening turmoil, were learning something approaching trust in each other. Almost in spite of themselves, they had become engaged in the process of dialogue that both Pope John XXIII in his public statements (and private communications with the two leaders) and Thomas Merton in his letters were advocating.

Thus it came to pass that in the most decisive hour of the Cuban Missile Crisis, when both sides and the world with them were falling into darkness, Nikita Khrushchev turned to his Foreign Minister, Andrei Gromyko, and said something totally shocking. Khrushchev said, "We have to let Kennedy know that we want to help him."[13]

Nikita's son, Sergei Khrushchev, has described that remarkable moment. He said that his father hesitated to use the word "help" in response to John Kennedy's plea for precisely that. In a secret meeting between Robert Kennedy and Soviet Ambassador Anatoly Dobrynin, RFK had specifically asked the Soviets for help to his brother, whom the U.S. military were pressuring relentlessly to bomb and invade Cuba. Khrushchev had been struck by JFK's appeal to the Soviets for help in holding off his own military chiefs. But when the Soviet leader did say the word "help" aloud, it forced him to ask himself: Did he really want to *help* his enemy Kennedy?

Yet Khrushchev and Kennedy had come to share a vision. In their secret correspondence the two men had agreed on Noah's Ark as a crucial symbol of their (and our) common predicament in the nuclear age.[14] They both believed that the precarious boat in which they and all of humanity were living amidst a sea of conflict had to stay afloat.

Khrushchev, who had suggested the Noah's Ark symbol to Kennedy, may have remembered that common vision, which summed up their mutual responsibility in the depths of their most awful conflict. After a short silence inspired by the sense of his word "help," Khrushchev repeated it to a wondering Gromyko: "Yes, help. We now have a common cause, to save the world from those pushing us toward war."

In that grace-filled connection, Nikita Khrushchev, his new partner John Kennedy, and the world with them, turned from darkness to dawn. When Khrushchev withdrew his Soviet missiles from Cuba, and Kennedy in turn pledged not to invade Cuba (and secretly promised to withdraw U.S. missiles from Turkey), neither side "won" in the missile crisis. In fact, each leader had made vital concessions to his Cold War opponent that dismayed the zealots in his own camp.

Half a world apart, in radical ideological conflict, both Kennedy in his call for help and Khrushchev in his response had transcended their Cold War interests. They had recognized their interdependence with each other and the world. They suddenly joined hands. After threatening to destroy the world, the two enemies turned to each other in desperation and grace. Instead of annihilation, they chose, in Khrushchev's words, "a common cause, to save the world from those pushing us toward war." Their willingness to turn at a critical point in history was the kind of miracle Merton was praying for. It brought profound consequences to both the world and themselves.

How does prayer work?

Thomas Merton gives no clear answer to that question in his letters or anywhere else, nor does any other spiritual writer. But

Merton knew that prayer takes many forms. He knew his Cold War Letters were a form of praying in darkness, a search for light with the companions he addressed, in a night of the spirit when everything seemed lost.

These letters to a global circle of correspondents are a prophetic invitation to *teshuvah, metanoia,* repentance—a call to each of us, and all of us, to turn together in a nonviolent direction, toward a new world before we burn up the old one. For it is we—not God or fate or political demons—who are on the verge of destroying everything and everyone, beginning with our own souls. What these letters say to us all, with truth and compassion, is that it is we who are responsible, we who must turn. Time is up. Do it or be done.

The *Cold War Letters* are Thomas Merton at his best, writing to us at our collective worst. Never before, perhaps, has a contemplative seen the darkness more clearly, nor been more powerless to act on what he saw. In these letters to a circle of correspondents that encompassed the world, the monk's perception and anticipation of the Missile Crisis is startling. He is not only a prophet, in the most demanding sense of the word, but a totally fearless explorer of our Cold War psyche. He plunges our warring heads into the cold waters of our fearful selves, and we feel as if we're drowning. In fact, we are. And we can be saved only by truth and a grace beyond grace.

In what he felt profoundly was a hopeless spiritual landscape, Merton hoped. He saw the death of the planet, and said it in these brilliantly dark letters. Yet he hoped in faith, and yearned for a light that would come upon us all. He knew as a certainty that nothing but a miracle could save us from ourselves.

He was right. The miracle came to pass. Through an act of grace in the depths of the Caribbean crisis, we were suddenly borne up by a light in the darkness that surpassed all understanding. The planet survived our Cold War demons—just barely.

Almost a half-century later, with our demons in command once again, we are ready to repeat our folly, this time in a total War on Terrorism. We are once again choosing our inevitable self-destruction, by a chain reaction of violence that may include nuclear weapons. We still have no sense of what saved us miraculously from ourselves back then, at the edge of history's black-out. Perhaps, in this present darkness, we can learn from Merton's letters written in the darkness of the Cold War. Perhaps we can begin to write our own letters to one another and to God in the way that Merton did, in the way that even Kennedy and Khrushchev with Pope John's guidance stumbled into doing, but with an acceptance now of our absolutely total dependence on grace, as the clock once again approaches midnight.

We were the cold in the Cold War, just as we are the terror in the War on Terror. We are also God's faith and hope—the Creator's reasons for putting us on this planet, God's faith in each of us, with the hope that we would choose finally to embody the love from which we came. Merton's call in writing these letters was to tell us that truth of the Cold War—with its prophetic equivalent today in the War on Terror—in such a way that we could, and can, begin to hear it. No writer of any letter has ever been more challenged.

Thomas Merton's "Cold War Letters" can take us back, as nothing else can, into that year from October 1961 to October 1962, a year of nuclear terror, utter despair, and overwhelming grace. If these letters can be understood now by even a few readers, they will help seed the ground for more miracles, equally necessary for our survival today.

Notes

[1] Thomas Merton to Etta Gullick, Oxford, October 25, 1961.

[2] Thomas Merton, "Chant to be Used in Processions around a Site with Furnaces," in *The Nonviolent Alternative,* edited by Gordon C. Zahn (New York: Farrar, Straus, Giroux, 1980), p. 262.

[3] Richard Reeves, *President Kennedy: Profile of Power* (New York: Touchstone, 1993), p. 250.

[4] Thomas Merton to Etta Gullick, Oxford, October 25, 1961. Cold War Letter 1.

[5] Thomas Merton, Preface to the "Cold War Letters," p. 6.

[6] Thomas Merton to the Editors, *Commonweal,* March 1962. Cold War Letter 49.

[7] Memorandum for Vice President Lyndon Johnson, "Notes on National Security Council Meeting, July 20, 1961," by Colonel Howard Burris, Johnson's military aide; reproduced in the article by Heather A. Purcell and James K. Galbraith, "Did the U.S. Military Plan a Nuclear First Strike for 1963?", *The American Prospect* (Fall 1994), p. 89.

[8] Dean Rusk, *As I Saw It* (New York: W. W. Norton, 1990), pp. 246-47.

[9] Thomas Merton to Archbishop T. D. Roberts, December 1961. Cold War Letter 9.

[10] Thomas Merton to Jim Forest, New York, January 29, 1962. Cold War Letter 25.

[11] Thomas Merton to Jim Forest, New York, April 12, 1962. Cold War Letter 69.

[12] *Foreign Relations of the United States, 1961-1963, Volume VI: Kennedy-Khrushchev Exchanges* (Washington: U.S. Government Printing Office, 1996). The private letter from Khrushchev to Kennedy that began their secret correspondence, written on September 29, 1961, is on pages 25-38. Kennedy responded on October 16, 1961. Ibid., pp. 38-44.

[13] Sergei N. Khrushchev, *Nikita Khrushchev and the Creation of a Superpower* (University Park, PA: Pennsylvania State University, 2000), p. 630.

[14] *Kennedy-Khrushchev-Exchanges,* pp. 35, 39.

Preface

William H. Shannon

Elsewhere[1] I have identified a period in Merton's life as "The Year of the Cold War Letters." It is not a calendar year, but a period in his life that extends approximately from October 1961 to October 1962. It was in the October 1961 issue of the pacifist monthly newspaper, *The Catholic Worker,* that Merton's first published article on war and peace, entitled "The Root of War Is Fear," appeared. In the summer of 1961 Merton had been struggling with the problem of violence in the world, especially the violence of war and the terrible threat of nuclear holocaust. It is difficult for us living in the twenty-first century to understand Merton's situation at the time. We live at a time when protest against war is a stance taken by any number of Catholic activists, including not a few priests. In the early 1960s Merton was alone. No Catholic priest or bishop (at least none well-known) had spoken out against war. Nor would people have expected this from a cloistered monk, let alone the author of *The Seven Storey Mountain.* But by 1961 Thomas Merton had journeyed a long way from the smug world-denying mentality that had characterized that 1948 best-selling autobiography (which, I must add, still remains, despite its deficiencies, a spiritual classic). More than a dozen years later, in 1961, Merton had reached the conviction that as a contemplative he had a mission to the world in which he lived. It was his duty to speak out against the moral evils that threatened the contemporary world; and to him the one evil that posed the greatest threat to the very existence of human civilization was war.

"The Root of War" was actually a chapter from a book of his *(New Seeds of Contemplation)* that was scheduled for publication in January 1962. The chapter was not something new, being simply an extended version of the same chapter in his earlier work, *Seeds of Contemplation.* Nor was it particularly startling—*except for three long paragraphs that Merton had append-ed to it*—in the copy he sent to *The Catholic Worker*. In three highly challenging, even inflammatory paragraphs (paragraphs not cleared with the censors of his Order!), he managed to sum up a whole program for opposing war and working for peace. Deploring a war-madness that had engulfed the whole world, and seemed to be rampant in the United States, he insisted that Christians had an obligation "to lead the way on the road towards nonviolent settlement of difficulties and toward the gradual abo-lition of war as the way of settling international or civil disputes." Practical steps must be taken: to preach peace, to teach nonvio-lence as a practical method of action. "We may not succeed in this campaign," he said, "but, whether we succeed or not, the duty is evident. It is the great Christian task of our time."[2]

With this article Thomas Merton entered definitively on his lonesome struggle against war with a vehemence that was sin-gle-minded and desperately serious. From then till the end of April 1962, he wrote a flurry of articles, as well as one book (*Peace in the Post-Christian Era*) about the Christian's responsi-bility to work for peace and for the outlawing of war. On April 26, 1962, he was informed by his abbot, Dom James Fox, that the Abbot General of the Cistercian Order, Dom Gabriel Sortais, had sent orders that he was no longer to publish books or articles on the issues of war and peace.

Merton obeyed the prohibition against publishing anything on war and peace. Nevertheless, he continued to write articles, which, while unpublished, were privately circulated in mimeo-graphed form among his friends. He even ventured two articles in 1963 in *The Catholic Worker* under pen names—Benedict Monk and Benedict Moore. The prohibition was eased somewhat after Pope John XXIII issued his encyclical *Pacem in Terris* in April 1963 and Merton did write some articles following the pub-lication of the encyclical. But it is still a fact that the period from October 1961 to October 1962 was the most vigorous, concentrat-ed, and productive period of Merton's writings on war and peace.

I have called this period "The Year of the Cold War Letters" because during this time Merton's many articles on war and peace were interlaced with a constant stream of letters to his friends in which he discussed the same topics. In the fall of 1961

Merton conceived the plan of putting together a book comprising selected letters of his own, written to a wide variety of people, and linked by the common themes of war and peace.[3] Not only did he conceive the book, he also decided on a title—"The Cold War Letters." It was a cleverly conceived plan, a way in which Merton could express his ideas without very much publicity coming his way. The letters would get to people who would be inclined to agree with his position and do something to implement it; at the same time there would be a minimal risk of their getting into the hands of those most opposed to his views. I have no information as to the precise time of Merton's decision but I believe it may well have been about the same time as his *Catholic Worker* article appeared. One indication is that the letters he selected began with October 1961 and ceased with October 1962; a second may be found in the letter he wrote on December 21, 1961, to W. H. ("Ping") Ferry of the Santa Barbara Center for the Study of Democratic Institutions. He asked Ferry if he would be willing to circulate some of his material in mimeographed form. "I am having a bit of censorship trouble," he remarked casually, and he made clear that getting his "stuff" around in this way would not require prior censorship. He then mentioned the Cold War Letters for the first time, as an example of material that could be circulated in this private fashion: "I have, for instance, some copies of letters to people—to make up a book called Cold War Letters. Very unlikely to be published." At that time Merton would have written only eleven of the letters that would eventually be included, yet the collection of "Cold War Letters" finally mimeographed consisted of forty-nine letters in its early edition (circulated in the late spring of 1962) and 111 in the final collection circulated in January 1963. To the final collection he added a formal preface.

What I am suggesting is that the "Cold War Letters" were not, as many have believed, an afterthought that came to Merton in the wake of the prohibition to publish on the topic of war and peace. Quite the contrary, the idea was a part of his thinking almost from the moment he decided to enter the "war on war." This may well suggest that the letters that eventually became part of this collection were written at least with some eye to their possible inclusion in the "Cold War Letters."

It is clear, then, that "The Year of the Cold War Letters" needs to be singled out as a unique year in the life of Thomas Merton. Articles on war and peace, interwoven with Cold War Letters, form a literary fabric out of which emerges a reasonably clear image of Thomas Merton, the peacemaker. The Cold War Letters were mimeographed and put together with a spiral binding. The letters were arranged in chronological order, and his correspondents were identified only by name initials and place. Sorting out the names and places called for a good bit of detective work. Letters that were part of a longer correspondence were normally easy to identify, but a single letter to a generally unknown correspondent often called for a bit of ingenuity and a lot of luck. Happily, after nearly a year of searching, I have been able to identify by name all the correspondents except one: W. D., Oyster Bay, Long Island, New York (Letter 50). Is there perchance a reader out there who recognizes W. D. in Oyster Bay? If there is, it would be wonderful to hear from you!

Why did Merton choose the title "Cold War Letters"? The term "Cold War" was coined by Walter Lippman in 1947 as a way of describing the atmosphere of suspicion and mistrust between the two super-powers that followed soon after the treaties that concluded World War II. It meant a condition in which war was waged, not by the physical armaments of hot war (though this was always a scary possibility), but with weapons that were psychological and rhetorical.

In the preface he wrote to the final edition, Merton related the letters to that confrontation between the United States and the Soviet Union that reached a climax in the Cuban Missile Crisis of October 1962. This crisis was precipitated by the presence in Cuba of Soviet missiles, capable of reaching the United States. On October 22, 1962, President John F. Kennedy ordered a blockade of Cuba. Six days later, October 28, Nikita Khrushchev ordered the ships carrying missiles to Cuba to turn around and head home. He also ordered the dismantling of the missile sites in Cuba.[4] In his preface Merton writes:

> These copies of letters, written over a period of a little more than one year preceding the Cuban Crisis of 1962, have been made for friends who might be expected to under-

stand something of the author's viewpoint, even when they might not agree with all he has said, still less with all he may have unconsciously implied.

These letters are published with the realization that they were written nearly a half century ago, but with the conviction that the very issues that Merton wrote about with such clarity and passion are the very issues we face in our time. We need to join Merton in opposing war-making and in voicing loudly and clearly the responsibility of all people of good will to commit themselves to the work of peace and to nonviolence as the only way to peace.

Finally, it needs to be pointed out that Merton's fertile mind simply could not be confined within the limits of a single topic, even one as important to him as war and peace. Hence not infrequently in these letters he branches off into other areas of concern to him that may have little to do with the main thrust of the Cold War Letters. Thus, the reader will often find in them a richness and a wisdom that go beyond the specific topics of war and peace.

Notes

[1] *Silent Lamp: The Thomas Merton Story* (New York: Crossroad, 1992), 209-224.

[2] For the full test of these paragraphs, see Thomas Merton, *Passion for Peace: The Social Essays* (New York: Crossroad, 1995), 11-13.

[3] Some of these letters were single letters to particular individuals; others were selected from more extensive correspondences. In the latter instances Merton did not restrict his letters simply to the topic of war and violence.

[4] Pope John XXIII was instrumental in resolving the standoff between the two super-powers. Through an intermediary Khrushchev had contacted the Pope, suggesting that a statement from him would give him a graceful way of withdrawing from this critical situation. On October 24, 1962, Pope John issued a strong appeal to world leaders begging "the heads of states not to turn a deaf ear to the cry of humanity: 'peace, peace.'" Khrushchev listened and four days later the Soviet ships turned around and returned home. See Thomas Cahill, *Pope John XXIII* (New York: Viking Penguin, 2002), 205-206.

Introduction

Christine M. Bochen

T he recent publication of Thomas Merton's *Peace in the Post-Christian Era,*[1] more than forty years after it was written, has focused renewed attention on Merton's prophetic critique of war and his witness to peace. *Peace in the Post-Christian Era* grew out of Merton's writings during the year, October 1961 and October 1962—a period during which Merton wrote a flurry of articles in which he spoke out against war and for peace. William H. Shannon has dubbed this period "the year of the Cold War Letters." By April 1962, Merton was forbidden by his superiors to publish on the subject of war. In obedience, he complied and the book was not published during his lifetime. Nevertheless, Merton had found other ways to get his message out: publishing a few pieces under a pseudonym; submitting some articles to small and obscure publications, not technically covered in the Order's ban; maintaining a wide-ranging correspondence; and compiling a collection of letters which he himself selected, had typed, mimeographed, and sent to his growing circle of friends and contacts. The first "edition" of forty-nine letters was completed in April 1962, the second edition of one hundred and eleven letters in January 1963. Disseminating the Cold War Letters became a way for Merton to continue his work of networking for peace.

Readers of Merton's letters, published in five volumes under the general editorship of William H. Shannon, have read individual letters, scattered throughout these volumes.[2] Here the Cold War Letters appear in a single volume—to be read as Merton himself intended them to be read. While he noted on the typescript of "Cold War Letters" that that they were "Strictly confidential. Not for publication," thus complying with the ban on his publishing on the subject of the war, the possibility of eventual publication must have occurred to Merton, as he observed in his Preface that the typescript had "none of the corrections, qualifications, and omissions which would be required before such a book could possibly be considered for general circulation, or even for any but the most limited and private reading."[3] Recognizing that the letters could be "open to all kinds of misinterpretation," Merton noted that there is "much that might have been modified since the letters were written and copied," admitting that they were written "in the heat of the moment, and when the moments of that year were often unusually fraught with excitement." This admission reflects not only his realization that his thinking was evolving but also his awareness of the volatile and hostile climate in which he was writing. He even found it necessary to assert that he "is not, never was, and never will be a Communist." Nevertheless, Merton unabashedly acknowledges that the letters are "biased by a frank hatred of power politics and by an uninhibited contempt for those who use power to distort truth or to silence it altogether."

Despite Merton's reservations about the letters, expressed in these caveats, the editors of this volume present the letters in the form in which Merton included them in the second mimeographed "edition," correcting only typographical errors, misspellings, and Merton's sometimes quirky punctuation; adding the occasional omitted word, and identifying names and references (these appear in brackets); and adding some explanatory notes. Our intent is to allow Merton to speak to contemporary readers as he spoke to the original recipient of each letter and to the small circle of readers to whom he sent the collected and mimeographed letters. What Merton considered a possible liability—the spontaneity and uncensored candidness of the letters as first written—is an asset to those of us who read and study Merton today. The urgency and immediacy of the Cold War Letters provides us with a body of work to be read alongside the more carefully nuanced, and perhaps more guarded statements in articles and essays, written with the knowledge that they would be read by censors.

The eighty-one original recipients of the Cold War Letters represent the wide range of Merton's contacts all over the world—he wrote to individuals in Argentina, Austria, Belgium, Brazil, Canada, England, Japan, and Pakistan—and testify to the ever-widening circle of friendships he built through his correspondence. Among those to whom Merton sent his "Cold War Letters" were peace activists such as Dorothy Day, James Forest, Jean Goss-Mayr and Gordon Zahn; fellow writers such as Lawrence Ferlinghetti, Czeslaw Milosz and Henry Miller; psychologists and psychoanalysts such as Erich Fromm, Karl Stern, and Joost Meerloo; scientists such as Leo Szilard; and old friends such as Robert Lax, Ad Reinhardt, and Edward Rice. The diversity of the recipients of these letters is matched by the variety of interests and concerns which Merton expresses in them. In addition to the central themes of war and peace, Merton addresses a host of other subjects such as faith and freedom, God and love, culture and literature. He engages in ecumenical and inter-religious dialogue. He celebrates the wisdom of Buddhism and Judaism and the contributions of Shakers and Mennonites. He reflects on mysticism and theology. He considers the challenges facing the Catholic Church and expresses his hopes for the Second Vatican Council. And so, while the Cold War Letters shed light on Merton's prophetic witness against war and his passion for peace, they also enable us to glimpse Merton the monk, the working writer, the contemplative, and the citizen of the globe.

Merton's Message

What was Merton's message? What did Merton say to those to whom he originally addressed the Cold War Letters and to those with whom he later shared mimeographed copies? What is Merton's message to those of us who read him today—almost a half-century later? Simply put, it is this: war is the most critical issue of our day and we need, with all the resources available to us, to work to abolish war and build peace. While this conviction and the moral imperative it entails inform all of Merton's writings on war and peace, there is a heightened sense of urgency expressed in these letters. The "abolition of war," Merton wrote to Etta Gullick, in October 1961, in Cold War Letter 1, "has become an urgent obligation . . . one task for me that takes precedence over everything else." Speaking out against war was for Merton nothing less than a vocation. He felt himself called to speak out, feeling that it was his duty to do so as a Christian and as a monk. Having answered the call to contemplation, he now heard the Spirit urging him to compassionate action. Merton's Cold War Letters document his response to the Spirit's call as do the host of essays and articles he wrote on war, violence, and racism. For Merton, contemplation and compassion were of a piece. His awakening to God's presence within him and within all people left Merton with no alternative but to work for peace in the two ways in which he could do so as monk and writer: he prayed and he wrote—the writing grounded in and informed by prayer, his prophetic vision clarified by a perspective honed in silence and solitude. Living physically apart from "the world," he was able to read the signs of the times with a clarity that astounded many of his contemporaries and continues to amaze contemporary readers. He saw what so many others in church and society could not: that humanity stands on the brink of self-destruction.

Two Ways of Seeing the World

A close reading of the *Cold War Letters* reveals that Merton's position against war and for peace is rooted in a thoughtful and critical consideration of two radically different ways of viewing the world and of living in it. One way is informed by a "Cold War mentality," the other by Christian humanism.

The "Cold War Mentality"

The "Cold War mentality" is "a highly oversimplified and mythical view of the world divided into two camps: that of darkness (our enemies) and that of light (ourselves)" and, while we see the enemy as "totally malevolent and totally dedicated to evil," we see ourselves as "totally innocent and committed, by our very nature, to truth, goodness, and light." Consequently, "everything the enemy does is diabolical and everything we do is angelic. His H-bombs are from hell and ours are the instruments of divine justice. It follows then that we have a divinely given mission to destroy this hellish monster and any steps we take to do so are innocent and even holy." There is no ambiguity about who is who and which is which. We are good and the enemy is evil. Merton saw this thinking for what it was: a dangerous charade. He saw what so many around him failed to see: that we and the "enemy" are more alike than not.

Already in the summer of 1961, when he wrote "A Letter for Pablo Antonio Cuadra" for publication in Latin America, he had argued that the similarities between the Soviet Union and the United States were greater than any differences between them. Drawing on the Book of Daniel, he named one superpower Gog and the other Magog.

"Gog is a lover of power, Magog is absorbed in the cult of money: their idols differ, and indeed their faces seem to be dead set against one another, but their madness is the same: they are the two faces of Janus looking inward, and dividing with critical fury the polluted sanctuary of dehumanized man."[4] The power of such a myth is seductive and enervating. It distorts our vision so that we cannot "see clearly what we have to resist," namely evil itself. Furthermore, "under the pressures of anxiety and fear, the alternation of crisis and relaxation and new crisis, the people of the world will come to accept gradually the idea of war, the idea of submission to total power, and the abdication of reason, spirit and individual conscience. The great peril of the Cold War is the progressive deadening of conscience."

"Cold War thinking" threatens to undermine our fundamental American values on a national and international scale. It puts the United States "in grave danger of ceasing to be what they claim to be: the home of liberty, where justice is defended with free speech, where truth is accessible to everybody, where everybody is alike responsible, enlightened and concerned, and where responsibility is sustained by a deep foundation of ethics," as we let our thinking be shaped by an aggressive and destructive policy. Writing to Ethel Kennedy in December 1961, Merton observed that "there are very dangerous ambiguities about our democracy in its actual present condition. I wonder to what extent our ideals are now a front for organized selfishness and systematic irresponsibility." When pragmatism trumps morality, all efforts to achieve success are deemed acceptable. In fact, the weapons themselves "dictate what we are to do," forcing us "into awful corners." Writing to W.H. "Ping" Ferry in March 1962, following the appearance of his controversial article, "Nuclear War and Christian Responsibility," in *Commonweal* (February 9,

1962), Merton is critical of the "Cold War assumptions" of one of his respondents. He writes: "The first and greatest of all commandments is that America shall not and must not be beaten in the Cold War, and the second is like unto this, that if a hot war is necessary to prevent defeat in the Cold War, then a hot war must be fought even if civilization is to be destroyed." Meanwhile, we toss around statistics and glibly talk of "first strikes" and "preemptive strikes"—paying no mind to the human cost of our actions and allowing ourselves to be "hypnotized by immediate military solutions."

An Incarnational Humanism

Viewing the world through a different lens, Merton offers his readers an alternative to the "Cold War mentality" as he envisions a world in which social and political actions are informed by regard for the dignity of the human person rather than by pragmatism and power-seeking and by a commitment to non-violence rather than recourse to armed conflict. This vision of a world in which people seek to resolve conflict through negotiation rather than military action is grounded in Merton's faith and contemplative vision. More precisely, it is a humanistic vision.

Merton's humanism is Christian: it is a humanism rooted in the Incarnation. Writing to Bruno P. Schlesinger in December 1961, Merton speaks of "the urgent need for Christian Humanism." Admitting that in using the word "humanism" he runs "the risk of creating wrong impressions," he clarifies what he means. "What is important is the fully Christian notion of man: a notion radically modified by the mystery of the Incarnation. This I think is the very heart of the matter." What is the basis of this Christian understanding of the human person? Merton suggests it is "rooted in the biblical notions of man as the object of divine mercy, and of special concern on the part of God, as the spouse of God, as, in some mysterious sense, an epiphany of the divine wisdom." Above all, it is a vision of the human person in Christ: "Man in Christ. The New Adam presupposing the Old Adam, presupposing the old paradise and the new paradise, the creation and the new creation."

Perhaps the most compelling and best-known expression of

Merton's Incarnational humanism is found in his account of his epiphany in Louisville at the corner of 4th and Walnut, first recorded in his journal and later expanded in *Conjectures of a Guilty Bystander*. Merton's description of this transformed and transforming vision of humanity is rightly hailed as a symbol of his "turning toward the world"—a dramatic experience at a corner in Louisville's business district on March 18, 1958, that signaled what had been a more gradual change in his vision of the world, a change that would express itself in the awakening of Merton's social consciousness and his commitment to speak out on war and a host of social issues. Celebrating his membership in the human race, Merton writes: "I have the immense joy of being *man,* a member of a race in which God himself became incarnate."[5] In the Incarnation, all humanity is transformed: people "are all walking around shining like the sun."[6] The "person that each one is in God's eyes" is who we truly are—with the "pure glory of God" shining in us.[7] The tragedy is that we fail to see ourselves as we all truly are. If only we could see each other as we really are, "There would be no more war, no more hatred, no more cruelty, no more greed."[8] But that seeing, Merton knew, cannot be imposed; it can only be received as grace, as a gift of God. Once received, this "seeing" transforms one's vision of humanity and prompts, as was Merton's experience, a realization of "our duty to mankind as a whole."

But this, Merton realized, is not how the human being is viewed—post-World War II, post-Auschwitz, post-Hiroshima. "The whole Christian notion of man has been turned inside out, instead of paradise we have Auschwitz." Coupled with this loss of the "Christian notion of man" is an evisceration of religion itself. Religion, Merton observes, has survived "as an abstract formality without a humanist matrix, religion apart from man and almost in some sense apart from God Himself (God figuring only as a Lawgiver and not as a Savior), religion without any human epiphany in art, in work, in social forms."

A Spiritual Crisis

While Merton was certainly cognizant of the complex political issues at play in the Cold War and in the arms race, he recognized that the problem facing the world in 1961–1962 was not primarily a political problem but rather a spiritual one. He decried the "spiritual obtuseness" of his generation and warned of "the gravity of the hour, spiritually speaking." The "awful issue of nuclear war" involves "much more than the danger of physical evil . . . What concerns me . . . is the ghastly feeling that we are all on the brink of spiritual defection." For Merton, that meant a "betrayal of Christ which would consist in the complete acceptance of the values and the decisions of callous men of war who think only in terms of mega-corpses and megatons, and have not the slightest thought for man, the image of God." In the "sudden, unbalanced top-heavy rush into technological mastery," we find ourselves bereft of "the spiritual means to face our problems." Though it need not be so, so it is.

If, as Merton saw it, the problem of war is, at its root, a spiritual problem, the solution must also be spiritual in nature. While prayer remained his "chief means," he realized it was not enough simply to pray for peace. What was needed was a spiritual transformation—a "complete change of heart." Only a radical conversion on the part of individuals and the human community could eradicate violence and inspire a search for alternative ways to address and respond to conflict. Without such a change of heart, without "a deep spiritual purification,"

> we all stand as prisoners of our own scientific virtuosity, ruled by immense power that we ought to be ruling and cannot. Our weapons dictate what we can do. They force us into awful corners. They give us our living, they sustain our economy, they bolster up our politicians, they sell our mass media, in short we live by them. But if they continue to rule us we will almost surly die by them. (CWL 17)

For Merton, spiritual transformation involves a conversion to non-violence. Drawing on the teachings of Gandhi and inspired by the witness of peace activists, Merton was, in the early 1960s, crafting an understanding of the Christian roots of non-violence which he would articulate so eloquently in "Blessed Are the Meek," an essay he wrote in 1966.[9]

His own Church was not immune from this spiritual crisis:

The Church, Merton wrote, "is full of a terrible spiritual sickness." Merton was appalled by the failure of Christians and particularly of his fellow Catholics to respond to the threat of impending war and nuclear devastation. The *Cold War Letters* captures his dismay at the passivity of Christians. He is dispirited by the Christianity of "individualism," of "formulas," and of "passive conformity," and deeply disturbed by the silence of the Catholic Church and its clergy. Only the Popes, it seems to Merton, had the courage to speak out against war: "It seems to me that the position of the Church, at least in this country, has become totally hardened and toughened, so that in spite of all the things that have been said by the Popes in favor of peace and disarmament, they are all now convinced that there is nothing for it but the 'realist' policy based on testing, stockpiling, etc." Writing to his friend Etta Gullick in December 1961, Merton expressed the wish

> that the Catholic position on nuclear war was held as strict as the Catholic position on birth control. It seems a little strange that we are so wildly exercised about the "murder" (and the word is of course correct) of an unborn infant by abortion, or even the prevention of conception which is hardly murder, and yet accept without a qualm the extermination of millions of helpless and innocent adults . . . I submit that we ought to fulfill the one without omitting the other.

For Merton, facing the "question of peace" was of such paramount importance that he did "not believe that anyone who takes his Christian faith seriously can afford to neglect it." Clarifying his position, he writes:

> I do not mean to say that you have to swim out to Polaris submarines carrying a banner between your teeth, but it is absolutely necessary to take a serious and articulate stand on the question of nuclear war. And I mean against nuclear war. The passivity, the incoherence of so many Christians on this issue and worse still the active belligerency of some religious spokesmen, especially in this country, is rapidly becom-

ing one of the most frightful scandals in the history of Christendom. (*CWL* 14)

The Challenge of Pacifism

The *Cold War Letters* shows Merton refining and nuancing his position on nuclear war, pacifism, and non-violence. He does not insist "that to be a Christian one must be a pacifist." In fact, he clearly states that he is not "a total pacifist" nor is he "an absolute pacifist." Writing to Dorothy Day, he confesses:

> It is true that I am not theoretically a pacifist. That only means that I do not hold that a Christian *may not* fight, and that a war *cannot* be just. I hold that there is such a thing as a just war, even today there can be such a thing, and I think the Church holds it. But on the other hand I think that is pure theory and that in practice all the wars that are going around, whether with conventional weapons, or guerila wars, or the Cold War itself, are shot through and through with evil, falsity, injustice, and sin so much so that one can only with difficulty extricate the truths that may be found here and there in the "causes" for which the fighting is going on. (*CWL* 86)

Merton goes on to assure Day that, "in practice," he is "with" her. Statements such as these reflect Merton's own struggle with the challenge of pacifism and the tension he felt between theory and practice. While he cautioned that he was "not theoretically a pacifist," it is clear that his heart was leading him in the direction of non-violence and peace. While he held on to the theoretical construct of "just war," he also realized that the reality of war and warfare demanded of him a more radical response.

By Way of Conclusion

Reading Merton's Cold War Letters more than forty years after they were written, I am struck by their timeliness and, sad to say, their continuing relevance. And I am moved by Merton's prophetic witness to another way of seeing and being in the world. Reading and responding to the signs of his times, Merton challenges contemporary readers to do the same and so to dispel the myths and illusions that too often define and inform our view of our world and ourselves.

Merton chose to end his collection of the "Cold War Letters" with a letter that ends with this line: "Every slightest effort at opening up new areas of thought, every attempt to perceive new aspects of truth, or just a little truth, is of inestimable value in preparing the way for the light we cannot yet see." Merton's Cold War Letters represents such an effort—challenging those who read them almost half a century later to join him "in preparing the way for the light we cannot yet see."

Notes

1 Thomas Merton, *Peace in the Post-Christian Era*, ed. Patricia A. Burton (Maryknoll, NY: Orbis, 2004).

2 Thomas Merton, *The Hidden Ground of Love: The Letters of Thomas Merton on Religious Experience and Social Concerns,* ed. William H. Shannon (New York: Farrar, Straus and Giroux, 1985); *The Road to Joy: The Letters of Thomas Merton to New and Old Friends,* ed. Robert E. Daggy (New York: Farrar, Straus and Giroux, 1989); *The School of Charity: The Letters of Thomas Merton on Religious Renewal and Spiritual Direction,* ed. Patrick Hart (New York: Farrar, Straus and Giroux, 1990); *The Courage for Truth: The Letters of Thomas Merton to Writers,* ed. Christine M. Bochen (New York: Farrar, Straus and Giroux, 1993); *Witness to Freedom: The Letters of Thomas Merton in Times of Crisis,* ed. William H. Shannon (New York: Farrar, Straus and Giroux, 1994). *Witness to Freedom* included Cold War Letters that had not been published in the first four volumes of selected letters. However, it should be noted that not all the Cold War Letters appear in their entirety in these five volumes of selected letters. In this book, they do.

3 In 1964, Merton included selections from thirty-five Cold War Letters as Part Three of *Seeds of Destruction* (New York: Farrar, Straus and Giroux, 1964), entitling the collection "Letters in a Time of Crisis."

4 *The Collected Poems of Thomas Merton* (New York: New Directions, 1997), 375.

5 Thomas Merton, *Conjectures of a Guilty Bystander* (New York: Doubleday & Co., 1965), 157.

6 Ibid.

7 Ibid., 158.

8 Ibid.

9 Thomas Merton, *Passion for Peace: The Social Essays,* ed. by William H. Shannon (New York: Crossroad, 1995).

Cold War Letters

(Strictly confidential.
Not for publication.)

PREFACE

These copies of letters written over a period of little more than one year preceding the Cuban Crisis of 1962, have been made for friends who might be expected to understand something of the writer's viewpoint, even when they might not agree with all he has said, still less with all that he may have unconsciously implied.

As a matter of fact, the letters themselves have been copied practically without change, except that the more irrelevant parts have been cut out. There have been none of the careful corrections, qualifications, and omissions which would be required before such a book could possibly be considered for general circulation, or even for any but the most limited and private reading. As it stands, it lies open to all kinds of misinterpretation, and malevolence will not find it difficult to read into these pages the most sinister of attitudes. A few words in a preface may then serve to deny in advance the possible allegations of witch hunters.

There is no witch here, no treason and no subversion. The letters form part of no plot. They incite to no riot, they suggest no disloyalty to government, they are not pandering to the destructive machinations of revolutionaries or foreign foes. They are nothing more than the expression of loyal but unpopular opinion, of democratic opposition to what seem to be irresponsible trends. Without such voices raised in opposition to grim policies and majority compulsions, democracy would be without meaning. The writer is then confident that the values of free speech and free opinion traditional in the western world are still not so far subverted by totalitarian thinking as to make these letters, even in their carelessness, and at times in their confusion, totally unacceptable.

There are certainly statements made in these pages which

the writer no longer holds just as they stand. There is much that might have been modified since the letters were written or copied. There are many expressions that the writer would be ready to withdraw or soften without more ado. The letters were written, as most letters are, in haste, in the heat of the moment, and the moments of that year were often unusually fraught with excitement. The perspective of these letters is then often distorted by indignation or by vehement protest. It is hoped that this may not cause them to be too grossly misinterpreted. Perhaps it is not out of place that those readers for whom these letters are not intended and of whose business they are none, may be asked politely to withhold their judgment. The author is not, never was and never will be a Communist. The author in fact detests every type of totalitarian coercion, under whatever form, palliated by whatever high-sounding and humanitarian excuse. These letters are, indeed, biased by a frank hatred of power politics and by an uninhibited contempt for those who use power to distort the truth or to silence it altogether. The somewhat belligerent tone—usually more belligerent than the writer himself would like it to be—should be heard against this background of easily aroused indignation, which the writer generally hopes is righteous. But of course such indignation is not always, in the event, as justified as one might hope.

What is the ground for the general protest uttered in these pages? It is the conviction that the United States, in the Cold War, are in grave danger of ceasing to be what they claim to be: the home of liberty, where justice is defended with free speech, where truth is accessible to everybody, where everybody is alike responsible, enlightened, and concerned, and where responsibility is sustained by a deep foundation of ethics. In actual fact it would seem that during the Cold War, if not during World War II, this country has become frankly a warfare state built on affluence, a power structure in which the interests of big business, the obsessions of the military, and the phobias of political extremists both dominate and dictate our national policy. It also seems that the people of the country are by and large reduced to passivity, confusion, resentment, frustration, thoughtlessness, and ignorance so that they blindly follow any line that is unraveled for them by the mass media.

There has been above all a tendency to insulation behind a thick layer of misinformation and misinterpretation, so that the majority opinion in the United States is now a highly oversimplified and mythical view of the world divided into two camps: that of darkness (our enemies) and that of light (ourselves).[1] The enemy is totally malevolent and totally dedicated to evil. We are totally innocent and committed, by our very nature, to truth, goodness, and light. In consequence of this, everything the enemy does is diabolical and everything we do is angelic. His H-bombs are from hell and ours are the instruments of divine justice. It follows that we have a divinely given mission to destroy this hellish monster and any steps we take to do so are innocent and even holy.

Now there is no question of the evil of communism, but the evil is more complex and more variable than we are willing to think. And furthermore our own economic and political system is not always either just or ideal.

In this confused and bellicose state of mind the country has drifted more and more toward war on a total and suicidal scale and has actually come so close to it that even the most cold blooded of her enemies were scared. (In parenthesis: the Cuba crisis does not by any means prove the effectiveness of nuclear deterrence, for the U.S. was not seriously deterred by Russia's missiles. The same indifference can work both ways, if it ever turns out that two powers, equally well-armed and equally excitable, find themselves face to face in another such predicament.)

It is a curious fact that those who insist that the only way to peace is the hard-nosed and stiff-necked way of missile rattling and nuclear threats, are developing a mentality that is insensitive to the realities of nuclear war, and indifferent to the missiles and menaces of the enemy. Indeed it is counted bravery and patriotism to ignore the realities of the situation or to shrug them off with a few platitudes about the number of mega-

---

[1] Thomas Merton explored this theme at some length, in the summer of 1961, in "A Letter to Pablo Antonio Cuadra Concerning Giants" in which he drew on the prophet Ezekiel to dub the U.S.S.R. and the U.S. Gog and Magog, respectively. See *The Collected Poems of Thomas Merton* (New York: New Directions, 1977), 372-391.

corpses we are ready to tolerate. Such thinking seems to be more prevalent in the United States than anywhere else except perhaps Soviet China, and obviously fanaticism of this type is able to dispose of the rationality which, it is assumed, will be "deterred" by H-bombs from rash and suicidal actions.

The protest in these letters is not, however, merely against the danger or the horror of war. It is not dictated by the fear that a few lives might be lost, or that property might be destroyed, or even that millions of lives might be lost and civilization itself destroyed. The protest is not merely against physical destruction, still less against physical danger, but against a suicidal moral evil and a total lack of ethics and rationality with which international policies tend to be conducted. True, President [John F.] Kennedy is a shrewd and sometimes adventurous leader. He means well and has the highest motives, and he is, without doubt, in a position sometimes so impossible as to be absurd. The same can be said of any national leader. I would not judge that any of the great ones today, even [Nikita] Khrushchev or Mao Tse-Tung are unexampled crooks or psychotics like [Adolf] Hitler.

Unfortunately there seems to me to be a general air of insanity about the whole conduct of public life today, even though the leaders are well-intentioned and "well-adjusted" men[2] and this is what makes it morally impossible for most people *even to consider objectively* the fact that war might no longer be a rational way of settling international differences. *It is taken for granted* that the mere idea of questioning recourse to war as a valid, rational and ethical means of settling problems, is not only absurd but may even be treasonable. There are not lacking moralists, Catholic theologians, who can argue that there exists a *moral obligation* to threaten Russia with nuclear destruction! In the opinion of the present writer such opinions are not only disgraceful, scandalous, and unchristian, but also plainly idiotic. They make far less sense than the measured mumblings of the theological experts who, in Galileo's day, did not want the earth to turn about the sun.

---

[2] See "A Devout Meditation in Memory of Adolf Eichmann" in *Raids on the Unspeakable* (New York: New Directions, 1966) for Merton's discussion of "insanity" passing as "sanity."

The writer is a Catholic, devoted to his Church, to his faith, and to his vocation. He does not believe that in differing from theologians like these, even when they may perhaps be bishops, he is turning against Christ or the Church. On the contrary he believes himself obliged in conscience to follow the line of thought which has been made quite clear by the modern Popes, particularly Pius XII and John XXIII, who have repeatedly pleaded for rational and peaceful ways of settling disputes, and who have forcefully declared that the uninhibited recourse to destructive violence in total war, nuclear or conventional, is "a sin, an offense and an outrage." (Pius XII)

The protest in these letters is then the same as the protest of Pope Pius XII who said that total and indiscriminate nuclear war would be "a crime worthy of the most severe national and international sanctions." (To World Medical Congress, 1954)

The appeal of these letters is the same as the appeal of Pope John XXIII repeatedly urging national leaders to "shun all thought of force."

It is the same as the appeal of Cardinal Meyer of Chicago in his Lenten-pastoral of 1962, where he said, "We are overcome by evil not only if we allow Communism to take over the world but if we allow the methods and standards of Communism to influence our own. If we adopt a policy of hatred, of liquidation of those who oppose us, of unrestrained use of total war, of a spirit of fear and panic, of exaggerated propaganda, of unconditional surrender, or pure nationalism, we have already been overcome by the evil."

To hold that nuclear war is an evil to be avoided at all costs is not the same as holding that one must make "peace at any price." Those who cling, with an almost psychotic obsessiveness, to the "red or dead" alternative,[3] as if no other choice could be possible, are simply admitting their incapacity to face the problem of our time in an adult and rational way. The greatest tragedy of our

---

[3] See Merton's essay by this title, "Red or Dead: The Anatomy of a Cliché," published in *Fellowship* (March 1, 1962) and in a pamphlet published by the Fellowship of Reconciliation: *Two Articles by Thomas Merton: The Root of War Is Fear & Red or Dead: The Anatomy of a Cliché* (Nyack, New York: Fellowship Publications, 1962). The article is reprinted in Passion for Peace: The Social Essays, edited by William H. Shannon (New York: Crossroad, 1995), 48-52.

time is not the mere existence of nuclear weapons but the apparent incapacity of men to think in terms that will enable them to deal with the problem of these weapons effectively.

It is certainly true that international cooperation must finally bring about the control and even the abolition of war, if the human race is to survive. It is of course equally true that this effort must proceed in such a way that it does not capsize in a sudden seizure of power by one of the great antagonists. How this is to be done, nobody can yet clearly see. But until really honest efforts are made surely nobody is going to even look at the problem squarely. We are living in a condition where we are afraid to see the total immorality and absurdity of total war. One reason for this incapacity is the fact that the whole nation is fattening on the profits of the war industries and on the production of fantastically expensive and complex weapons that are obsolete almost before they are produced.

The burden of protest in these letters is simply that such a state of affairs is pure madness, that to accept it without question as right and reasonable is criminally insane and that in the presence of such fantastically absurd and suicidal iniquity the Christian conscience cannot keep silent.

The Letters

1. To E.G. [Etta Gullick], Oxford [c. October 25, 1961]

I know you have been patient with me as a bad correspondent. I owe you replies for two or three wonderful letters and several cards. I was very interested in your marvelous trip through the Balkans, your visit to the Patriarch at Istanbul. It must have been most impressive. I hear he is wonderful. A friend of mine in New York has written back and forth and published magazine articles on him. He is very cordial. I hope the chapel in Oxford will be a success. God bless you for it.

Thanks especially for the *Downside Reviews* with C.F. Kelley's excellent articles. These are very fine and I like them a lot. But do you realize that in sending me his address you did not give the name of any town? California is a big place, you know! Could you look again, please? I am not in a great rush to write to him as I have an awful stack of letters to answer.

One thing that has kept me very busy in the last few weeks is the international crisis. It is not really my business to speak out about it but since there is such frightful apathy and passivity everywhere, with people simply unable to face the issue squarely, and with only a stray voice raised tentatively here and there, it has become an urgent obligation. This has kept me occupied and will keep me even more occupied, because I am now perfectly convinced that there is one task for me that takes precedence over everything else: working with such means as I have at my disposal for the abolition of war. This is like going into the prize ring blindfolded and with hands tied, since I am cloistered and subject to the most discouragingly long and frustrating kinds of censorship on top of it. I must do what I can. Prayer of course remains my chief means, but it is also an obligation on my part to speak out in so far as I am able, and to speak as clearly, as forthrightly, and as uncompromisingly as I can. A lot of people are not going to like this and it may mean my head, so do please pray for me in a very special way, because I cannot in conscience willingly betray the truth or let it be betrayed. The issue is too serious. This is purely and simply the crucifixion over again. Those who think there can be a just cause for measures that gravely risk leading to the destruction of the entire human race are in the most dangerous illusion, and if they are Christian they are purely and simply arming themselves with hammer and nails, without realizing it, to crucify and deny Christ. The extent of our spiritual obtuseness is reaching a frightful scale. Of course there is in it all a great mercy of God Whose word descends like the rain and snow from heaven and cannot return to Him empty: but the demonic power at work in history is appalling, especially in these last months. We are reaching a moment of greatest crisis, through the blindness and stupidity of our leaders and all who believe in them and in the society we have set up for ourselves, and which is falling apart.

Thanks especially for the [E. I.] Watkin book [*Poets and Mystics* (London: Sheed and Ward, 1953)]. I read first the chapter on Julian [of Norwich], whom I love dearly. Then [Augustine] Baker. It is an admirable chapter and certainly one needs access to unpublished material to really learn B's mind on active contemplation, etc. It is splendid. Many thanks and God bless you.

2. To J.H. [John C. Heidbrink], Nyack, N.Y. [October 30, 1961]

Thank you for your good letter of October 25. I am glad Dorothy Day and the CW [*Catholic Worker*] got in touch with you. I am very anxious to be in touch with anyone who is working for peace at this hour. I do not think that Catholics realize the situation at all. They seem to be totally unaware of the gravity of the hour spiritually speaking, quite apart from the physical danger. It may very well be that we are faced with a temptation to a total interior apostasy from Christ, while perhaps maintaining an exterior rectitude of some sort. This is frightful. In this event, I feel that the supreme obligation of every

Christian, taking precedence over absolutely everything else, is to devote himself by the best means at his disposal to a struggle to preserve the human race from annihilation and to abolish war as the essential means to accomplish this end. Everything else must be seen in this perspective; otherwise it loses its Christian significance at a time like this.

Since this is my attitude I am of course ready to help you in any way that I can. Unfortunately I am in an extremely ambiguous and difficult position. Everything I write, unless it is to appear in "some small publication with limited appeal," is subject to a censorship which can drag out as long as two or three months, and then all sorts of trivial objections are raised to everything that is not purely a matter of pious homilies for the sisters on how to arrange the veil during meditation.

3. To A.A.L. [Paulo Alceu Amoroso Lima], Rio de Janeiro [November 1961]

It was a great pleasure to receive your letter [dated November 1, 1961], and above all, do not apologize for writing to me in Portuguese. Dom Teodoro, from São Bento in São Paolo, who made his novitiate here under me, taught me the language after his profession here (Fr. Bede) and I enjoy very much reading it, though it would probably be impossible for me to write it very coherently. It is a language I delight in, and it has really become the one I like best. It is to me a warm and glowing language, one of the most human of tongues, richly expressive and in its own way innocent. Perhaps I say this speaking subjectively, not having read all that may have enlightened me in some other sense. But it seems to me that Portuguese has never yet been used for such barbarities as German, English, French, or Spanish. And I love the Brazilian people. I keep wanting to translate Jorge de Lima. I have the poems of Manuel Bandeira and Carlos Drummond de Andrade and several others. I like them and read them all.

Now as to the topic of your letter. I believe it is very important that we exchange ideas from time to time. This is a crucial and perhaps calamitous moment in history, a moment in which reason and understanding threaten to be swallowed up, even if man himself manages to survive. It is certainly an age in which Christianity is vanishing into an area of shadows and uncertainty, from the human point of view. It is all very well for me to meditate on these things in the shelter of the monastery: but there are times when this shelter itself is deceptive. Everything is deceptive today. And grains of error planted innocently in a well-kept greenhouse can become giant poisonous trees.

Everything healthy, everything certain, everything holy, if we can find such things, they all need to be emphasized and articulated. For this it is necessary that there be communication between the hearts and minds of men, communication and not the noise of slogans or the repetition of clichés. Communication is becoming more and more difficult, and when speech is in danger of perishing or being perverted in the amplified noise of beasts, perhaps it becomes obligatory for a monk to try to speak. There is therefore, it seems to me, every reason why we should attempt to cry out to one another and comfort one another, in so far as this may be possible, with the truth of Christ and also with the truth of humanism and reason. For faith cannot be preserved if reason goes under, and the Church cannot survive if man is destroyed: that is to say if his humanity is utterly debased and mechanized, while he himself remains on earth as the instrument of enormous and unidentified forces like those which press us inexorably to the brink of cataclysmic war.

Yes, we should try to understand [Fidel] Castro together. This is a significant and portentous phenomenon, and it has many aspects. Not the least, of course, is the fact that Castro is now about to become a figure with a hundred heads all over Latin America. One aspect of it that I see is the embitterment and disillusionment of the well-intentioned man who was weak and passionate and easily abused: perhaps mentally sick. The man who like all of us wanted to find a third way, and was immediately swallowed up by one of the two giants that stand over all of us. The United States could have helped him and could indeed have saved him: but missed its chance. Castro remains not as a knife pointed at the U.S. but as a big question mark in the very foundations of North America's "democracy." I do not know if I sent you the letter about the Giants ["A Letter to Pablo Antonio Cuadra Concerning Giants"], but perhaps I did. It may be on a boat somewhere. You will tell me what you think of it.

It is indeed supremely necessary for us to try to think together a little of the Church in the Americas. This is an enormous obligation. There is much activity but not so much thought, and in any case the activity may have come late. I do not know what I can contribute, but the issue has been close to my heart for several years. I have thought much of it and prayed much also.

As for yourself, tell me anything you want, and I will reply as I can: but perhaps the mere fact that I will listen to you with all my heart may itself be of some help. We are all nearing the end of our work. The night is falling upon us, and we find ourselves without the serenity and fulfillment that were the lot of our fathers. I do not think this is necessarily a sign that anything is lacking, but rather is to be taken as a greater incentive to trust more fully in the mercy of God, and to advance further into His mystery. Our faith can no longer serve merely as a happiness pill. It has to be the Cross and the Resurrection of Christ. And this it will be, for all of us who so desire.

4. To M.S. [Maynard Shelly], Newton, Kans. [December 1961]

Thank you for your kind letter of Nov. 14. I am looking forward to receipt of the copy of *The Mennonite* [edited by Maynard Shelly] which contains my poem about the extermination camps ["Chant to be Used in Processions around a Site with Furnaces"]. I am happy that you saw fit to use it and am proud to appear in your magazine.

Certainly it is most necessary for all to realize that the terrible situation in the world today is a vivid sign in which the mercy of God seeks to spell out the truth of our sins and win us to repentance. The agonizing thing is to see how inexorably all mankind, even with the best and most honest of intentions, remain blind and indifferent to the light which is offered them. If we only knew how to read the "signs of the times." It seems that even the faithful who have sincerely clung to the Gospel truth, and are not just Christians for social reasons and for prestige, have lost their sensitivity to these things. I am personally deeply shocked and grieved by the way many of my fellow Catholics, including priests, seem to take it for granted that nuclear war against Russia is permitted as a "lesser evil." It is unbearable, in such a connection, to hear echoes of the voice of Caiphas who thought also that deicide was a "lesser evil," that one man might perish for the people. What has become of us, and what will become of us, now that we are so desperately blind? At least we have been promised that "for the sake of the elect those times will be shortened" [Matthew 24:22].

Surely we ought to see now that repentance means something far deeper than we have suspected: it can no longer be a matter of setting things right according to the norms of our own small group, the immediate society in which we live. We have to open our heart to a universal and all-embracing love that knows no limits and no obstacles, a love that is not scandalized by the sinner, a love that takes upon itself the sins of the world. There must be total love of all, even of the most distant, even of the most hostile. Without the gift of the Holy Spirit this is mere idealism, mere dreaming. But the Spirit who knows all things and can do all things, He can be in us the power of love that heals, unites, and redeems, for thus the Blood of Jesus Christ reaches all men through us.

It is with these thoughts in mind that I tell you what respect and reverence I have for the Mennonite tradition of peaceful action and non-violence. Though not a total pacifist in theory myself, I certainly believe that every Christian should try to practice non-violence rather than violence and that some should bind themselves to follow only the way of peace as an example to the others. I myself as a monk do not believe it would be licit for me ever to kill another human being even in self-defense and I would certainly never attempt to do so. There are much greater and truer ways than this. Killing achieves nothing. Finally, though as I said in theory I would still admit some persons might licitly wage war to defend themselves (for instance the Hungarians in 1956), yet I think that nuclear war is out of the question, it is beyond all doubt murder and sin, and it must be banned forever. Since in practice any small war is likely to lead to nuclear war, I therefore believe in practice that war must be absolutely banned and abolished today as a method of settling international disputes.

5. To E.F. [Erich Fromm], Mexico City [December 1961]

I am deeply grateful for your two letters, and glad to hear the new book [*May Man Prevail*] is coming along so well. Indeed it is to some extent heartening that there is such a current of sanity welling up on all sides. Yet not as encouraging as it might be, because though people in general have preserved a great deal of the old energy and health in striving for a society based on truth, the sickness is awfully deep-rooted, and most of all in those who make everybody move in the direction they want. I am more and more baffled by the mystery of this great insidious force that has the whole world by the neck and is forcing it under water in spite of all its good and self-preservative reactions. The situation certainly makes the psalms we chant in choir each day most eloquent. Erich, I am a complete Jew as far as that goes: I am steeped in that experience of bafflement, compunction, and wonder which is the experience of those who have been rescued from tyranny only to renounce freedom and in confusion and subjection to worse tyrants, through infidelity to the Lord. For only in His service is there true freedom, as the prophets would tell us. This is still the clear experience of the Jews, as it ought to be of the Christians, except that we were too sure of our freedom and too sure we could never alienate it. Alas, for hundreds of years we have disregarded our sonship of God and now the whole world is reaping the consequences. If only Christians had valued the freedom of the sons of God that was given them. They preferred safety and the Grand Inquisitor.

The Catholics in the peace movement we are now starting are not the most influential in the country by any means, quite the contrary. Some of us are of an already notoriously pacifist group, the Catholic Worker, tolerated by all as a sign that we can find a mansion for beats in the Church as well as for the respectable. There are a few priests, no bishops. The English

Catholics are more articulate. There is a fine little book which I hope to include in toto in the paperback, by Catholic intellectuals in England, edited by Walter Stein, Merlin Press . . . It is called *Nuclear Weapons and Christian Conscience.*[4] You would like it, and will see it in the book if I can get permission.

Incidentally we very much want you to send us the article you are finishing now for *Commentary* [on civil defense].[5] That would be much better for our purpose anyway than the *Daedalus* one, though we do need a good piece on disarmament. Can you suggest any? What we lack is a good article on the positive and constructive side, a suggestion for a possible policy of peace, what to *do*.

Today I received a curious letter from a priest in Italy to whom I had sent an article on Christian pacifism and the obligation to resist this pressure towards war and disaster. He sent it back, or rejected it for the magazine to which I had sent it, saying that in Italy there was a kind of war psychosis and everybody was easily depressed by this sort of thing and it was better to keep them optimistic by showing them the bright side. I am not condemning him, because they have been through horrors I have been spared, and they are doubtless quite aware that they can do nothing themselves, for they cannot change our policies. Yet I am disturbed by this prevalent attitude in Europe. I wrote a poem about Auschwitz ["Chant to be Used in Processions around a Site with Furnaces"] which was just the truth, awful as it is. A good French Jesuit friend of mine simply couldn't read it, and another told me that a Jewish friend of his who had been in the camps would never write like that, but would just turn to love "stressing the positive side of things." I am perfectly willing to admit that when things have a definitely positive side to them, it should be stressed. They told Jeremiah to stress the positive side of things, too. It seems to me that there has never been such a black

---

[4] First published in England in 1961, this book was published in the United States under the title *Nuclear Weapons, A Catholic Response* (New York: Sheed and Ward, 1962).

[5] Merton included "The Question of Civil Defense: A Reply to Herman Kahn" by Erich Fromm and Michael Macoby in *Breakthrough to Peace: Twelve Views on the Threat of Thermonuclear Extermination* (New York: New Directions, 1962).

avalanche of negation in human society, and that if there is evil someone should point to it. It is not that I mind sentimental people telling me I am a pessimist, but people whose judgment I otherwise respect in many ways say I am too much of a pessimist. Perhaps there is much in what they say, but at the same time I cannot feel quite easy with the attitude of so many Christians, priests and monks included, who at the present time are totally occupied in small points of patristic theology, of liturgy, of changing forms of observances, etc. Nor can I be satisfied with the happy making attitude of my friend's magazine in Italy. There the whole idea is to stress the warm, expansive, positive aspect of Catholic life, the charity, the fraternal unity of Catholic actionists, their hopeful approach to problems: but what problems? Secondary ones mostly. Or if they approach the big ones, it is in a secondary sort of way. "There ought to be peace." In the long run I find the whole thing smells slightly of the engineering of consent we are used to over here. The creation of the hopeful image, the optimistic cover story.

Again, I think people have wholly failed to take into account the objectively evil force (I say objectively with reservations, meaning that it transcends subjective good will), which makes use of and manipulates the best intentions of optimists and turns them to evil, in spite of the hopeful image they have created for themselves. I would call this for want of a better word a demonic force. People ignore it completely because they know that they themselves, subjectively, want only "the good." They do not realize that the good they want is rooted in negation and injustice, that it depends on the vast cruelty of an alienated society that is *kept* alienated with deliberation.

The other possibility is that by being "pessimistic" and looking at the dark side, pointing to the evil, I am only helping the process of evil along by collaborating with it, getting people used to it in some new way, perhaps even my pessimism equals a kind of acceptance of the worst disasters as a foregone conclusion when there is still a clear way out. All these questions float about in my mind, but my personal conviction is that when everybody else in my Church (except the Popes who have after all spoken quite clearly condemning nuclear annihilation bombing) seems to want to stay silent and perplexed, or worse still encourages nuclear war as the "lesser evil," it has become my clear duty to speak out against this crime and to denounce the steps taken to perpetuate it, while refusing all cooperation and trying to get others to do the same. If there is anything positive I can do, I wish I knew what it is. Any suggestions you have will always be welcome.

The poem of [Yevgeny] Yevtushenko ["Babi Yar"] moved me very deeply.[6] I have already come in contact with him, and this poem represents a distinct growth. It is a great crime when, in our day, so many men are feeling in their hearts this warm and profound need for identification with "the stranger" everywhere, governments should deliberately stifle the little spark of human love and enlist all our psychic energies to fill their mass movements, perverting and crushing our souls when they could and should grow so freely and so well. It is a world in which there could and should be a universal state, and if the men who made the policies wanted it, a world government could be created. They don't want it. What can you do?

6. To J.T.E. [Msgr. John Tracy Ellis], Washington, D.C. [December 7, 1961]

The thing that strikes me is that at a time where there are formidable and very basic issues at stake, some of our official minds can waste time and create confusion over things that are quite secondary: and yet thereby divert valuable energies that could go into more constructive work. It is absolutely crucial for the Church in America to have enough freedom of movement to deal with the unique and large problems of our country in a healthy and productive way. As you know, one of the things that

---

[6] Yevtushenko's poem commemorated the victims of a Nazi massacre at Babi Yar, a ravine outside of Kiev, in Ukraine, in September 1941. Yevtushenko emphasized the fact that 33,000 Jews were among the nearly 100,000 victims, thus challenging official Soviet policy of the time to make no distinction between Jewish victims and other Soviet citizens. As a result Yevtushenko's poem became a *cause célèbre*. This and his outspoken criticism of the Stalinist legacy led, in 1963, to his being banned from travel outside the Soviet Union.

most bothers me is the attitude of so many American Catholics to nuclear war. They make no distinction between out and out pacifism which refuses to serve even in a "just war" and the Christian obligation, pointed out by the recent Popes, to avoid the criminal tragedy of nuclear annihilation of civilian centers, even for the best of causes. Apparently much popular thought in this country simply goes along with the immoral and secularist attitude that since Communism is evil we can do anything we like to wipe it out and thus prevent it from gaining ground and overwhelming us. This awfully short-sighted and completely unchristian attitude may well result in complete disaster for the Church. For one thing, the result might be that Russia and the U.S. would knock themselves out and leave the whole world at the mercy of Red China. The west of Europe would of course evaporate into the bargain. What would be left of Christianity? What would be the attitude of conscientious non-Christians toward survivors of a Body that had urged such a crime in the name of religion? The hour seems to me to be extremely grave.

7. To L.F. [Lawrence Ferlinghetti], San Francisco, Calif. [December 1961]

J. [Laughlin] forwarded your letter to me, and I am sorry to hear that you have been sick. All my friends have been in hospitals, operated on, diagnosed as about to die, God alone knows what. We are all cashing in our chips, so it seems, except that for my part I am still standing, though hungry.

About the *Journal*[7]: don't think I was personally embarrassed by it. But as I rather expected, Fr. Abbot [Dom James Fox] took a good look at it and decided that from now on I am not to contribute any more to it. That is the only thing I regret. I admit that I am not much dazzled by the approach most of the writers take. I mean I can get along from page to page without getting swept off my feet with enthusiasm. Not that I am mad at dirty

---

[7] Merton's Auschwitz poem, "Chant to be Used in Processions around a Site with Furnaces," was published in the first issue of *Journal for the Protection of All Living Beings*.

words, they are perfectly good honest words as far as I am concerned, and they form part of my own interior mumblings a lot of the time, why not? I just wonder if this isn't another kind of jargon which is a bit more respectable than the jargon of the slick magazines, but not very much more. And I wonder just how much is actually *said* by it.

However, that is not what I mean, because I thought a lot of the stuff was real good, like especially the one about David Meltzer's baby getting born. This was fine. And a lot of good in the Robt Duncan, which I liked mostly. I liked very much your beautiful Haiti and best in the whole book was Nez Perce. So there. I haven't read the Camus yet but him I like always. Yet I don't think it was what one might have expected, as a lot of the material was not very near the target, and I am inclined to doubt the reality of the moral concern of a lot of these people who are articulate about the question of war in your *Journal*. And I think that is one reason why you can't get the other ones to commit themselves. I don't know if there is anything they are apt to mean about a problem as big as this. However, they are all much more human and more real than the zombies who have all kinds of facts about deterrence and finite deterrence and all out non-survivability and all in first strike ballistic preemption plus as distinguished from massive plus plus retaliation plus.

As regards the Christianity Buddhism thing[8]: both [D. T.] Suzuki and I ended up hanging in various trees among the birds' nests. I am not insisting upon anything, least of all affectivity. That remark was a journalistic kind of remark, referring to the way Christianity and Buddhism look to people who are very definite about being one or the other and very sure that the metaphysic of one excludes the metaphysic of the other. This is all quite probably so. But Zen is beyond metaphysics and so, as far as I am concerned, is the kind of Christian experience that seems to me most relevant, and which is found in [Meister] Eckhart and the Rhenish mystics and all the mystics for that matter. I agree theoretically that there is a complete division

---

[8] "Wisdom in Emptiness: A Dialogue between Daisetz T. Suzuki and Thomas Merton" first appeared in *New Directions in Prose and Poetry* 17, edited by James Laughlin (New York: New Directions, 1961), 65-101.

between the two approaches: one personalistic, dualistic, etc. the other non-dualistic. Only trouble is that Suzuki's very distinction between God and Godhead is dualistic, and his lineup of Buddha vs. Christ is also dualistic, and when he starts that he forgets his Zen. He can forget his Zen too if he wants to or has to, no law saying you have to remember your Zen every minute of the day. It seems to me the Cross says just as much about Zen, or just as little, as the serene face of the Buddha. Of course the historic, medieval concern with the expression of feeling and love in the Crucified Christ is nowhere near Zen, it is Bakhti or however you spell it [Bhakti], and that is another matter. But essentially the Crucifix is a non-image, a destroyed image, a wiped out image, a nothing, an annihilation. It just depends what you are looking at and who you are that looks at it. So the Zens say burn all the Buddhas, and they come out with the same thing in the end, as far as the destruction of the image is concerned.

What I do think matters is liberty. The complete freedom and unlimited, unrestricted quality of love, not its affectivity. This I think the Zens are after in their own way too, though more intellectual about it. And note that Zen is full of affectivity too, look at the Zen paintings: plenty compassion, humor, comment, all sorts of stuff which in the west we would frown at calling it literature.

8. To B.S. [Bruno P. Schlesinger], Notre Dame, Ind. [December 13, 1961]

I have taken a little time to get around to your letter of November 10th about the Program for Christian Culture at St. Mary's [College, Notre Dame, Indiana]. This is a very important question and I am afraid I will not entirely do justice to it, but at least I can set down a few thoughts that occur to me, and hope for the best.

First of all, the urgent need for Christian Humanism. I stress the word humanism, perhaps running the risk of creating wrong impressions. What is important is the fully Christian notion of man: a notion radically modified by the mystery of the

Incarnation. This I think is the very heart of the matter. And therefore it seems to me that a program of Christian culture needs to be rooted in the biblical notions of man as the object of divine mercy, and of special concern on the part of God, as the spouse of God, as, in some mysterious sense, an epiphany of the divine wisdom. Man in Christ. The New Adam, presupposing the Old Adam, presupposing the old paradise and the new paradise, the creation and the new creation.

At the present time man has ceased entirely to be seen as any of these. The whole Christian notion of man has been turned inside out; instead of paradise we have Auschwitz. But note that the men who went into the ovens at Auschwitz were still the same elect race, the object of the divine predilection . . . These perspectives are shattering, and they are vital for Christian culture. For then in the study of Europe and European Christianity, Latin Christianity, we come up against a dialectic of fidelity and betrayal, understanding and blindness. That we have come to a certain kind of "end" of the development of western Christianity is no accident, nor yet is it the responsibility of Christian culture, for Christian culture has precisely saved all that could be saved. Yet was this enough? These are terrible problems and I am sure no one can answer. In a word, perhaps we might profitably run the risk, at least those who are thinking about the course behind the scenes, not just of assuming that Christian culture is a body of perfections to be salvaged but of asking where there was infidelity and imperfection. And yet at the same time stressing above all the value and the supreme importance of our western Christian cultural heritage. For it is the survival of religion as an abstract formality without a humanist matrix, religion apart from man and almost in some sense apart from God Himself (God figuring only as a Lawgiver and not as a Savior), religion without any human epiphany in art, in work, in social forms: this is what is killing religion in our midst today, not the atheists. So that one who seeks God without culture and without humanism tends inevitably to promote a religion that is irreligious and even unconsciously atheistic.

It would seem that the a-cultural philistinism of our society were the preferred instrument of demonic forces to finally eviscerate all that is left of Christian humanism. I am thinking of an appalling item read in our refectory yesterday in which we were informed that at last religion was going to be put on the map in America by the "advertising industry." Here with a sublimely cynical complacency we were informed that now everybody would be urged in the most shallow, importunate, tasteless, and meaningless ways, that they had to go to some Church or Synagogue or conventicle of some sect. Just get into the nearest dam conventicle as fast as your legs can carry you, brother, and get on your knees and *worship*; we don't give a hoot how you do it or why you do it, but you got to get in there and worship, brother, because the advertising industry says so and it is written right here on the napkin in the place where you eat your fallout lettuce sandwich. Sorry if I sound like a beatnik, but this is what is driving intelligent people as far from Christianity as they can travel. Hence in one word a pretended Christianity without the human and cultural dimensions which *nature* herself has provided, in history, in social tradition, etc., our religion becomes a lunar landscape of meaningless gestures and observances. A false supernaturalism which theoretically admits that grace builds on nature and then proceeds to eliminate everything natural; there you have the result of forgetting our cultural and humanistic tradition.

To my mind it is very important that this experiment is being conducted in a Catholic women's college. This is to me a hopeful sign. I think women are perhaps capable of salvaging something of humanity in our world today. Certainly they have a better chance of grasping and understanding and preserving a sense of Christian culture. And of course I think the wisdom of Sister Madeleva, [C.S.C.], [President of St. Mary's College], has a lot to do with the effectiveness of this experiment and its future possibilities. The word wisdom is another key word, I suspect. We are concerned not just with culture but also with wisdom, above all.

Here I might mention someone who I think ought to be known and consulted as a choragos for our music, and that is Clement of Alexandria. In fact I think one might profitably concentrate a great deal of attention on the Alexandrian school, not only the Christians, but all that extraordinary complex of trends, the Jewish and Gnostic and neoplatonist, Philo above all, and then the desert Fathers too, just outside. And Origen. And the Palestinians who reacted against Alexandria, and the Antiocheans. Here we have a crucially important seed bed of future developments. How I wish I could be there to talk with you [about] all of this, and try to give conferences on it perhaps, but that is out of the question.

But the whole question of Christian culture is a matter of wisdom more than of culture. For wisdom is the full epiphany of God the Logos, or Tao, in man and the world of which man is a little exemplar. Wisdom does not reveal herself until man is seen as microcosm, and the whole world is seen in relation to the measure of man. It is this measure which is essential to Christian culture, and whatever we say or read it must always be remembered. I could develop this more, but have no time. I could refer you to a booklet that is being printed in a limited edition by Victor Hammer on this. I will ask him if perhaps he would consent to send the college a copy. If there is no end of money to spend on books, perhaps the library would want to buy it from him, as he only prints editions of fifty or sixty and makes his living on the proceeds. The booklet is my *Hagia Sophia*,[9] which might or might not have something to say that would be relevant. I hope I don't sound commercial, but probably do, alas.

Mark Van Doren was here talking about liberal education recently. He would be a good man to consult. He stresses the point that liberal education is that which frees an (adult) mind from the automatisms and compulsions of a sensual outlook. Here again we rejoin the Alexandrians and Greeks. The purpose of a Christian humanism should be to liberate man from the mere status of *animalis homo (sarkikos)* to at least the level of *rationalis (psychicos)* and better still, spiritual, Gnostic or pneumatic.

---

[9] Sixty-nine copies of the first limited edition of *Hagia Sophia* were numbered at the press (Lexington, Kentucky: Stamperia Santuccio, 1962). Merton included "Hagia Sophia" in *Emblems of a Season of Fury* (New York: New Directions, 1963), 61-69. The prose poem is reprinted in *The Collected Poems of Thomas Merton* (New York: New Directions, 1977), 363-372.

9. To J.R. [Archb. Thomas Roberts, S.J.], London
[December 1961]

First let me thank you for your kind letter of November 15th, and the copy of your letter to His Eminence. I do not have a totally clear picture of the situation, but clear enough to understand something of the essential problem, and to feel, with you, deep concern. For here, in this whole tormented problem in which we are all involved, and you more than most, it is not merely the rights of this or that person, but the honor and holiness of the Church as the guardian of truth and the minister of mercy and salvation to men. I have no hesitation in agreeing with you that I must expect a small amount of what has been visited on you. I think this is going to be the *only* visible fruit of most of our protests in favor of peace, honesty, truth, and fidelity to the Law of Christ. This is of course to me a shattering and totally disconcerting question, and I do not hesitate to admit to you that it reaches down into the very foundations of my life and, but for the grace of God, might shake them beyond repair.

Do you mind if I give you a little news of my own very small problems? As I may or may not have indicated, and as you certainly know very well: the situation in this country is extremely serious. It amounts in reality to a moral collapse, in which the policy of the nation is more or less frankly oriented toward a war of extermination. Everybody else claims not to "want" this, certainly. But step by step we come closer to it because the country commits itself more and more to policies which, but for a miracle, will make it inevitable.

This gradual progress is accepted with fatalistic indifference or ignored in a spirit of irresponsibility and passivity. The most scandalous thing of all, and this has been stated very explicitly by some few sane people who are still pointing to the danger, is that the Church and her clergy have been almost completely silent. In some cases, statements that have been made have tended rather to promote an atmosphere of hatred and irresponsibility, like the famous Fr. [L. C.] McHugh, of your Society [of Jesus], with his advice to take a revolver into your shelter with you and kill anyone else who tries to get it.[10] Such is the climate in which we are now living in America.

In this situation I have felt that it would be a matter of fidelity to my vocation as a Christian and as a priest, and by no means in contradiction with my state as a monk, to try to show clearly that our gradual advance towards nuclear war is morally intolerable and even criminal and that we have to take the most serious possible steps to realize our condition and do something about it.

The question is, what does one do?

At present my feeling is that the most urgent thing is to say what has to be said and say it in any possible way. If it cannot be printed, then let it be mimeographed. If it cannot be mimeographed, then let it be written on the backs of envelopes, as long as it gets said. But then of course, what is the purpose of saying things just for the sake of saying them, without the hope of their having any effect? Am I not reduced to doing what they demand of me, to sit in silence and make no protest?

I realize of course that if I were a holier person, if I had been more faithful to God's will all along the line, if I were less undermined by my own contradictions, I would have much more of the needed strength and clarity. Perhaps the Lord wants me to keep silence lest by my writing I do more harm than good. I don't know. And it seems impossible to get a clear idea of what ought to be done. One thing I do not do: try to tinker with the big machine. If it runs in its own inhuman inexorable way, that is the affair of the machine and the mechanics. I am not a mechanic and it is none of my business.

10. To E.K. [Ethel Kennedy], Washington, D.C. [December 1961]

I liked very much the president's speech at Seattle which encouraged me a bit as I had just written something along those same lines. The interview granted to Izvestia was great also. We

---

[10] In response to Fr. McHugh's "Ethics at the Shelter Doorway," published in the September 30, 1961, issue of *America,* Merton wrote "The Machine Gun in the Fallout Shelter," published in *The Catholic Worker* under the title "Shelter Ethics" in November 1961.

need more and more of that. Every form of healthy human contact with Russia and above all China is to be encouraged. We have got to see each other as people and not as demons. Today as I write the President is in South America. I hope all goes well. I am working on some projects to help further the cause of peace, and thought I might tell you of some of the ideas that have been crystallizing out as I do so.

It seems to me that the great problem we face is not Russia but war itself. War is the main enemy and we are not going to fully make sense unless we see that. Unless we fight war, both in ourselves and in the Russians, and wherever else it may be, we are purely and simply going to be wrecked by the forces that are in us. The great illusion is to assume that we are perfectly innocent, peace-loving and right while the communists are devils incarnate. I admit they are no angels and they have been guilty of some frightful crimes against humanity. They are without doubt a terrible menace, and a permanent one, to the safety and sanity of the human race. I admit also that we must not go to the extreme of condemning ourselves without reason. We have made mistakes and will make more of them, but I hope we can learn to be a bit more realistic about all that, as long as we avoid the biggest mistake of all: plunging the world into nuclear war by any deliberate decision of our own. I think also it is tremendously important for us to work out a collaborative control scheme with the USSR to check on various possible accidents that might trigger a nuclear war.

Why is war such a problem to us? I do not pretend to be able to give a reason for everything under the sun, but if I am to be consistent with my own experience and my religious beliefs, as well as with the crying evidence that is all around us, one main reason is our moral decline. As a nation we have begun to float off into a moral void and all the sermons of all the priests in the country (if they preach at all) are not going to help much. We have got to the point where the promulgation of any kind of moral standard automatically releases an anti-moral response in a whole lot of people. It is not with them above all that I am concerned, but with the "good" people, the right-thinking people, who stick to principle all right except where it conflicts with the chance to make a fast buck. It seems to me that there are very dangerous ambiguities about our democracy in its actual present condition. I wonder to what extent our ideals are now a front for organized selfishness and systematic irresponsibility. The shelter business[11] certainly brought out the fact that some Americans are not too far from the law of the jungle. If our affluent society ever breaks down and the façade is taken away, what are we going to have left? Suppose we do have a war, and fifty million people are left to tell the tale: what kind of people are they going to be? What kind of a life will they live? By what standards? We cannot go on living every man for himself. The most actual danger of all is that we may some day float without realizing it into a nice tight fascist society in which all the resentments and all the guilt in all the messed-up teenagers (and older ones) will be channeled in a destructive groove.

This may sound pretty awful. You know of course that I am not trying to sit back and judge the whole country. These things are in every human being, and they have always been, and will be. But I feel strongly that in the condition in which we now live there is no adequate control for these unpleasant and dangerous forces, and that people are much too ready to give up trying to control them rationally, in order to line up with some kind of a group that will provide an "outlet," along with guns, uniforms, and a special kind of salute.

The President [John F. Kennedy] can certainly do more than any one man to counteract this by word and example, by doing everything that can help salvage the life of reason, by maintaining respect for intelligence and humanist principles without which freedom is only a word.

It think it is going to be of greatest importance, in the next few months and years, if Americans can regain their healthy respect for reason, for the light of intellect, and get rid of this shallow contempt for "eggheads." They must learn to respect thought and stop idolizing psychopathic goofs. God knows, this is going to take a miracle. There are plenty of wise and sane men in the country, and they are able to be articulate. They can do a tremendous amount. I think for example of the group out of Santa Barbara, the Center for the Study of Democratic

---

[11] See footnote 10 above.

Institutions.[12] They have done a lot of serious and enlightened work. They can do much more.

There are people around like Senator [J. William] Fulbright who, it seems to me, has the right kind of ideas and works courageously in the right direction. But you can't do that without being regarded as a Red. The people who fail to see the value of our best liberal traditions, and who attack every moderate as a fifth columnist, are the ones who are really undermining the country and preparing it for ruin, if anyone is.

Anyway, these are not easy times to live in, and there are no easy answers. I think the fact that the President works overtime at trying to get people to face the situation as it really is may be the greatest thing he is doing. Certainly our basic need is for truth, and not for "images" and slogans that "engineer consent." We are living in a dream world. We do not know ourselves or our adversaries. We are myths to ourselves and they are myths to us. And we are secretly persuaded that we can shoot it out like the sheriffs on TV. This is not reality and the President can do a tremendous amount to get people to see the facts, more than any single person. If he can get the country to face reality and accept it and try to cope with it on a sober basis, without expecting miracles at every turn, we may begin to get ourselves together. But for this one has to have motives and principles, and that is just what too many people have thrown overboard.

I personally wish the Church in America and everywhere were more articulate and definite about nuclear war. Statements of Pius XII have left us some terribly clear principles about this. We cannot go on indefinitely relying on the kind of provisional framework of a balance of terror. If as Christians we were more certain of our duty, it might put us in a very tight spot politically but it would also merit for us special graces from God, and these we need badly.

---

[12] Wilbur H. Ferry, to whom Merton addressed four of the Cold War Letters, served as vice-president of the Center for the Study of Democratic Institutions from 1954 to 1969.

11. To D.D. [Dorothy Day], New York [December 20, 1961]

I have read your latest "On Pilgrimage" in the December CW [*The Catholic Worker*] and I want to say how good I think it is. In many ways I think it is about the best thing I have seen that came out of this whole sorry shelter business. What you say in the beginning is clear and uncontrovertible. You make one unanswerable point after another, though I don't claim that people are not going to answer you and some may get quite hot about the fact that you want to point out that [Fidel] Castro may have had good intentions and have been in actual fact less wicked than our mass media want him to have been. People who are scared and upset use a very simple logic, and they think that if you defend Castro as a human being you are defending all the crimes that have ever been committed by Communism anywhere, and they feel that you are threatening them.

But as Christians we have to keep on insisting on the distinction between the man, the person, and the actions and policies attributed to him and his group. We have to remember the terrible danger of projecting on to others all the evil we find in ourselves, so that we justify our desire to hate that evil and to destroy it in them.

The basic thing in Christian ethics is to look at the *person* and not at the *nature*. That is why natural law so easily degenerates, in practice and in casuistry, to jungle law which is no law at all. Because when we consider "nature" we consider the general, the theoretical, and forget the concrete, the individual, the personal reality of the one confronting us. Hence we can see him not as our other self, not as Christ, but as our demon, our evil beast, our nightmare. This, I am afraid, is what a wrong, unintelligent, and unchristian emphasis on natural law has done.

Persons are known not by the intellect alone, not by principles alone, but only by love. It is when we love the other, the enemy, that we obtain from God the key to an understanding of who he is, and who we are. It is only this realization that can open to us the real nature of our duty, and of right action.

To *shut out* the person and to refuse to consider him as a person, as an other self, we resort to the impersonal "law" and "nature." That is to say we block off the reality of the other, we cut the intercommunication of our nature and his nature, and we consider only our own nature with its rights, its claims, its demands. And we justify the evil we do to our brother because he is no longer a brother; he is merely an adversary, an accused.

To restore communication, to see our oneness of nature with him, and to respect his personal rights and his integrity, his worthiness of love, we have to see ourselves as similarly accused along with him, condemned to death along with him, sinking into the abyss with him, and needing, with him, the ineffable gift of grace and mercy to be saved. Then instead of pushing him down, trying to climb out by using his head as a stepping stone for ourselves, we help ourselves to rise by helping him to rise. When we extend our hand to the enemy who is sinking in the abyss, God reaches out for both of us, for it is He first of all who extends our hand to the enemy. It is He who "saves himself" in the enemy who makes use of us to recover the lost groat which is His image in our enemy.

It is all too true that when many theologians talk about natural law, they are talking about jungle law. And this is not law at all. It is not natural either. The jungle is not natural. Or rather, perhaps the true primeval life is natural in a higher sense than we realize. The "jungles" which are our cities are worse than jungles, they are sub-jungles, and their law is a sub-jungle law, a sub-sub natural law. And here I refer not to those who are considered the lowest in society, but rather those who exercise power in the jungle city, and use it unscrupulously and inhumanly, whether on the side of "law and order" or against law and order.

And yet, as a priest and as one obligated by my state to preach and explain the truth, I cannot take occasion from this abusive view of natural law to reject the concept altogether. On the contrary, if I contemn and reject *en bloc* all the ethical principles which appeal to the natural law, I am in fact undercutting the Gospel ethic at the same time. It is customary to go through the Sermon on the Mount and remark on the way it appears *to contrast with* the mosaic law and the natural law. On the contrary, it seems to me that the Sermon on the Mount is not only a supernatural fulfillment of the natural law, but an affirmation of "nature" in the true, original Christian meaning: of nature as assumed by Christ in the Incarnation. As a remote basis for this, we might consider Colossians 1:9-29, noting especially that we humans who were at enmity with one another are "reconciled in the body of His flesh." Christ the Lord is the Word Who has assumed our nature, which is one in all of us. He has perfectly fulfilled and so to speak transfigured and elevated not only nature and the natural law which is, in its most basic expression, treating our brother as one who has the same nature as we have. Now here is the point where our ethical speculation has gone off the rails. In the biblical context, in the context of all spiritual and ancient religions that saw this kind of truth, the good which man must do and the evil he must avoid according to the natural law must be based on an experience or a realization of connaturality with our brother.

Example: if I am in a fallout shelter and trying to save my life, I must see that the neighbor who wants to come in to the shelter also wants to save his life as I do. I must experience his need and his fear just as if it were my need and my fear. This is not supernatural at all, it is purely and simply the basis of the natural law, which of course has been elevated and supernaturalized. But it is per se natural. If then I experience my neighbor's need as my own, I will act accordingly, and if I am strong enough to act out of love, I will cede my place in the shelter to him. This I think is possible, at least theoretically, even on the basis of natural love. In fact personally I am sure it is. But at the same time there is the plentiful grace of God to enable us to do this.

Now, to approach casuistry: if the person who threatens the life of my children, say, is raving mad: I have a duty to protect my children, it may be necessary to restrain the berserk guy by force . . . etc. But my stomach revolts at the casuistical approach to a question like this at a time like this.

My point is this, rather, that I don't think we ought to simply discard the concept of the natural law as irrelevant. On the contrary I think it is very relevant once it is properly understood. Matthew 5:21-26 is, to my way of thinking, a vindication of human nature because it is a *restoration* of human nature. I admit that this view of nature is perhaps not that of the scholastics but rather that of the Greek Fathers. But it is to my way of thinking more natural, more in accord with the nature of man, to be non-violent, to be not even angry with his brother, to not say "raca," etc. But we cannot recover this fullness of nature without the grace of God.

In this peculiar view, then, the natural law is not merely what is ethically right and fitting for fallen man considered purely in his fallen state: it is the law of his nature as it came to him from the hand of God, the law imprinted in his nature by the image of God, which each man is and must be in his very nature. Hence the natural law is the law which inclines our inmost heart to conform to the image of God which is in the deepest center of our being, and it also inclines our heart to respect and love our neighbor as the image of God. But this concept of nature is only comprehensible when we see that it presupposes grace and calls for grace and as it were sighs and groans for grace. For actually our contradiction with ourselves makes us realize that without grace we are lost.

In a word, then, I want with my whole heart to fulfill in myself this natural law, in order by that to fulfill also the law of grace to which it leads me. And I want with my whole heart to realize and fulfill my communion of nature with my brother, in order that I may be by that very fact one with him in Christ. But here, as I said in the beginning, I must rise above nature, I must *see the person* (this is still possible to nature "alone") and I must see the person in Christ, in the Spirit.

12. To E.D. [Edward Deming Andrews], Pittsfield, Mass. [December 21, 1961]

Forgive please this very long delay in thanking you for the copy of *Shaker Furniture* which will remain a highly valued possession in the novitiate library. I believe it is of the highest importance for the novices to see these things, and get used to this wonderful simplicity. This wordless simplicity, in which the works of quiet and holy people speak humbly for themselves. How important that is in our day when we are flooded with a tidal wave of meaningless words: and worse still when in the void of those words the sinister power of hatred and destruction is at work. The Shakers remain as witnesses to the fact that only humility keeps man in communion with truth, and first of all with his own inner truth. This one must know without knowing it, as they did. For as soon as a man becomes aware of "his truth" he lets go of it and embraces an illusion.

I am so glad you liked [the translation of] Clement [of Alexandria]. If it ever gets printed, I will gladly send you a copy.[13] New Directions is not in a hurry to decide because we are working on a more urgent project, a book of articles against nuclear war [*Breakthrough to Peace* (New York: New Directions, 1962)].

Speaking of Clement and Alexandria, you know of Philo Judaeus, the Jewish Platonist who flourished in that city. He has a very intriguing book, *De Therapeutis* (which I have not yet found and read). In this book he speaks of Jewish monastic communities in Egypt in which there are some similarities with the Shakers. Particularly the fact that they were contemplative communities of men and women, living separately and joining in worship, though separated by a partition. It would seem there might be many interesting facts in this book, and I recommend it to your curiosity. Alexandria remains a fascinating place, and I am sure that more study of the intellectual and spiritual movements that flourished there will prove very rewarding.

13. To J.C. [Msgr. Josiah G. Chatham], Jackson, Miss. [December 1961]

I think that in this awful issue of nuclear war there is involved much more than the danger of physical evil. The Lord knows that is enormous enough. What concerns me, perhaps this is pride, is the ghastly feeling that we are all on the brink of a spiritual defection and betrayal of Christ, which would consist in the complete acceptance of the values and the decisions of the callous men of war who think only in terms of mega-corpses and

---

[13] This letter of Merton to E. D. Andrews is one of thirty-five Cold War Letters that Merton included in *Seeds of Destruction* (New York: Farrar, Straus and Giroux, 1964). In *Seeds*, Merton notes that he is speaking of the translation of Clement. For the translation and Merton's accompanying essay, see *Clement of Alexandria: Selections from the Protreptikos* (New York: New Directions, 1962).

megatons, and have not the slightest thought for man, the image of God.

I know the moral theologians are very wise in their circumspect avoidance of self-commitment to anything but very "safe" positions. But all of a sudden it seems to me that these safe positions yawn wide open and where they open is right into the depths of hell. That is not what I call safety. The German clergy, the German Catholic press, even the German bishops, some of them, got in there behind Hitler and said that his war was just. They urged all the faithful to give the Vaterland everything they had. This they did in order, in some measure, to try to keep peace with a tyrant who threatened to destroy the Church. Their action did nothing whatever to keep men like Fr. [Max] Metzger from being executed,[14] or to save hundreds of priests and religious from Dachau. How much can we trust our moral theologians in a context like that? How much can we trust men who complacently urge the faithful to go along with these disastrous preparations that will involve the murder of millions of innocent and helpless people on both sides? The word murder is not exaggerated. The Popes have practically used it, and have used very strong language urging us to do everything to preserve peace. But because it is possible to assert that they have not condemned nuclear war, we can simply ignore all this, we think, and we can go along with the secular forces that sweep us irresistibly over the falls. And no one raises his voice. This is the frightful scandal to people outside the Church, and to very intelligent and responsible and wise people, people who are to my mind *naturaliter Christiani.* Certainly when the Patriarch of Moscow or rather his representative takes advantage of his position in the World Council of Churches to get in a few licks for the Red foreign policy and back it up with a swing at the Vatican, we have no difficulty in seeing that the Russian Church is in some measure sold out to the Kremlin, though there is still a tremendous amount of good in the heroic Russian Orthodox Christians who have held on.

---

[14] Father Max Metzger was executed by the Nazis in 1943. See Merton's "Testament to Peace: Father Metzger's Thoughts about the Duty of the Christian," first published in *Jubilee* in March 1962 and reprinted in *Passion for Peace: The Social Essays,* edited by William H. Shannon (New York: Crossroad, 1995), 53-55.

You will say that the whole problem is terribly complex, that there are no simple solutions, that we have to be realistic, and that at the moment there is no alternative to a policy based on this threat of nuclear extermination. Maybe. But we have got to get busy and find an alternative, and act as if there were a possible alternative, or else it is going to be too bad for us not only physically but even morally. One does not have to have the explicit intention of becoming a war criminal in order to be one. One just has to do what is flagrantly unjust and wrong, no matter for what good end. The Church of the Crucified Christ cannot be saved from disaster by murder. Even if it could be, we are not allowed to resort to it.

I just cannot in conscience, as a priest and a writer who has a hearing with a lot of people, devote myself exclusively to questions of devotion, the life of prayer, or monastic history, and act as if we were not in the middle of the most serious crisis in Christian history. It is to me incomprehensible that so many other writers and theologians and what not simply ignore this question, or, if they treat it, do so in a manner that encourages people to line up with a frankly godless and pragmatic power bloc, the immense wealth and technical capacity of which is directed entirely to nuclear annihilation of entire nations, without distinction between civilians and combatants.

14. To E.G. [Etta Gullick], Oxford [December 22, 1961]

This new book on Gregory of Nyssa by Danielou and Musurillo[15] has been sent me for review by Scribners. I wonder if it is published in England. It is excellent, as far as I have gone with it. A good clear introduction by Danielou and plenty of the best texts, though unfortunately they are all from the old Migne edition and not from the new critical edition of Werner Jaegher. I am sure your friend there will know about this. I hope to do an article on it. As for the man who said my essay on the desert

---

[15] From *Glory to Glory: Texts from Gregory of Nyssa's Mystical Writings,* edited by Jean Danielou and Herbert Musurillo (New York: Charles Scribner's Sons, 1961).

fathers[16] was not "sufficiently Eastern," well, is there any reason why it should be "Eastern"? Is it not enough that I am a Westerner who has some appreciation of the East? Since when does a person have to climb out of his own skin and put on that of somebody else? This is the kind of nonsense that is prevalent everywhere in the Church, I regret to say: people conforming to their little party lines and to the slogans of their movements for this and that. Let us not lose our perspective. It will not help the reunion of East and West if everybody in the west becomes eastern and everybody in the east, then, logically, becomes western. All that is needed is for us to really reach a deep understanding of one another.

The question of peace is important, it seems to me, and so important that I do not believe anyone who takes his Christian faith seriously can afford to neglect it. I do not mean to say that you have to swim out to Polaris submarines carrying a banner between your teeth, but it is absolutely necessary to take a serious and articulate stand on the question of nuclear war. And I mean against nuclear war. The passivity, the incoherence of so many Christians on this issue, and worse still the active belligerency of some religious spokesmen, especially in this country, is rapidly becoming one of the most frightful scandals in the history of Christendom. I do not mean these words to be in any sense a hyperbole. The issue is very grave.

It is also, of course, very complex. Certainly I do not say that to be a Christian one must be a pacifist. And indeed there is the awful obstacle that in some schools of thought a Catholic "cannot be a conscientious objector." This is still open to debate even on the theoretical plane. In practice, since there is every reason to doubt the justice of a nuclear war and since a Christian is not only allowed but obliged to refuse participation in an unjust war, there is certainly every reason why a person may on the grounds of conscience refuse to support any measure that leads to nuclear war, or even to a policy of deterrence.

I do think you ought to read something about it. A book put out by the Merlin Press in London, and edited by Walter Stein,

---

[16] See *The Wisdom of the Desert: Sayings from the Desert Fathers of the Fourth Century* (New York: New Directions, 1961).

a professor at Leeds, is very solid. There is a really good essay by a professor or whatever you call a lady-don at Somerville, G.E.M. Anscombe. Do you know her? I think her contribution to this book makes a world of sense. The book is *Nuclear Weapons and Christian Conscience* [New York: Sheed and Ward, 1962]. I hope to use all the material in a collection I am editing here [*Breakthrough to Peace* (New York: New Directions, 1962)]. There will be a lot of other things, too, by people like Lewis Mumford, whom you must have read at one time or other.

What is worst about the Catholic silence on this subject (the Popes have certainly spoken out) is the idea that moral theology *obligates* one, almost, to take the lowest and most secularized position. We have actually got to the point where moralists are almost saying in so many words that the Sermon on the Mount is unchristian and that the Christian way of "sacrifice" is to bow one's neck under the sweet yoke of pharaoh. This, I submit, is going pretty far and it smells somewhat of sulphur.

One would certainly wish that the Catholic position on nuclear war was held as strict as the Catholic position on birth control. It seems a little strange that we are so wildly exercised about the "murder" (and the word is of course correct) of an unborn infant by abortion, or even the prevention of conception which is hardly murder, and yet accept without a qualm the extermination of millions of helpless and innocent adults, some of whom may be Christians and even our friends rather than our enemies. I submit that we ought to fulfill the one without omitting the other.

Enough of this unpleasant topic, but I feel that it is quite necessary to speak plainly. It is impossible not to be in some way involved in the evil, but we must be very careful that we are not passively involved, or willingly involved: but that we are doing what we can to disengage ourselves from cooperation in mass murder and to remain Christian in so far as this is possible when so many issues are muddled and obscure.

15. To J.B. [Jeanne Burdick], Topeka, Kans. [December 26, 1961]

What I said about the disinterested love of God represented my interest, at that time, in the medieval Platonic tradition, running through Sts. Augustine and Duns Scotus, and including the Cistercian monks. A monastery is supposed to be a "school of charity" (i.e. disinterested love). A school of *agape* rather than *eros*. Disinterested love is also called the "love of friendship," that is to say a love which rests in the good of the beloved, not in one's own interest or satisfaction, not in one's own pleasure. A love which does not exploit, manipulate, even by "serving," but which simply "loves." A love which, in the words of St. Bernard, simply "loves because it loves" and for no other reason or purpose, and is therefore perfectly free. This is a spiritual ideal which also has secular counterparts in the courtly love of the Provençal poets, and there is a whole interesting literary tradition, which finally gets lost in the sand.

The ideal of disinterested love is one that in one form or other crops up in all mystical religion. It is, in a very intellectual form, found in the offprint on Zen which I sent you. It is found in wonderfully rich and charming human expression in the mysticism of the Hassidim, Jewish tzaddiks of Poland and Central Europe. (Read [Martin] Buber)

The way I would express it now, is in purely religious and symbolic terms. That we should "love God" not merely to convince ourselves that we are good people, or to get a warm glow of peace, or to fit in with an approving group, or to get rid of anxiety, but to throw all that to the winds, and anxiety or not, even though we realize the utter depth of our inadequacy, to realize that this simply does not matter in the "eyes of God" for, as we are, with our misfortunes and needs, "we are His joy" and He delights to be loved by us with perfect confidence in Him because He is love itself. This is of course not capable of being put in scientific language, it is religious symbol. But if you will be patient with it, and stay with it, I think you will find it is the most fundamental symbol and the deepest truth: at least I am trying to express that which is deepest and most essential. My own symbol may be very poor. But that is the way I would put it. It is not that we have to sweat and groan to placate an austere Father God in our own imagination, but rather to realize, with liberation and joy, that *He is not that at all.* That in fact He is none of our idols, none of our figments, nothing that we can imagine anyway, but that He is Love Itself. And if we realize this and love Him simply and purely in order to "please Him," we become as it were His "crown" and His "delight" and life itself is transformed in this light which is disinterested love.

Freud did not think much of mysticism which was described as "an oceanic feeling" and I think in a way he was rather right in his suspicion of it, though he was a great old puritan that man! Oceanic feeling is not something that has to be rejected just because it might suggest a danger of narcissism. But pure love, disinterested love, is far beyond the reach of narcissism and I think even old Freud would have caught on that this was an equivalent of mature and oblative love in the ordinary psychophysical sphere.

I hope these few words from me will be of some help. The rest may be found perhaps in the offprint.[17] Suzuki is an interesting and splendid mind, and a great Buddhist. And I enjoyed trying to keep up with his Zen, which after all does have some parallel in the western tradition. Disinterested love opens a way to the understanding of both.

16. To R.L. [Robert Lax], New York [December 1961]

Here is at my side your exceedingly ribald Christmas card in many foreign languages inciting to joy.

Here without feet running in the sand or on the burning deck beneath the whips here amid the wolves we meditate on joyeux noel.

Here with the ship of state already half submerged and with waters up to beard standing nobly in the tottering captain's bridge.

---

[17] "Wisdom in Emptiness: A Dialogue between Daisetz T. Suzuki and Thomas Merton," *New Directions in Prose and Poetry* 17, edited by James Laughlin (New York: New Directions, 1961). The essay was reprinted in *Zen and the Birds of Appetite* (New York: New Directions, 1968).

We Santa Claus salute you.

Jubilee should move to Chile, or to Tierra del Fuego. There is joy, if also hunger and cold, in Tierra del Fuego. There is no need to live in a hole in Tierra del Fuego, though perhaps there also a two week hole would maybe turn out useful. Here I am told on good authority the guys who go down into the holes they will find that while they crank the hand blower the blower will be melted by the heat of the firestorms. Some fallout shelter.

Did you hear about the scientist who built himself a very fine fallout shelter for thirty dollars made out of railroad ties and along came an ordinary every day grass fire which burned out his house and garage and gutted his scientific shelter. It seems to me that there must be a moral in this somewhere. It seems to me that there must be a moral in a lot of the funny things that people are saying somewhere. But the noise of the announcers leaves no more time or peace to hunt for a moral.

If *Jubilee* moves to Chile and if *Pax* moves to Chile there will be no more purpose in wearing yourselves out putting out a magazine. This also has its advantages as any editor can readily see. You can spend most of your time dancing in the mists, while of course being very careful not to slip off the rocks into the perpetually wintry sea. You may occasionally visit the seals and sea-lions. You may light your houses with lamps of whale blubber. You may write poems in Fuegian. There will be little reason to do much else. But this at least has its points.

Well let's see what is the news of the monastery? Today on the Feast of the Holy Innocents, Father Innocent got up and preached a sermon all about Sartre and generally quite favorable, whereas he was expected to preach rather on the Holy Innocents. This met with some disfavor and I believe that Fr. Innocent is about to be immolated in one way or another. Of Fr. Innocent, a wise Benedictine once said, *"Nomen est omen,"* but he didn't know the half of it. Fr. Innocent hasn't read Sartre any more than anybody else around here and kept calling him "Sarter." Anyway it was an interesting sermon and nobody slept. Apart from that all that has happened is a great controversy about this year's Christmas Crib which looks more like the window of Bonwit Tellers than like the window of a third avenue pawnshop.

The guys at the Catholic Worker have said nothing about using the bit from Clement of Alexandria[18] to which you now have exclusive rights in English and Fuegian. You have it first and last.

Hoopsa boyaboy hoopsa. Watch out for the fires. Don't look at the fireball. We Santa Claus, up to the snout in ashes, salute you. I hope to miss most of the fun by eating large quantities of fallout celery. Eat your strontium spinach and you will be too weak to look at the fireball. All the Santas salute you. Ding Ding. Take cover.

17. To C.L. (Clare Boothe Luce), New York [December 1961 or January 1962]

What can I say about those three utterly magnificent books. Especially the Giotto. I cannot remember when I have seen anything so fine as this last, and yet we have lived in a time when marvelous things are produced. I remember most of the Giottos from Santa Croce, especially St. Francis before the soldan [sultan] which for some reason hit me very hard and has always stayed with me. Now that I am very interested in Moslems, and have contact with some,[19] I think I understand the reason why. But what the book gives that nothing else can is the appreciation of all the marvelous detail. It is an unending pleasure for me and for the novices, and we are all still wondering at it.

Thank you, then, for having added to our Christmas this wonder. And it has been a marvelous Christmas for me. The darkest in my life and yet in many ways the clearest and most radiant. Dark of course because of the situation we are all in. And radiant because one comes to understand that the darkness is there for a reason also. That the Light has come into darkness which has not understood it: this we have known long since. But we have not known all the implications. Nor have we understood

---

[18] *Clement of Alexandria: Selections from the Protreptikos: An Essay and Translation by Thomas Merton* (New York: New Directions, 1962).

[19] In 1961 Merton had begun corresponding with Abdul Aziz. See *The Hidden Ground of Love,* edited by William H. Shannon (New York: Farrar, Straus and Giroux, 1985), for Merton's letters to Abdul Aziz.

the immense depth of the mystery which we nevertheless know by rote: that the Light not only shall and will triumph over the darkness, but already has. This is not a spiritual bromide, it is the heart of our Christian faith. Have you ever read the English mystic Julian (sometimes wrongly called Juliana) of Norwich? I will write to you about her some time. She is a mighty theologian, in all her simplicity and love.

Though "all manner of things shall be well," we cannot help but be aware, on the threshold of 1962 that we have enormous responsibilities and tasks of which we are perhaps no longer capable. Our sudden, unbalanced top-heavy rush into technological mastery has left us without the spiritual means to face our problems. Or rather, we have thrown the spiritual means away. Even the religious people have not been aware of the situation, not become aware until perhaps too late. And here we all stand as prisoners of our own scientific virtuosity, ruled by immense power that we ought to be ruling and cannot. Our weapons dictate what we are to do. They force us into awful corners. They give us our living, they sustain our economy, they bolster up our politicians, they sell our mass media, in short we live by them. But if they continue to rule us we will also most surely die by them. For they have now made it plain that they are the friends of the "preemptive strike." They are most advantageous to those who use them first. And consequently nobody wants to be too late in using them second. Hence the weapons keep us in a state of fury and desperation, with our fingers poised over the button and our eyes glued on the radar screen. You know what happens when you keep your eye fixed on something. You begin to see things that aren't there. It is very possible that in 1962 the weapons will tell someone that there has been long enough waiting, and he will obey, and we will all have had it.

It shows what comes of believing in science more than in God. The business about Pharaoh in Exodus is not so far out after all, is it? Bricks without straw, and more than that. Faith is the principle of the only real freedom we have. Yet history is full of the paradox that the liberation of the mind of man by Christianity did a great deal to make the development of science possible too. Yet you can't blame all this on the Bible or on the Greeks or on the Council of Nicea (which brought into the spotlight the meaning of the Person). There was also too much underground that we didn't know about, I presume.

I don't want to waste your time philosophizing. But I do want to say this one thing. We are in an awfully serious hour for Christianity, for our own souls. We are faced with necessity to be very faithful to the Law of Christ, and His truth. This means that we must do everything that we reasonably can to find our way peacefully through the mess we are in. This is becoming harder and harder every day and success seems less and less likely. Yet we remain responsible for doing the things that "are to our peace." ("Jerusalem, Jerusalem, if thou hadst known the things that are for thy peace . . . and now there shall not be left of thee a stone upon a stone.") [Luke 19:42-44]

We have to be articulate and sane, and speak wisely on every occasion where we can speak, and to those who are willing to listen. That is why for one I speak to you. We have to try to some extent to preserve the sanity of this nation, and keep it from going berserk which will be its destruction, and ours, and perhaps also the destruction of Christendom.

I wanted to say these few things, as we enter the New Year. For it is going to be a crucial year, and in it we are going to have to walk sanely, and in faith, and with great sacrifice, and with an almost impossible hope.

It will be my prayer for you that all these graces and many more will be yours. And I want, once again, to say thanks for everything. The light and serenity of Giotto make me very ashamed of what happened to the Christian heritage, but there is no use in that. There is no use in being despondent about anything, it is a waste of time and a waste of hope. Our treasure of hope is so small that we cannot afford to let any of it fall out of our hands.

18. To W.S. [Walter Stein], Leeds, England [December 1961 or January 1962]

I have your letter of the 12th and am glad to hear from you. As I said in the letter to the people of the Merlin Press, I found the book edited by you [*Nuclear Weapons and Christian Conscience* (New York: Sheed and Ward, 1962)] very impressive.

What struck me most was the fact that the level was high, the thinking was energetic and uncompromising, and I was stimulated by the absence of the familiar clichés, or by worn-out mannerisms which have served us all in the evasion of real issues. For example (without applying these criticisms to any other book in particular), I was very struck by the superiority of your book over *Morals and Missiles* [by F. H. Drinkwater (London: J. Clarke, 1959)] which nevertheless had some good things in it. But *Morals and Missiles* had that chatty informality which the Englishman of Chesterton's generation thought he had to adopt as a protection whenever he tried to speak his mind on anything serious. Thank God you have thrown that off, because it emasculates a lot of very good thought.

At the moment, the publisher here is hesitating a bit because he finds your book "hard" but I am going to give him the business on that. It is necessary that for once a book be a little hard. We are submerged in all kinds of confused journalism on this awful issue, and there is very little thought. I do hope however to get some very good things. Lewis Mumford has said some of the clearest and most pointed moral judgments on nuclear warfare that have been uttered in this country and I hope [to include] at least one possibly two fine essays of his. Erich Fromm is a psychiatrist whom you may or may not know. He is a leftist and is outspoken, appearing in all sorts of places, and operating from Mexico. He has a good book out called *May Man Prevail.* I'll send you a copy because I think I can dig up an extra one somewhere. There are several essays the publisher especially wants, about the effects of bombs and the uselessness of civil defense measures. Most of the material at this end is about the psychology of the present nuclear crisis in this country, not that I want it to be this way. And I am hoping to get something constructive about a way toward peace. The title of the book is provisionally "The Human Way Out"[20] though I am afraid there is not yet a

---

[20] "The Human Way Out" became *Breakthrough to Peace,* published by New Directions in 1962. Merton proposed the idea for the book in a letter to James Laughlin, dated October 30, 1961. See *Thomas Merton and James Laughlin: Selected Letters,* edited by David D. Cooper (New York: W.W. Norton, 1997), 183.

great deal about the way out, except for the moral principles in your collection. I am of course going to hold out for the inclusion of your whole book in this anthology, and I think the publisher will see the point of it. He ought to come down here in a couple of weeks and we will come to our conclusions then.

Many of us here feel that 1962 is going to be awfully critical. Humanly speaking, the mentality of this country, as I now understand it, is about as bad as it could be. Utterly sinister, desperate, belligerent, illogical. We will either press the button or become fascists, in which case the button will be pressed all the more inevitably later on. The one hope is that a lot of people who have more sense are protesting and there is a real communication going on among them which is quite heartening. But one wonders just what can be done, when the country is in the grip of the business-military complex that lives on the weapons and is dominated by them. We have actually reached the state where our weapons are telling us what to do. We are guided and instructed [and] nurtured by our destructive machines.

I am seriously wondering if the efforts some of us are making (a belated formation of an American Pax group, etc.) can have more than symbolic value. This may sound pessimistic, and of course it is. But it is not so pessimistic that it excludes the dimensions of a real hope: a hope that is not seen. What is seen seems to me to be more or less hopeless, at the moment. The debacle is at hand, and it is a question of helping to save what God wills to save, not of preserving present structures that seem to me to be doomed. For the very effort to preserve them is what is bringing on the disaster. However, I do not pretend to weigh and measure things on such an enormous scale. I think our first duty is to preserve the human measure and to stay on the level where judgment is pertinent and does not become pure hubris. That is what the essays in your book and their judgments seem to me to affirm clearly and sanely: the human and the Christian measure.

Do believe that it is a satisfaction for me to be in touch with you and to share with you some effort and some concern at this time. I say this because everything else seems to me to be without solidity and almost without meaning. I keep you in my Masses and prayers. The protection of God is surely over us and He will guide us. May we be faithful to His guidance.

19. To J.G.M. [Jean Goss-Mayr], Vienna [January 1, 1962]

Your very welcome letter has been received and I have been waiting for some time to get the documents which were sent under separate cover. I have not yet received these but at least I want to send a word of acknowledgment for your letter. It is very good to be in touch with you. I will send you a few things which you may or may not be able to use in *Der Christ in der Welt*. I can read German sufficiently well to profit by this if you send it.

It is sometimes discouraging to see how small the Christian Peace movement is, and especially here in America where it is most necessary. But we have to remember that this is the usual pattern, and the Bible has led us to expect it. Spiritual work is done with disproportionately small and feeble instruments. And now above all when everything is so utterly complex, and when people collapse under the burden of confusions and cease to think at all, it is natural that few may want to take on the burden of trying to effect something in the moral and spiritual way, in political action. Yet, this is precisely what has to be done.

At times it seems almost humanly impossible, in the fluid, obscure and ever-changing movement of words and secular ideologies, to find stability and clarity, and even to formulate the problems we face. I think your efforts to state the questions clearly and place them before the Church, particularly before the Council, is of the greatest importance. The fact that the Church, while opposing war in a general way, says nothing very definite about the acute and present problems, is to many people quite disconcerting. Of course, they do not realize how complex the problem is, nor do they know that the Church does not always have to proceed by formal definitions in everything that she does.

I believe it is very important for Catholics to take a clear stand for nuclear disarmament, on some practical basis. But there again we get into the political maelstrom.

One of our great problems is to see clearly what we have to resist. I would say that at the moment we have to understand better than we do the Cold War mentality. If we do not understand it, we will run the risk of contributing to its confusions and thereby helping the enemies of man and of peace. The great danger is that under the pressures of anxiety and fear, the alternation of crisis and relaxation and new crisis, the people of the world will come to accept gradually the idea of war, the idea of submission to total power, and the abdication of reason, spirit, and individual conscience. The great peril of the Cold War is the progressive deadening of conscience. This of course is a process which was already well under way after World War I, and received a great impetus during the second war.

No one knows what this year will bring. The mentality of this country is deeply disturbing. But in the past year, the awful nonsense about the fallout shelters has finally awakened resistance and articulate opposition on the part of many intelligent people. This is a healthy reaction, but I do not know where it will go. The book I am editing will, I hope, contain very many interesting and compelling articles. I hope to use all those that were in the English collection edited by Walter Stein [*Nuclear Weapons, A Catholic Response*], which you have doubtless seen, and which is superb. I will look forward to seeing the material you have sent. Where I may not be able to print some of it, I will use it for my own instruction and guidance. I rely very much on your help and friendship. Send me anything you think will be of service to the cause of peace, and pray that in all things I may act wisely. God bless you always. I keep you in my Masses and prayers.

20. To S.T. [Sr. Therese Lentfoehr, S.D.S.], Wisconsin [January 11, 1962]

As for the "extreme groups": they are going to be a difficult problem for the country and may do much harm. The people are in most cases so sincere, even so naïve. The mixture of naiveté, outraged innocence, and hidden violence can become terrible though. It is very important that the rest of the country, especially Catholics who have retained some sense of perspective in these matters (there are still some), should not merely execrate them, and not merely accept them with passive indifference. If there is any way in which we can help them, keep communication patiently open with them, get a little truth through, make an occasional effective plea for tolerance and reason, then we should try it. If they get the impression that they have been given up in despair by the rest of the human race then they will complete the rejection of others which they have almost completed anyway, and will become entrenched in their self-righteous conviction that they are permitted every form of hatred, every form of injustice, every form of cruelty in the name of God and country. This is of course the price we pay for something like the Cold War. If it goes on much longer, the price is going to get much higher. And either the Cold War is going to go on, or it is going to turn into something worse.

My own objective is not to crusade wildly for anything, even for peace, but to try to develop an infinite patience and understanding, even though there is little hope of doing anything once you have them. The stuff I have written so far about peace does not have this tone. Pray that I may be what God wants me to be. St. Francis knew what this was all about. In a certain way I see the utter impossibility of my even attempting to take the road he took, and I do not think of the problem in those terms in any case.

21. To G.Z. [Gordon C. Zahn], Chicago, Ill. [January 11, 1962]

Your article ["The Case for Christian Dissent"] reached me the other day and I read it immediately. It is very fine indeed, and I think it will be one of the most powerful and telling contributions to the anthology [*Breakthrough to Peace*]. [James] Laughlin was a little hesitant about the chapter from the book which I passed on to him, but wait until he sees this. He is to come down next week and we will go over all the material. I think we have a lot of superb things. The greatest problem will be to get everything together and not have to make the book too big or exclude anything really worthwhile.

In any case I am deeply grateful, and I am glad to hear that the book itself (your book) [*German Catholics and Hitler's War*] is coming along well. Frank Sheed is a good and courageous publisher. I wish you success with it, and look forward to seeing a copy. It certainly will upset some people. We have to face the fact that we have traveled a long way from the real Christian center. Centuries of identification between Christian and civil life have done more to secularize Christianity than to sanctify civil life. This is not a popular idea. I wonder if anyone in our time has really faced it in a satisfactory way without either too much evasion, too total and too oversimplified a rejection of the secular and the temporal, or too complete a submission to it? The problem is enormous, and of course your article, and your book, go right to the heart of it. We have been too ready to assume that if it could all be worked out in theory we could then apply the theory to practice. On the contrary, if we do not practice what we are already supposed to know and believe, Christian social thought will never really bite into the big and urgent problem (except speculatively).

[Franz] Jagerstatter is to me a moving symbol of a lonely isolated Christian who was faithful to his conscience, in the supremely difficult question of the most real and the highest kind of obedience.[21] In the case of St. Thomas More we have obscured the issue by talking as if he had been obedient to the Pope and not to the King. Safe and cozy. There was nothing safe or cozy about it, and the Pope was miles and miles away.

This is only a short note, but I hope a very appreciative one.

22. To S.E. [Sr. Emmanuel de Souza y Silva, O.S.B.], Petrópolis, Brazil [January 16, 1962]

The poems of Dom Basilio [Penido, O.S.B., Abbot of the Monastery of Olinda] are quite charming. The Advent one was particularly good. But I have not yet read them all, nor the clippings that you sent. I have them still. I hate to rush through things, and I have so much to read at the moment. One has to read much in order to be able to think at all clearly on the problems of the time, and they are very great. There is so little said, people seem exhausted with the labor of coping with the complications of this world we live in. Yet it is absolutely necessary

---

[21] Gordon Zahn's In Solitary Witness: The Life and Death of Franz Jägerstätter (New York: Holt, Rinehart and Winston, 1965) recounted the story of a Catholic layman in Austria executed by the Nazis for refusing to serve in Hitler's army.

that we do so. We have to take responsibility for it, we have got to try to solve the problems of our own countries while at the same time recognizing our higher responsibilities to the whole human race. It is in a time like this that we are forced to have a Christian view of society at the risk of failing to be Christians altogether. And yet I remain a contemplative. I do not think there is a contradiction, for I think at least some contemplatives must try to understand the providential events of the day. God works in history, therefore a contemplative who has no sense of history, no sense of historical responsibility, is not a fully Christian contemplative: he is gazing at God as a static essence, or as an intellectual light, or as a nameless ground of being. But we are face to face with the Lord of History and with Christ the King and Savior, the Light of the world, who comes forth from the Father and returns to the Father. We must comfort Him in the awful paradoxes of our day, in which we see that our society is being judged. And in all this we have to retain a balance and a good sense which seem to require a miracle, and yet they are the fruit of ordinary grace. In a word we have to continue to be Christians in all the full dimensions of the Gospel.

I know that this is a very critical time especially for Brazil. I hope that the crisis will be weathered and that those who have given themselves so generously, at last, to the task of Christian social action, will not be frustrated and deprived of their hopes. Meanwhile here we are trying to start a small Catholic movement against war. It is hard to say whether the danger of nuclear war is really as great as it seems, but in any event there is no doubt whatever that a most destructive cataclysm is possible and perhaps even probable.

Certainly there is a great danger everywhere of extreme movements. Here in the U.S. also there are many people who are upset and tormented and who think they have to allay their anxieties by looking for communists everywhere except where they are, and as a result they make life very unpleasant and difficult for the more liberal minded people who still stand for peace and for a reasonable way of solving the problems of the country. I would not be terribly surprised if in a few years this country found itself under a dictator of some sort. I think [President] Kennedy is all right, and his brother [Robert F. Kennedy] is a good man. I know his brother's wife [Ethel Kennedy]. They are reasonable people, and probably as good as anyone we have at the moment. In a word I think Kennedy is fairly capable, but that is perhaps because he represents a favorable contrast with [President Dwight] Eisenhower who, with his whole administration, was a complete failure and did much harm to the country. Though Eisenhower himself is a very fine person. As a president he was zero. However let us hope that Kennedy may be able to rise above his own level and grow into a great president, for we certainly need one. Some of his cabinet are pretty good men too. But the task is enormous, and the dangers are very great. I do not at all like the mentality of this country at present. People are trying to convince themselves that nuclear war is reasonable and that it makes sense trying to consider it as a real possibility, not just as something inconceivable. This is a very dangerous step, for if this country comes to accept nuclear war as a reasonable solution to anything, we are very likely to have one. This would be disastrous for all of us. In which case we might just as well prepare for the end of our civilization and of all that it stands for.

These next few years are going to be quite crucial. However I think we have to be careful what we say about developments, careful about the guesses we make in public, careful about the possibilities we consider. We are going to need to learn a prudence which does not belong to the mass mind.

I must close now, with every blessing to you and to all my good friends in Brazil. And I mean to get those articles off to you today, registered.

23. To J.F. [John Cuthbert Ford, S.J.], Washington, D.C. [January 1962]

You may see an article of mine ["Nuclear War and Christian Responsibility"] in the *Commonweal* [75 (February 9, 1962)] these days. This too I regret to say, is a bit sweeping and shows something of the lack of perspective from which I necessarily suffer to some extent. It was written before I got in touch with you and I have not had an opportunity to make changes, expecting it to appear from issue to issue. Since it is in the

Commonweal, however, I think the readers will know how to qualify the statements to some extent. If not, well, they will find people to tell them, I am sure!

I suffer from my limitations, and I wish I were more of a professional, because an increased sophistication and a deeper experience of the problems and methods would help me serve the truth much better: and of course that is what I want to do. But I must say this: I am very deeply concerned with what seems to me to be the extreme reticence and hesitation on the part of Catholics who might take a position for peace, or for a more positive and constructive approach to world problems, when there seem to be quite a few irresponsible voices, which have great influence on some of the faithful, giving the impression that the Church needs and even wants a kind of nuclear crusade against the godless communists. I do not claim to be an expert in world affairs, but the superficial knowledge that I have of the arms race and of present day military policies and the power involved in them, shows me that there is not much chance of the things we want to defend actually surviving a nuclear war—even a "limited" one which would necessarily affect at least some cities.

It is for that reason that I believe that I am obliged, out of fidelity to Our Lord and to my priestly and religious vocation, to state very definitely some alternative to this awful passivity and lotus eating irresponsibility which, in the end, delivers us all over bound hand and foot into the power of political forces that know nothing of God or morality, whether natural or divine. Sure, the theologians are divided, and the bishops rely on the theologians. But can't the theologians and the bishops say something? Can't there be some constructive and courageous discussion? Can't there be more show of genuine concern? Father, my heart is very sick with the feeling that we don't give the impression of caring at all what happens to man, the image of God. We seem to be concerned more with abstractions. Of course I know we are all warmly devoted to those around us and to our students, penitents and whatnot. But as other Christs we should have universal horizons and we should not be limited by any dividing line whatever. We should be just as concerned about man in Russia and man in China as about man in America. How is it possible that we should, with equanimity, toss around statistics and estimates of deaths running into the millions and then proceed to justify these deaths, and even justify them on the basis of our Christian faith and loyalty to the Church? I know you agree with me that there is something terribly wrong somewhere.

I know of course that vehement zeal is not enough, there has to be wisdom. And I know that perhaps the zeal of those with whom we do not agree may in the end contain elements of Christian charity too.

Personally, I sense the danger of a kind of political tussle between various Catholic opinions, a tussle in which men may be more concerned with persuading authority to approve their view, than with establishing the truth in all simplicity. I am not trying to put forward a view which I will then foist off on some authority. (I don't think I would have much chance anyway, as I do not know the ropes.) All I want to do is say as much as I can reasonably say for the point of view which seems to me just and in accord with the law of Christ, and thereby perhaps stir up a little interest and articulate participation in the issue.

We all need leadership and the guidance to which one might apply the popular cliché of "creative." I don't think the theologians in this country are anywhere near fulfilling this kind of function, and I pray the Holy Spirit may inspire you all to be something more than spectators and get in the game. Otherwise people like me may simply ruin the game for our side.

This is a sort of manifestation of a frustrated conscience, and at the same time a reassurance that I am not going to do anything rash (at least I hope not). And I hope I haven't been rash already. And I know I am going to have to simmer down and take the long view, and be careful that my own nature and its frustrations do not make this crucial issue merely a subjective outlet, which of course would be tragic. I have got to learn not to take my own zeal too seriously, and not to be carried away by rhetoric.

But of one thing I am convinced: the vital importance of a forceful and articulate Catholic position, in this country, in favor of peace, rather than the permissive and silent attitude that seems to prevail at the moment. We seem to be able to get excited over everything but the important problem. We are deeply involved in a movement towards a war of annihilation which certainly promises to be criminal, and the Pope certainly seems to fear this.

Father, I am trying your patience. But I do so knowing that you are interested not only for my own sake but for the sake of the Church. And I know you will have wise advice to give me. I do need opportunities for some kind of dialogue. One cannot develop correct views of issues like this, in a vacuum. So I trust your charity to bear with me.

24a. To M.B. [Mary Childs Black], Williamsburg, Va. [c. January 24, 1962]

I need not tell you how I would love to be there on February 2nd. There are few earthly desires I cherish more than the desire to see the Shaker spiritual drawings in the original. I am still hoping that the collection may find its way out here. It is with great regret that I must decline your kind invitation. I never obtain permission to travel that far or indeed to travel at all merely for a "social" occasion. This would be called a social occasion I suppose. Though to me it would be more.

Recently though I did have the happiness to get to the old Pleasant Hill Shaker Community near here, and even took some photographs which came out quite well and I hope I will be able to use them in a little photo essay on the place and on the Shakers.[22] The ideas have not crystallized out yet, and one must give them time. I know Edward Andrews will be interested though.

This much I can do: share with you all a few of the thoughts that are at work in my mind about the Shakers and their deep significance, which manifests itself in a hidden and archetypal way in their art, craftsmanship, and in all their works. Their spirit is perhaps the most authentic expression of the primitive American "mystery" or "myth": the paradise myth. The New World, the World of renewal, of return to simplicity, to the inno- cence of Adam, the recovery of the primeval cosmic simplicity,

---

[22] See Thomas Merton, *Seeking Paradise: The Spirit of the Shakers*, edited with an Introduction by Paul Pearson (Maryknoll, NY: Orbis Books, 2003).

the reduction of divisions, the restoration of unity. But not just a return to the beginning, it is also an anticipation of the end. The anticipation of eschatological fulfillment, of completion, the New World was an earnest and a type of the New Spiritual Creation.

In the secular realm this consciousness was of course very pronounced, the consciousness of the pioneer and later of the business man who thought that America could literally be the earthly paradise. The belief that there was nothing impossible, that all goodness and all happiness was there for the asking. And in the poor of other lands, America existed as the place where they thought gold could be picked up on the streets.

For the Shakers, it was a different consciousness, for at the same time they saw the deceptiveness of the secular hope, and their eyes were open, in childlike innocence, to the evil, the violence, the unscrupulousness that too often underlay the secular vision of the earthly paradise. It was a paradise in which the Indian had been slaughtered, and the Negro was enslaved. In which the immigrant was treated as an inferior being, and in which he had to work very hard for the "gold" that was to be "picked up in the streets."

The Shakers realized that to enter into a genuine contact with the reality of the "paradise spirit" which existed in the wonderful new world, they had to undergo a special kind of conversion. And their conversion had this special, unique, wonderful quality in that it, more than any other "spirit," grasped the unique substance of the American paradise myth, and embodied it in a wonderful expression. For myths are realities, and they themselves open into deeper realms. The Shakers apprehended something totally original about the spirit and the vocation of America. This has remained hidden to everyone else. The sobering thing is that their vision was—eschatological! And they themselves ended.

Note: Merton repeats the number 24—assigning it to the next letter as well as the previous one.

24b. To V.H. [Victor Hammer], Lexington, Ky. [c. January 25, 1962]

As for brainwashing, the term is used very loosely about almost anything. Strict technical brainwashing is an artificially induced "conversion," brought about by completely isolating a person emotionally and spiritually, undermining his whole sense of identity, and then "rescuing" him from this state of near collapse by drawing him over into a new sense of community with his persecutors, now his rescuers, who "restore" his identity by admitting him into their midst as an approved and docile instrument. Henceforth he does what they want him to do and likes it, indeed finds a certain satisfaction in this, and even regards his old life as shameful and inferior.

In the loose sense, any mass man is a "brainwashed" man. He has lost his identity or never had one in the first place, and he seeks security, hope, a sense of identity in his immersion in the pressures and prejudices of a majority, speaking through TV, newspapers, etc. Having no real power or meaning in himself he seeks all in identification with a presumably all-powerful and all-wise collectivity. Whatever the collectivity does is right, infallible, perfect. Anything, approved by It, becomes legitimate and even noble. The worst crimes are virtues when backed up by the all-powerful collectivity. All that matters is to be part of the great, loud mass.

It seems to me that the great effort of conscience that remains for modern man is to resist this kind of annihilating pressure, this defection, in every possible way. The temptation comes unfortunately from very many angles, even seemingly good sources. The Cold War is the deadly influence that is leading western man to brainwash himself.

When the process is completed there will be nothing left but the hot war or the decline into totalitarian blindness and inertia, which also spells hot war in the end. The prospects are very dark, aren't they? Yet I think that perhaps some providential accident may happen that will wake everyone up. Some kind of plague of radiation, perhaps, something unexpected and unforeseen that will force people to their senses. But can we say we have done anything to deserve this? I hardly think so. Fortunately, if we only got what we deserved, we would never have very much of anything good. God is not simply just, He is also and above all merciful. I wish that this had not been so thoroughly forgotten.

The clipping was interesting, and I had already started a note to Carolyn [Hammer] which had that book included in a short list of other items. The French situation is very disturbing indeed. Much evil can come of this. Everyone expects De Gaulle to get it this year some time, and I wonder how long he can survive. He has been a good man in many ways, yet perhaps mistakenly Messianic too. But what could any reasonable human being have done with Algeria? If he goes, then France goes too. And this may be the spark that will finally ignite everything. The next few months will tell us a thing or two. And the next three years, or four: well, to call them fateful is putting it so mildly as to be ridiculous.

I wonder if there is going to be much left of the Western World by 1984, to fulfill George Orwell's prophecies.

Meanwhile, we have only to be what we are and to retain the spirit and civilization which we are blessed with, and to keep as human as we can.

25. To J.F. [James Forest], New York [January 29, 1962]

It is really quite providential that the Peace article ["Nuclear War and Christian Responsibility"] I wrote for the *Commonweal* Christmas issue was held up by the censors and is now appearing this week [February 9, 1962], in conjunction with the General Strike for Peace. I do hope it helps even a little bit. Anyway, my heart goes with it, and I am with you all in spirit. I am glad that in that article I explicitly mentioned the point that all people, the ordinary people, the ones who don't want war, the ones who get it in the neck, the ones who really want to build a decent new world in which there will not be war and starvation, these should know the power of their witness against war, and the effect that they can have by protest and refusal of cooperation in immoral war efforts.

Of course the tragedy is that the vast majority of people do not understand the meaning of this kind of witness. In their pitiful blind craving for undisturbed security they feel that agitation for peace is somehow threatening to them. They do not feel at all threatened by the bomb, for some reason, but they feel terribly threatened by some little girl student carrying a placard, or by some poor workingman striking in protest. Somehow they feel that it is after all possible for people to change their mind and revise their whole attitude towards a setup that has its enormous disadvantages but—at least it is "what we are used to, and please God don't ask us to get used to something else." Unfortunately the bomb is going to impose a terrible adjustment on those who may be left around to adjust. And it is with this that people want to defend themselves. We have to have deep patient compassion for the fears of men, for the fears and irrational mania of those who hate us or condemn us.

My Mass on February 1st, the Feast of St. Ignatius Martyr of Antioch, will be for all of the strikers everywhere in the world and for all who yearn for a true peace, all who are willing to shoulder the great burden of patiently working, praying, and sacrificing themselves for peace. We will never see the results in our time, even if we manage to get through the next five years without being incinerated. Really we have to pray for a total and profound change in the mentality of the whole world. What we have known in the past as Christian penance is not a deep enough concept if it does not comprehend the special problems and dangers of the present age. Hairshirts will not do the trick, though there is no harm in mortifying the flesh. But vastly more important is the complete change of heart and the totally new outlook on the world of man. We have to see our duty to mankind as a whole. We must not fail in this duty which God is imposing on us with His own hand.

The great problem is this inner change, and we must not be so obsessed with details of policy that we block the deeper development in other people and in ourselves. The strike is to be regarded, I think, as an application of spiritual force and not the use of merely political pressure. We all have the great duty to realize the deep need for purity of soul, that is to say the deep need to possess in us the Holy Spirit, to be possessed by Him. This takes precedence over everything else. If He lives and works in us, then our activity will be true and our witness will generate love of the truth, even though we may be persecuted and beaten down in apparent incomprehension.

I got a beautiful letter from a nun in Haiti, talking about the people there. Maybe they are among the very poorest on the face of the earth. One feels that Christ is almost visible among them, in them, in their poverty, in their abandonment, their destitution: why does no one look to see the face of Christ and come to Him with help? But meanwhile His Heart has assumed all their sorrow, all the injustice done to them, and while He will comfort them, He will also do what He does, in mystery, to restore the balance, the violated order.

God was seemingly never more absent from the world and yet His Christ, the Word, is walking about all around us all over the face of the earth, and in a terrible hour.

26. To W.H.F. [Wilbur H. Ferry], Santa Barbara, Calif. [January 30, 1962]

I have just received your two letters and the other items. I have just read the article you indicated in *Worldview*. We have our Catholic Herman Kahns and I think they are the majority. As far as I can see this is the more or less accepted view of many theologians and perhaps of the majority of the U.S. It is stated with much more subtlety and humanity by John Courtney Murray, and there is one Jesuit, Fr. John Ford, who takes exception to it and is more over our way. But this man Fr. Mahon is a crusader and franker expression of all that lies behind the suave surface of Murray's argument. Here are my remarks, without much preparation, spontaneously.

1. Fr. Murray has a good, reasonable, clear mind, makes all kinds of clear distinctions, is learned in his theology. Underlying his thought is a basic assumption that somehow everything is quite reasonable, that military men are not extremists really, that we are all human, sensible and tolerant, that we all mean pretty well. And that the Reds don't mean pretty well at all. Hence what we need is to make it quite clear that we are ready at any time to engage in a *limited war,* a reasonable war, a nice kind of war, in which the limits set down by Catholic moral theology and Pius XII are respected by the Pentagon. The Pentagon

will always be ready to give Fr. Murray and any other Catholic full assurance that they have no intention of doing anything that is not "limited" in some way or other.

2. The emphasis on limited war as a military possibility, of course it is possible, isn't it? It is what the government intends, isn't it? Well, the reason for that is that if a war is limited then no Catholic can possibly object to it in conscience. The Popes have said strong things about all-out war, they have even called it a sin. Hence there might be trouble if one started out right away on an all-out basis, wouldn't there? But it is clear that a limited war is licit, hence every Catholic has a moral obligation to support it, hence *that* is in the bag. Just let's remember please that this war is going to be limited. Limited to countries. Some of the continents will not be directly hit, they will only get fallout. But the effects of the bombs will not be beyond control. On the contrary, we will know very well that when we explode a bomb over or near Leningrad, that the blast and fire will affect Leningrad while the fallout will affect Helsinki, Riga, Warsaw, Berlin, etc., etc., or, if the wind is wrong, well, Archangel, etc. We have full control. This is a limited war. And this Fr. Mahon, he likes to look at it principally as the destruction of *property*. If you think of the destruction of property, the ruin of buildings, then one who objects to the destruction is nothing but a pragmatist, he puts material things (buildings) before spiritual things (the spiritual desert which will result under Communism). This is in line with the primitive Christian ethic which stated that one should at all costs destroy the potential persecutor of the faith. One should under no circumstances allow oneself to give witness to the faith by suffering persecution. This must remind us to put aside "romantic notions of the Church of silence," etc. He definitely prefers "a world of smashed buildings and smashed skulls, to a Soviet World without God or freedom." That is a lovely touch, isn't it? Smashed skulls. We are not fighting with H-bombs, only with clubs. Real limited war, isn't it. Limited to clubs all of a sudden. There is a kind of magic in this kind of moral theology, don't you think?

3. The real thing that they are all getting at is the justification of preemptive first strike. The game is this. Traditional Catholic morality about the just war says that under no circumstances can a war of aggression be accounted just. At best it must be a war of

defense. But of course the missile armed with the nuclear warhead gives overwhelming advantage to the man who strikes first. Consequently we have to have that first strike at all costs, and the Christian thing to do is to adjust traditional moral teaching so that it becomes licit for us to attack if we want to. We have to be able to take "anticipatory retaliation" if we are "sufficiently provoked."

This is the beauty of the new theories. Gone forever is all this nonsense about patiently sustaining injuries, which is not even good for the individual Christian any more and never was any good for the state (even though Pius XII said the state was just as much obliged to practice charity as the individual was). One does not have to be attacked. One just has to be "provoked." Who decides what constitutes provocation? The standard, our Fr. Mahon frankly admits, is sufficient as long as the one provoked is "subjectively" certain that he has been provoked. I take it this means all we need is to feel provoked. Hence the thing to do is to drop all cultivation of any kind of virtue that would make us suppress feelings of provocation. Let us realize that anger is virtuous, and that it provides us with a sensitive barometer that registers provocation a whole lot sooner than patience would. This will bring our moral teaching and practice right up to the minute. "The combatant must be subjectively certain of the justice of his fighting and of its efficacy."

4. Justice and efficacy. Ah, now we come to the heart of the new theory. Traditional teaching on war taught that a condition for just war was the moral certitude that one could actually achieve something by going to war. This meant two things. One that there was no disproportion between the destruction on one hand and the good achieved on the other and that there was really after all some good to be achieved. The modern popes have of course said that they did not think war was a just and reasonable means of settling international disputes, and declared that we should not resort to it any more. That it resulted not only in great physical evil (even conventional weapons did this), but greater spiritual evil.

All this goes by the board with the new theory. Efficacy? Sure, what is more efficacious than ICBM's armed with H-bombs. Here you really have efficacy for the first time in all its purity and simple strength. Naked, streamlined efficacy, no?

This is what the Pope wants. "It is interesting to note that he speaks of efficacious self defense," says our mentor. "May we not assume then that in using the expression efficacious self defense in the year 1956 he is using the term in a modern context"? Not only may we assume this, but as loyal followers of the Papal teaching we go right ahead and declare it. The Pope, ahead of his times as always, was looking forward to the theory of counterforce and preemptive strike, counterforce with bonus, you know, ten percent of the missiles take out the chief cities . . . This is what is necessary to make the thing efficacious.

5. We will, in short, prove our disobedience to the Holy See by twisting the words of the Popes around to make them mean exactly what they did not mean, and doing exactly what the Popes warned us not to do. We will be blindly loyal to our Christian obligations and we will get in there with the nuclear first strike and wipe Russia off the map. Then our troubles will be over, we can sit back and Christianity will have the whole world at its feet. And all as the result of an innocent little limited war fought with a preemptive club.

The funny thing about this reasoning is that it makes me vomit. Possibly I am not a good Catholic. I guess that is really the trouble. I haven't learned how to go into this kind of mental gymnastics yet. But I guess they are going to teach me after they see the article I have in the *Commonweal*. I will have to beef that up a little more, as it is to be in the book.[23] Already one of the censors in horror has denounced me as a pacifist, just because I don't believe in all-out war. The Pope too is a pacifist, except of course he can get away with it, being old and probably soft in the head, the way he comes out with sentimental nonsense about having absolutely no recourse to violence. But patience, nobody listens anyway. Nobody even knows that he said that, and really few care.

---

[23]Merton would go on to expand "Nuclear War and Christian Responsibility," published in *Commonweal* 75 (February 9, 1962), in "We Have to Make Ourselves Heard," in "Peace: A Religious Responsibility," and, finally, in a chapter in the manuscript of *Peace in the Post-Christian Era,* the book Merton was forbidden to publish during his lifetime. It was published thirty-six years after his death (Maryknoll, NY: Orbis Books, 2004).

This time I want to try to answer you immediately. I think you are quite right, and that the ideas that have come to you are true. You should accept them in peace and in humility and ask for the patience and perseverance to cooperate with the truth that has been shown to you. It is a long and weary business, and very difficult because it means being in conflict with good people who mean well but who are radically wrong in their view of things.

It seems to me that the darkness that has troubled you, and the same darkness which many good people and souls of prayer suffer these days, comes from one very serious source. Without wanting to be in conflict with the truth and with the will of God, we are actually going against God's will and His teaching. We are actually refusing Him what He asks of us as Christians, while at the same time proclaiming to heaven and earth that we are the best Christians. We are however, without knowing it, adhering to a Christianity that is scarcely Christian. It is infected with worldly values, and it is corrupted by love of wealth and power. In fact the Christianity which we have subtly substituted for the will of God and for true Christian tradition is really the Christianity of the rich, the powerful, the selfish. It is a Christianity of individualism, of greed, of cruelty, of injustice, which hides behind specious maxims and encourages a kind of spiritual quietism. It is a Christianity of formulas, which are to be accepted blindly and repeated without understanding, a Christianity of passive conformity, in which under the name of obedience we are often brought into subjection to the most worldly influences and powers.

It is quite natural that a Christianity such as this should encourage hatred and revenge, and be immersed in the most confused and absurd of political complexities. You must be very careful of a false and noisy zeal that talks loudly about plans for action and conquest. Some of the religious Orders specialize in this kind of zeal, but it is dangerous and misleading, especially at the present moment. Also there is a great danger that those who have had a little inconvenience to suffer, have spent some time in prison, may imagine themselves confessors of the faith and thereafter infallible in all their judgments, so that their hatred and desire for revenge, which may be quite natural and understandable, appears to them to be the voice of God Himself. These people, without meaning to, and in all good faith, will do much harm. They will spread hatred, darkness, and confusion, while thinking to serve the cause of God. You must pray for them every day, and ask God to give all such people much light and help. You must pray that we may all be truly humble and docile to the Holy Spirit in order that we may come to appreciate the grave realities of our time and understand our true task.

Many Catholics make the mistake of thinking that the problems of our time are very clear cut, that there is no difficulty in seeing the truth, and that since the just cause is very evident, we need only to apply force in order to achieve justice. But precisely this illusion that everything is "clear" is what is blinding us all. It is a serious temptation, and it is a subtle form of pride and worldly love of power and revenge. Only if we are humble and contrite of heart and admit that there is much wrong in our so-called zeal, will we merit from God the light to understand our problems. We are at present doing little or nothing to merit this light, because we do not think we need it, we think everything is quite clear. Unfortunately the opposite is the case. Everything is dark and uncertain, and we need light as a pure gift from God. Unless He gives this light, we will be in terrible darkness and will go forward to tragedy for ourselves and everybody.

The great error of the aggressive Catholics who want to preserve their power and social status at all costs is that they believe this can be done by force, and thus they prepare the way to lose everything they want to save. On the contrary, the force that preserves the Church is love and patience and suffering and courage to overcome cruelty and violence. So many Catholics think this is "defeatism." They dismiss it without even thinking about it. This is natural, they have never really been taught these things. It has been totally overlooked. This oversight is now having terrible consequences. We will be asked to give an account of our ignorance of the most basic teachings of the Gospel.

Read carefully the wonderful statements of the Popes, especially all the Christmas Messages of Pius XII and John XXIII. Have you read *Mater et Magistra* [Encyclical of Pope John XXIII, promulgated on May 15, 1961]? These have wonderful and inexhaustible teachings for our meditation, and above all they need to be put into practice. How are these teachings received? The right-wing Catholic who thinks only in terms of power and political pressure dismisses the teaching of the Pope as "private opinion" without authoritative force. And the theologian who accepts them, nevertheless twists them around so that they end up saying the opposite of what the Pope meant.

I must stop now. God bless you. I will always keep you more than ever in my prayers. I will send you a few things to read. Do not be impatient or in a hurry to become a "militant" of another kind. Wait and learn in silence. We will see what comes next.

28. To E.E. [Elsa Engländer], Linz, Austria [February 4, 1962]

I was happy to hear from you again and have very much enjoyed the beautiful book of Austrian Churches, *Glanz des Ewigen*. Like you I feel many pangs of nostalgia over the wonderful unappreciated grace of the civilization that is inexorably perishing all around us. Austria has been such a wonderful rich and living source of this European Christian culture. Mozart represents for me all the purest and best in the Austrian and Christian genius, and those unabashed excesses of baroque attempt to keep up with his inexhaustible imagination. They do not of course succeed, but they have their charm and their boldness. I admire especially the daring of baroque that was not afraid to risk terrible lapses of taste, and yet managed almost always to come off with some marvels of ingenuity and playfulness. In former days I found it hard to take seriously but now I think nevertheless its significance grows on me. I suppose it is terribly out of fashion. As for the older Austrian churches, especially the earliest ones of all, they are simply enchanting. So your gift has given me great pleasure and made me secretly homesick for the Europe I shall never see again.

And, as you say, the poignancy of the situation is accentuated by the physical danger of destruction.

There is no question that we live in an age of revolutionary change, perhaps even of cataclysm. We cannot simply cling to the past, yet we must advance into the future while trying to preserve what is relevant and vital in the past, in so far as we can. It is of the greatest importance that we advance peacefully. If by miscalculation or accident, or even by the pride and fury of men, war breaks out again, then there is every danger that nothing at all will be left of what was valuable and great in Europe. And all the wonderful possibilities of North America will be destroyed. It is a shame that we have such great capabilities and so little wisdom.

I keep you in my masses and in my prayers. May the love of Christ protect your heart and may you rejoice in His peace. But in our time it is not possible to have a peace that is altogether without sorrow nor should we even desire it, for sorrow is salutary in such an age.

29. To J.T.E. [Msgr. John Tracy Ellis], Washington, D.C. [February 4, 1962]

One of the main points I am trying to make [in "Nuclear War and Christian Responsibility" (*Commonweal* 75, February 9, 1962)] is that I think our theology ought to stand above political issues a little more than it does, and that we ought to be making every effort to clarify the moral principles instead of to explain them in such a way that they seem to favor some altogether limited and immediate political purpose that seems to us to be good. I think this is the case with some of our theologians and nuclear war. I note that in *Theological Studies* in the last couple of years they seem to be wanting in every possible way to squeeze around the traditional limitations of the "just" war in order to show that by Catholic standards a preemptive nuclear attack is really only defense.

Now this seems to me to be quite fatal both to theology and to political sanity. Actually it seems logical on a certain level, but only because on that level we have already abdicated from a really Christian and traditional view of war and accepted the unprincipled opportunism of the secularist. In fact what we are trying to do is to find pretexts for nuclear attack, and if that is the case, then I think it is a very grave defection. In reality the issue does not hinge so much on principles, which remain relatively clear, but on states of mind and interpretation of fact. And a lot of moral judgments are being made on the basis of assumptions about military policy that to even the most casual observer appear to be without the slightest foundation. It seems to be quite gratuitous to assume that a war will be a limited nuclear war, when all our policies are built on all-out war, and then, what happens is that we proceed to justify limited war, in order without explanation or justification to slide right into all-out war and assume that it too has been justified.

This is the way moral thought seems to have evolved in World War II. You start out by saying that a given situation is morally acceptable. This leads to all sorts of consequences which should have been foreseen but were not. These consequences, by traditional standards are immoral, (e.g. Hiroshima) but they are accepted as an accomplished fact, and then justified post factum.

It seems to me we are doing that now. We are arguing: a limited nuclear war is licit. We realize that a nuclear war might become an all-out war of annihilation, but we hope that it won't, and at the same time we prepare for the fact that it might be saying that it after all might be justified too. Meanwhile, the Pentagon has not consulted us anyway. And having conditioned our people for a limited war, we then precipitate them into an all-out war. And we refuse them any appeal to their own conscience. They have to abide by the decisions of "legitimately constituted authority." The results are likely to be terrible. And maybe your man in *Réalités* may be correct after all about that "last chance." I am glad the Holy Father has fixed the date for the Council. He evidently seems perturbed about the international situation and wants to get the Council under way before it is too late. I feel personally that the trouble in France is so dangerous that it may be the thing that finally precipitates a general war. De Gaulle might get assassinated, for instance, and the Reds take advantage of the chaos to seize power. Then . . .

I am sorry to say that the pessimism of your friends in Rome rings a bell with me too.

Note: There is no CWL 30.

31. To J.F. [James Forest], New York [February 6, 1962]

I was very moved by your account of the civil disobedience at the AEC [Atomic Energy Commission building]. It must have been very significant for you indeed. I am extremely happy that the letter reached you right there, and that too seems to be significant and a great grace for me. At the same time you speak of the violence and resentment of the bureaucrats leaving work and making a point of kicking people out of the way. This is no surprise and also it raises certain questions.

One of the most problematical questions about non-violence is the inevitable involvement of hidden aggressions and provocations. I think this is especially true when there are a fair proportion of non-religious elements, or religious elements that are not spiritually developed. It is an enormously subtle question, but we have to consider the fact that in its provocative aspect, non-violence may tend to harden the opposition and confirm people in their righteous blindness. It may even in some cases separate men out and drive them in the other direction, away from us and away from peace. This of course may be (as it was with the prophets) part of God's plan. A clear separation of antagonists. And perhaps now we have to see that this may be all we can do: simply clarify the issue.

Anyway we can always direct our action towards opening people's eyes to the truth, and if they are blinded, we must try to be sure we did nothing specifically to blind them. Yet there is that danger: the danger one observes subtly in tight groups like families and monastic communities, where the martyr for the right sometimes thrives on making his persecutors terribly and visibly wrong. He can drive them in desperation to be wrong, to seek refuge in the wrong, to seek refuge in violence.

The violent man is, by our standards, weak and sick. Though to us at times he is powerful and menacing in an extreme degree. In our acceptance of vulnerability, however, we play on his guilt. There is no finer torment. This is one of the enormous problems of the time, and the place. It is the overwhelming problem of America: all this guilt and nothing to do about it except finally to explode and blow it all out in hatreds, race hatreds, political hatreds, war hatreds. We, the righteous, are dangerous people in such a situation. (Of course we are not righteous, we are conscious of our guilt above all, we are sinners: but nevertheless we are bound to take courses of action that are professionally righteous and we have committed ourselves to that course.)

This is not for you so much as for myself. We have got to be aware of the awful sharpness of truth when it is used as a weapon, and since it can be the deadliest weapon, we must take care that we don't kill more than falsehood with it. In fact, we must be careful how we "use" truth, for we are ideally the instruments of truth and not the other way round.

Anyway I am very happy with all you say in the letter and glad that things have clarified themselves for you in action. This is essential, because the business of remaining mired down in a mass of words exhausts the spirit and leads nowhere. It is a wonderful grace to have the opportunity to simply speak by work and suffering and witness, and you have every reason to keep saying the Magnificat.

32. To J.F.S. [Frank J. Sheed], New York [February 1962]

It has taken me a little time to get around to answering your letter, because I did not want to just dash off a hasty note. Certainly it is important to explain this matter if it is causing comment and upsetting some people, hence I will try to do so.

I can see that the leaflet,[24] being cheaply printed, and perhaps circulated in a random and irresponsible seeming way, might cause suspicion in some minds. It is put out by a very poor group of Catholics who, however, number among them some quite saintly people. The leaflet consists largely of part of a chapter from a book, and doubtless those who read it in the context of the book will find it less surprising. Added to that are a few introductory paragraphs which were written in the heat of the moment when I was shocked by the highly regrettable public statement of a Jesuit Father[25] who seemed to be advising people to be completely ruthless and selfish and keep others out of their

---

[24] *Two Articles by Thomas Merton: The Root of War & Red or Dead: The Anatomy of a Cliché* (Nyack, New York: Fellowship Publications, 1962) 12.

shelter with a gun if necessary. There you have the background.

I know that this whole unpleasant issue of war is a delicate one to handle. I know too that people are very upset, and excitable, and that it is difficult to keep a straight perspective when discussing such a critical problem. It is very unfortunate that many people think that the mere fact of hesitating to approve an all-out nuclear war makes a man by that very fact a communist.

Now this is the real danger I am getting at. We have got to try to keep our heads and judge this war problem with traditional moral standards. We have got to remember that such standards still exist. Even some of our clergy are stretching things quite far. I personally believe it is my duty to explain and spread the clear teaching that has been given by the Popes for the last twenty years, and they have stated very forcefully what our duty is. Of course they have not condemned nuclear war formally, but they want us to be extremely careful and to try at all costs to find some other way of settling international problems.

It does not seem to me that this fact is clearly realized in America, and consequently I have felt obliged to state my opinion, and to call attention, where possible, to what the Popes have said. The most recent utterance is that of John XXIII, last Christmas, when he spoke in the most solemn terms, both pleading and warning national leaders and publicists to shun all thought of force.[26]

It is certainly true that Communism presents an immense danger. It is a terrible menace to the Church and to free society. But that does not mean that the only answer is nuclear war. We have a choice between the arduous and sacrificial path of negotiation and the insane course of destruction. Public opinion is still very important. As Christians we are bound to make our choice in the light of God's will as expressed by the teachings of the Church. It is true that there is a lot of loose talk and debate. A witless pacifism is no answer. There is no question of just giving

---

[25] Merton is referring to Father L.C. McHugh, S.J. who published "Ethics at the Shelter Doorway" in *America* on September 30, 1961. Merton responded with "The Machine Gun in the Fallout Shelter," published as "Shelter Ethics" in *The Catholic Worker* (November 1961).

[26] In his first Christmas Message (December 23, 1961), Pope John XXIII said that in order to build international peace, it "is necessary . . . to overcome certain erroneous ideas: the myths of force, of nationalism or other things that have prevented the integrated life of nations."

up. We have to seek and find the sane middle path, to protect our faith and our freedom while at the same time keeping peace.

In conclusion, I assure you quite solemnly that I am in no sense communistic or subversive, and have no intention of ever going in that direction. God bless you.

33. To E.R. [Edward Rice], New York [February 10, 1962]

The article of Fr. M.A. [Michael Azkoul] is quite good, and it touches on the main theme of eastern Christian spirituality, deification. There is nothing strange about this theme, which is in fact common to both the Eastern and the Western Fathers. The fact that he presents it as something that might arouse opposition (and of course it might) tends to provoke opposition, and also to create a kind of uneasiness in the non-theological general reader, as if there "might be something the matter with it, but I'll just go along with it anyway because now we have to be nice to the Eastern Christians." This would do more harm than good probably.

Also he does bring up the question of uncreated energies in a way that might require a lot more introduction. Here you do have something that can be and is disputed, but once again it is presented in an abrupt way, with a whole lot taken for granted, so that the reader has no way of getting properly oriented and once again realizes, rightly this time, that he has picked up a hot potato. There are no instructions about what he is supposed to do next.

On the whole, then, though this is a good article on a good subject, the approach is such that I don't see how you can profitably use it. It will, as it stands, create uneasiness and confusion more than enlightenment. At least that is how it looks to me.

I think you should have an article on this subject from a reputable and well-known Catholic theologian sympathetic to the East, and then follow that with some such article, but again I think it should be by an Orthodox theologian of some weight, like probably Ivan [John] Meyendorff. In short I think you ought to arrange a two-part treatment of this theme, showing the basic agreement of the East and West regarding deification as the summit of the Christian life. And also showing that it does not mean anything wacky either.

Could you please send a dozen copies of the last issue [*Jubilee*], air freight or however you do it, to Ernesto Cardenal in Nicaragua? It has to go by air or else it gets carried around in a freighter through the Panama Canal. . . .

I have still no news from the censor about that peace article. Probably it got the axe finally. I have a couple of others which are also getting the axe right now. Except that I am getting one censored in England, where it may have more chance.

Sending a poem. I originally sent it to *Catholic Worker* and I suppose they will want it, so it is just a poem for fun, but if you have some special use for it, and can work it out with CW, go ahead. I don't think you will want to use this. Can't print everything twice. Unless Bob wants it for *Pax*.

How did [William G.] Congdon's exhibit go? He says he is coming down here.

Merry Septuagesima to everybody. Circumdederunt me dolores mortis, etc.

34. To B.S. [Bruno P. Schlesinger], Notre Dame, Ind. [February 10, 1962]

It was kind of you to send me the remarkably good essay ["The Scope of Christian Culture"] by Fr. [George] Tavard. I have read it with considerable interest and will discuss it with the novices here. He is clear and positive and I think he says very much that can be helpful.

Certainly it is first of all important to realize that Christian culture poses a question, and constitutes a problem. Too often we start out with the assumption that all the answers are quite clear, and that we of course are the ones who know them. That everybody else is malicious or ignorant, and that all that is required is for everyone to listen to us and agree with us in everything from faith to table manners and taste in art. Then the world will be all right.

This attitude, as I feel, together with Fr. Tavard, is precisely the most fatal and the most absurd we can possibly take. It assumes that "Christendom" is as much a reality today as it was in the 13th century, or at any rate after the Council of Trent, and that Catholic culture is the culture of those who are obviously and aggressively Catholic in the American sense of the word. We have failed to see that in that sense of the word, we have come to be living contradictions. The "Catholic" who is the aggressive specimen of a ghetto Catholic culture, limited, rigid, prejudiced, negative, is precisely a non-Catholic, at least in the cultural sense. Worse still, he may be anti-Catholic in the cultural sense and perhaps even, in some ways, religiously, without realizing it. Do you think this is too bold and too sweeping a statement? I know it would shock and hurt many, but still I think there is a lot of truth in it. And I think we sometimes obscurely realize it and this contributes no little to our guilt and aggressivity.

I don't suppose you know or read Henry Miller, and I hasten to assure you that I do not read all of him. But in one of his books of essays he has a most interesting comparison between French and American Catholics, and I think that paradoxically he may in some ways have a better intuitive grasp of what a Catholic ought to be than many "Catholics."

In any case I think Fr. Tavard's analysis is very acute, especially as regards the "cosmic" demands for catholicity. I agree too, of course, as anyone with eyes and ears must inevitably agree, that "Christendom" has ceased to exist and that we are *bel et bien* in the post-Christian era. Unless we realize this fact, we cannot possibly make sense out of our situation and its claims upon us. Nor is it reasonable to expect the troubles of the world to be settled all of a sudden by miraculous mass conversions to what, for better or for worse, we actually have now in the way of Christian life, culture, etc., on top of our faith. We just simply do not deserve this, nor would it be merciful of God to bring such a thing about. On the contrary, I am quite sure He wants to teach us much, our *Paidagogos,* and to teach us precisely by the exigencies of our terrible situation.

At one point I would amplify and clarify what Fr. Tavard has said: where he discusses Marx. He does not make clear the inner spiritual potentialities hidden under the surface of the Marxian dialectic and the genuine pretensions to humanism that Marx himself expressed. The subordination of man to the technological process is not something that Marx accepts with unqualified satisfaction. On the contrary it is, for him, the danger and the challenge of a technology based on profit. He thought that the ultimate challenge was for man to free himself of his machines and gain control over them, thus breaking the bonds of alienation and making himself the master of his history. The early essays of Marx recently published by Erich Fromm (Praeger), have some interesting possibilities in the way of the kind of dialogue Fr. Tavard suggests. For in these early essays, in which he concentrates on the problem of alienation, there is a very clear demand for the kind of dimension that can only be supplied by wisdom. Marx himself was uncertain and ambiguous in his treatment of this, but in any case he finds himself compelled to toy with the idea of human nature on which to base his humanism. Now of course to what extent his latent existentialism destroyed or fulfilled this is a question for experts. But in recent discussions among the "revisionists" in those iron curtain countries where the strict dogmatism of the Marxians is questioned, points like this are always agonizingly close to the surface.

Hence I would offer this as a further contribution to the question: if there is to be a collaboration between the Christian humanist and the technological humanist, based on the latter's eventual realization of the need for wisdom, this is going to require as of now a living and radical dialogue between Christian thinkers of the West and revisionist Marxists in the East. How this is to be brought about the Lord alone knows. It is however vitally important.

Meanwhile, thanking you again, I can at least assure you all that I think much of this great issue in my prayers. I am sending you under separate cover a few items that might be relevant in one way or another. As to the *Hagia Sophia* piece, I have decided to mimeograph it for those who cannot afford the limited edition.[27] I am sending you a copy. If the library stills feels inclined to invest in the limited printed edition, which will be exceptionally good looking, they may write to Victor Hammer [in] Lexington, Kentucky.

---

[27] *Hagia Sophia,* limited edition of sixty-nine (Lexington, Kentucky: Stamperia Santuccio, 1962).

35. To K.S. [Karl Stern], Montreal [February 1962]

I was very happy to hear you had written something about peace. If possible please send me a copy at once, as I might be able to include it in an anthology of such essays [*Breakthrough to Peace*] which we are putting out, my publisher and I. We have got a lot of very fine things, and I would like very much to have something of yours. There is a first class little book that has just come out in England, *Nuclear Weapons and the Christian Conscience*, edited by Walter Stein, which you may know.

In the United States things are by no means hopeful and as you point out it is the Catholics who give evidence of the worst moral insensibility. In a collection of articles on nuclear war presumably from a "religious" point of view, the first breath of religious fresh air after some fifty pages of pure secularism dressed up in clerical garb, was from a Rabbi who finally spoke as if he knew something about the relation of ethics to the holiness of God.

The tragedy of Catholics, or rather of some clerics, here, is that they are still clinging to the illusion that they can foster some kind of living unity between Christianity and anti-Christian society. Their efforts at compromise and at bringing about a marriage between the living and the dead result in the most ghastly travesties of religion and religious culture. The current infidelity is to fawn on those who despise religion and to provide them with scraps and rags of a religious justification for their inhumanity, and to kiss their feet until they kick us in the face. Right up until now they do it. Such was the policy in Hitler's Germany. At all costs the state must not be displeased with us Christians. We are loyal, we are loyal. We love Caesar. We will turn all our people over to Caesar for any purpose whatever, and in return, let Caesar permit us to run our stupid little newspapers and hold our little cultural and political picnics . . . It is a grave and tragic situation.

I was pleased to hear about the memorial to Fr. [Max] Metzger and of your devotion to him. I hear that there has been a plea to Rome for his process to begin and that the plea comes from Jews.

I am reading Jeremias a lot and working on the Old

Testament. And last summer I met a wonderful guy from Winnipeg, a Rabbi S . . . [Zalman Schachter], a fine great Hasid who has become a warm friend. I wish you knew him.

I was glad to hear about your trip. It may have brought you up to date on some of the news of the past two or three years. Things which started and went awry, but no matter. If you are ever likely to be down this way, be sure to let me know.

God bless you always. K-. Thanks for your prayers and friendship, I value them in the depths of my heart and keep you in my Masses.

36. To J.N. [James Roy Newman], Washington, D.C. [mid-February 1962]

Cordial thanks for your letter and for the clipping from the *Washington Post*. I think that was one of your best letters and enjoyed it immensely. In return I am sending a modest proposal of my own, which may or may not make the pages of the magazine to which it was sent.

The Rule of Folly[28] contains some excellent things, and above all the dissection of Herman Kahn. Your title is all too literally correct. The way people are working their way up to the most fabulous of all decisions is nothing short of fantastic. It would be unbelievable if anyone wrote it in a novel, before it came to happen. This is to me a source of inexhaustible and disheartening meditations. And yet they grimly confirm a lot of basic assumptions of my own. One thing that is to me especially significant is the role played by blind, deaf, and dumb faith in all this. An abject, superstitious, proto-African credulity that worships the magic oracle of the computer, and tactfully, reverently fails to observe that the thing gives out what has been put in. And as a result of the mystic numbers, people rush forth and fall over themselves to dig these holes in the backyard. It would be utterly farcical if it did not involve real, simple, and on the whole quite good people, with their families and their poor, tragic aspi-

---

[28] James Roy Newman, *The Rule of Folly,* with Preface by Erich Fromm (New York: Simon and Schuster, 1962).

rations to remain human in spite of everything. But everything conspires against it.

I am exercised about some of the things that are being said about "other worlds" sending us messages, a few beeps to teach us their language followed by "the equivalent of a volume of the encyclopedia." Mr. N. - please, for the love of God, tell me how to build a shelter that will protect me from these hurtling volumes of the Encyclopedia Martiana. I am not afraid of fallout, but I am a man of books and I dread of all things these huge volumes. I know how much concentrated frightfulness they can contain and indeed I have contributed to two of them recently. I fear that the Lord is about to punish me in a manner that fits my crime. I am planning an encyclopedia shelter, then, in the woods near here. But don't tell anyone.

I am also evolving a private theory that specially intelligent animals, like seals, dolphins, gorillas, etc., are really the remains of smart civilizations that blew themselves up before us. A few people had the brains to turn into dolphins. If you can tell me how one gets enrolled in the guild of the dolphins, or if you foresee that some new creature is lining up for the future and applications are acceptable . . . I am rather tired of being a human, and would enjoy being a nice, quiet, civilized fish, without political affiliations.

By the way, I got two copies of *The Rule of Folly*. I will pass the extra one along to someone who can profit by it, and am grateful for both.

37. To Z.S. [Rabbi Zalman Schachter], Winnipeg [February 15, 1962]

Many things: first I sent the books to Joe [Manella] at the Kibbutz. I want to know a lot more about this Kibbutz.

Then too we will be looking for you August 8th. There may possibly be a Jesuit friend of mine, a poet, D.B. [Daniel Berrigan], here around then. If there is you will like him. He has contacts with a boy in Chicago [Karl Meyer] who may come down at the same time, and who went on the San Francisco to Moscow peace walk [sponsored by the Committee for Nonviolent

Action]. When he got to Russia he offered to stay there as a hostage for peace but they didn't want any hostage for peace.

Rabbi S. [Steven Schwarzschild] wrote two good letters and sent some offprints of excellent things of his. I especially liked one on silence and prayer, and will be writing to him soon.

Guess what, I just got through reading *The Last of the Just*.[29] I think it is a really great book. It has helped crystallize out a whole lot of things I am thinking about.

Chief of these is of course no news to anyone: that the Jews have been the great eschatological sign of the twentieth century. That everything comes to depend on people understanding this fact, not just reacting to it with a little appropriate feeling, but seeing the whole thing as a sign from God, telling us. Telling us what? Among other things, telling Christians that if they don't look out they are going to miss the boat or fall out of it, because the antimony they have unconsciously and complacently supposed between the Jews and Christ is not even a very good figment of the imagination. The suffering Servant is One: Christ, Israel. There is one wedding and one wedding feast, not two or five or six. There is one bride. There is one mystery, and the mystery of Israel and of the Church is ultimately to be revealed as One. As one great scandal maybe to a lot of people on both sides who have better things to do than come to the wedding.

And of course it is in no sense a matter of shuttling back and forth institutionally. Each on our side, we must prepare for the great eschatological feast on the mountains of Israel. I have sat on the porch of the hermitage and sung chapters and chapters of the prophets out over the valley and it is a hair-raising experience is all I can say.

Therefore I am not at all surprised that you like *The New Man*,[30] the best parts of which are Old Testament parts.

When the Christians began to look at Christ as Prometheus . . . You see what I mean? Then they justified war, then they justified the crusades, then they justified pogroms,

---

[29] André Schwartz-Bart's *The Last of the Just* (New York: Bantam/Atheneum House, 1960), a novel of the Holocaust, was originally published in France.

[30] Thomas Merton, *The New Man* (New York: Farrar, Straus & Cudahy, 1961).

then they justified Auschwitz, then they justified the bomb, then they justified the Last Judgment: the Christ of Michelangelo is Prometheus, I mean the Christ in the Sistine Chapel. He is whipping sinners with his great Greek muscles. "All right," they say, "if we can't make it to the wedding feast (and they are the ones who refused) we can blow up the joint and say it is the Last Judgment." Well, that's the way it is the Judgment, and that's the way men judge themselves, and that's the way the poor and the helpless and the maimed and the blind enter into the Kingdom: when the Prometheus types blow the door wide open for them.

Enough. More some other time. May we enter into the Kingdom and sit down with Abraham and Isaac and Jacob and the Holy One, Blessed be His Name, to Whom Abraham gave hospitality in the Three Strangers.

38. To J.H. [John C. Heidbrink], Nyack, N.Y. [February 15, 1962]

Thank you for the tearsheets of "Red or Dead." I assume you don't want me to return them. I have just sent them off in a letter to E.F. [Erich Fromm]. In the note about the author, I presume there is no point in trying to make any changes and I do not wish to. I must observe that perhaps it would have been better with no mention of the Order. Not that it is important. It is only a very small point. But remember here we are in the realm of Byzantine and highly formal niceties, and in writing for *Fellowship* I am acting as a detached individual while the Order so to speak looks the other way. And I am greatly relying on it looking the other way, for this will continue to be more and more important as we go on.

I think then in my relations with *Fellowship* it would be just best if I were, so to speak, taken for granted as part of the scenery, not requiring an introduction or an explanation, but I just happen to be on the scene somehow . . .

You speak about Una Sancta:[31] definitely it ought to be start-

---

[31] Una Sancta is an ecumenical movement begun in 1939 to promote Christian unity. Fr. Max Metzger was a founder of the movement.

ed in America and I think it will. Things are moving along much more promisingly than one would have dreamed even five years ago. There is much to hope for, and I am quite sure that all it takes is for those at the Catholic end who are officially approved for this kind of work, to take cognizance of such a desire and then do what needs to be done. For Protestants and the Orthodox are long since ready and there is nothing holding them back.

I have had a lot of good reactions from the little piece on Fr. [Max] Metzger.[32] Do you know of K.S. [Karl Stern], the psychiatrist and author? He speaks of having long "prayed to" Fr. Metzger every day. Evidently he knew him in Germany. S. should write for you. Do you want me to mention it? I will.

As far as ecumenism and related "movements" go: I have no capacity to do anything that would even hint at organization. I am, once again, "not really there" or rather if I happen on the scene, it is understood that nobody has adverted to the fact and this is the only way in which I can remain there. Even the small amount of work that I am able to do here has been reduced and cut down to the minimum, and consists in nothing more than giving a few informal talks to groups who come, or chatting for a while with visitors. I had, by the way, a wonderful talk with Douglas and Mrs. Steere, the very day your last letter arrived.

The whole thing is this: I have in no sense whatever any mandate or approval or mission in the Church to work for ecumenism or for anything else. What I do I do purely as an isolated and articulate member of the clergy, whose actions are tolerated and within certain limits "approved" by Superiors so long as I do not involve them in embarrassing situations or long explanations. Hence the point is that you must always be very careful not to say anything that involves any institution to which I belong, except I assume it is legal to say I am a Catholic.

I agree with you that work must be done to clarify the prac-

---

[32] Merton wrote two articles on Fr. Metzger: "Testament to Peace: Father Metzger's Thoughts About the Duty of the Christian," *Jubilee* 10 (March 1962) and "A Martyr for Peace and Unity: Father Max Joseph Metzger (1887-1944)," published in *The Non-Violent Alternative,* edited by Gordon C. Zahn (New York: Farrar, Straus and Giroux, 1980).

tical meaninglessness of arguments based, in a purely theoretical and speculative way, on the "just war" theory.

The great danger is that by isolating oneself from the unpleasant facts, one can spin out a theory that justifies almost any form of nuclear war. Within a very limited and even arbitrary set of suppositions and assumptions, one may end up by concluding "authoritatively" (with a theologian's authority, which cuts ice with bishops) that nuclear war "can be justified."

This theoretical statement having been generally accepted and blessed, the Christian is left at the mercy of anything that may be decided by the military according to an entirely different and more drastic set of assumptions.

The moralist may sweetly and benignly bless a nuclear war which he supposes involves only a few five-megaton H-bombs directed at missile launching sites while the Pentagon is in reality contemplating massive high megatonic terroristic attacks on bases and cities indiscriminately, plus a little chemical and bacteriological hors d'oeuvre to make it go down nice.

By the way, "Target Equals City"[33] and "Christian Action [in World Crises"] have been submitted to the censors but not yet passed, so if you print them before I get the green light there may be trouble. However I refer you to the recent *Commonweal* with an article of mine ["Nuclear War and Christian Responsibility"] which you can pick up if you want. There is a longer and more complete version which you may want to print as a pamphlet, perhaps. That will be in the collection I am editing, and maybe in *The Catholic Worker.*

No matter whether "Red or Dead" shows up with "The Roots of War," I leave that to you. The Shelters for the Shelterless campaign seems to be to be very eloquent as well as fruitful.

Really, [Aldous] Huxley is a great man. I would like to see his ms. about his wife, very much. If you write to him do please

---

[33] "Target Equals City" was not published during Merton's lifetime. As William H. Shannon notes in introducing the article in *Passion for Peace,* this article "more than any other brought the directive from the Abbot General, the highest authority of the Order, that Merton was to write nothing more on the issue of war and peace" (Thomas Merton, *Passion for Peace: The Social Essays,* edited by William H. Shannon [New York: Crossroad, 1995], 227).

give him my regards and remind him of the great esteem and affection I have for him. I have a feeling he thinks that having become a hardened Roman and a monk into the bargain, I have drifted far from any common ground with him, but this is not so.

Did I by the way send you the offprint of the discussion I had with Suzuki about Zen ["Wisdom in Emptiness, A Dialogue: D.T. Suzuki and Thomas Merton" (*New Directions* 17 (1961)]? I will, if I did not already do so.

I am returning the Pamela Frankau piece. It is good but it could be a lot better. I have no suggestions as to who might do an American version. The English business of being a bit non-committal gives an impression they are not fully serious. That is one of the things I like about Walter Stein and Co: they are definitely serious and show it.

Whether or not I can do anything about Una Sancta I can always be a sounding board and a prompter, as well as an encourager. And we can always have our own Una Sancta underground. This is what I think my real mission is, an ecumenical underground, that reaches out everywhere, to Buddhists and the Lord knows where.

39. To W.H.F. [Wilbur H. Ferry], Mexico [February 17, 1962]

I envy you the sunny, dusty lanes, but why go spoil it all with Jules Romains [French author]. Anyway I hope you are having a nice rest.

I am stimulated greatly by the little book on the problem of abundance, and also by your essay on justice in economic life. Certainly your essay is completely "Catholic" in the best sense and it seems to me to fit in perfectly with *Mater et Magistra* [Encyclical of Pope John XXIII, 1961], which is a document full of good sense. There is no catholicity without this basic good sense, and where it is lacking, or where it is evaded, under the pretense of being "more human" or (usually) more "realistic," then everything begins to split open and fall apart.

Yes, I kept a copy of that letter on the "just war" bit [Cold War Letter 26] and it will probably be one of those I intend to get together informally for those who are likely to be interested as well as discrete.

Certainly the greatest danger today is to assume that we have to accept society and its ills as a divinely given and final reality to which our thinking must be adjusted, without any attempt to change anything according to deeper standards. That way, we just let "society" push us along, and we forget that we are society. That if we do not strive to build and guide society according to reason and to conscious principles, then it will lead us and sink us by the power of our own unconscious forces, with a little help from the devil.

To simply suppose that everything works along automatically and nicely and that it is just a question of sweetly adjusting individual greeds together so they form a composite bliss of fulfillment, is what has got us where we are, and is leading us to the final splendid flash.

MacMillan just offered me a ten thousand dollar advance for a small book on peace. I mean the publisher, not the British politician. This shook me and pleased me, not that I can do anything with ten thousand dollars but it shows people are serious about it. Any suggestions? Of course this is quite apart from J's [James Laughlin] anthology [*Breakthrough to Peace*] which has taken a nap while he has been in Florida selling his aunt's circus.

Dust lanes of Sonora! Well, enjoy them!

40. To R.L. [Robert Lax], New York [February 1962]

Dear Major Smithfield,

Indeed the poem of Nick the Gosling is a very fine poem, Major. I think you crazy, Major, if you givem this poem to Swami's revista. This very fine poem, sharpie poem, sharpie poem, much knowledge of monkhouse, I am amazed, heretic yes, dancer yes yes, I am swept away by this very fine poem of Nick your agent on Sinai. It was on Sinai then he get these black lights? Major, my advice to you is to publish this poem so dam fast they cannot see you for smokes, O major.

Furthermore since the cries go up incessantly that there is

in *Pax* no variety, then I feel this is a further ragione for publish this magnificent sequels.

What cry? You balk, what variety? What goes? What goes up?

What cry? Cry of "Hola, no variety in papst."

"Helas, helas, my prince, my prince helas."

"My o my, no varieties."

"I am extinguished with weariness from always that same poem in Paps."

What goes? It goes up. They cry goes up. "Always the same damfool poem."

Which way is up? Relativity is up. Astronarts is up. Apes is up. Russians is up.

As regards up, when I look into ces espaces infines, am I afraed? What is space? What is infamous space?

I look into space and I figurativel or otherwise see: stars, apes, Russians.

Who is afraid of apes or Russians, or Mister Powers release shortly after?

Up in the air is the all seeing eye of some instrument.

But it makes no variety in Paps. For this reason I commend the magnanimous poems of Harry O'Garfield your agent from Dublin.

(The cry also goes up in Dublin.)

Yrs in deep thought
Harvey Cucumerario

Poscraps: We have here entering a fine calypso singer from St. Lucia Westindies but he refuse to bring his guitar.

41. To S.S. [Rabbi Stephen Schwarzschild], Boston, Mass. [February 24, 1962]

Thanks for your two very good letters. I am happy that Z— [Rabbi Zalman Schachter] sent you my texts on peace, for they have brought us into contact and have brought me your fine offprints which I have very much enjoyed. The one on "Speech and Silence before God" is wonderful and very close to my own heart. Thank you for it.

As a matter of fact I had also read your essay in *Worldview,* the collection of essays on nuclear war, gathered around the rather dubious witness of good Fr. M. [Max Metzger]. I felt that yours was the only voice that really spoke with a full and unequivocally religious note and really was loyal to the holiness of Him who is All Holy. It seemed to me that the others were not listening to His demands, and that from the book as a whole He was absent.

His absence among religious people, among religious groups, His absence where it is claimed that He is worshipped, is something terrifying today. Or said in the utter extreme, because it is not His wrath, exactly, it is His loneliness, His lostness among us. That He waits among us unknown and silent, patiently, for the moment when we will finally destroy Him utterly in His image . . . And leave Him alone again in the empty cosmos.

It is the terrible power that He has given to man, that man can isolate himself and blast himself irrevocably into an outer darkness where he is separated from Him Who is nevertheless everywhere. I cannot believe that this is designed to be irrevocable, but so we are told and so perhaps it is. How can it be? There are dimensions that we are not capable of investigating.

But at any rate let us finally have pity on Him, that we may return to ourselves and have pity on one another.

Certainly I think the unutterable pity of the fate of the Jews in our time is eschatological, and is a manifestation of the loneliness and dejection of God, that He should bring upon Himself so much sorrow and suffer it in His Beloved People. In this He is speaking to us who believe ourselves, in His mercy, to have been adopted into His Chosen People and given, without any merit, the salvation and the joy promised to the Sons of Abraham. But we on the other hand have been without understanding and without pity and have not known that we were only guests invited to the banquet at the last minute.

We have not lived up to our share in the promise and we have not been to Israel, as we were meant to have been, a consolation. It is terrible to see how little we have been that, so little that the irony is almost unbearable. Who notices this?

Certainly let us consider a statement. Though I am not crazy about all these statements (some however have been very good). I would much rather I had a chance to be parachuted on to one of those Pacific (may He forgive us) islands and sit there protesting against the next test. I do not think these words count much any more, nobody reads words. And also there still remains one crazy reservation: because I think guerilla warfare is not illegitimate. I think that people like the Hungarians, like the Jews in Israel, have a right to recourse to that kind of protest and self-protection. Hence I cannot make a statement that would leave South Americans presumably without right of action against Communists down there. At the same time, I realize what form self-defense would take: the mercenary fascist army . . . Alas. Perhaps we can discuss this more. I am not clear.

I am not worthy yet to write about the mystery of Judaism in our world. It is too vast a subject. I wish I could. Maybe some day. If there is anything I say *en passant* that happens to make sense to you, you can quote it if you like. The article will have to be a thing of the future, if God wills us to have a future on this earth. (I do not doubt that He does, but sometimes the chances are a little disconcerting.)

42. To M.A. [Mother Angela Collins (Mother Angela of the Eucharist), O.C.D.], Louisville, Ky. [February 1962]

The issue about Civil Defense concerns not only you but the whole community and since my opinion has been implicitly asked, I would like to clarify.

Certainly I would think it would be very important for everyone to take any *effective* steps to protect themselves against a nuclear attack and its effects. I suggest that if the Louisville Carmel wants to be protected effectively against nuclear war, . . . well, you might move to New Zealand.

Look: the problem is this. An awful lot of poor well-meaning people have been simply "had" by this nonsense about fallout shelters. The ignorance and well-meaning mistakes that have occurred have been monumental. First of all, the estimates of nuclear radiation, on which this whole program is based, are purely a guess as to the *kind of attack* that would occur. The estimates of the dangerous radiation have been figured out in terms of a ridiculously small attack, with small bombs. A fallout shelter in Louisville might be of some use if the nearest target hit were say, Chicago. Perhaps Cleveland. But if Louisville or Fort Knox got hit, then you and we have simply had it. No fallout shelter will be of any use whatever within twenty to fifty miles of a target hit by a big bomb. The H-bomb is an *incendiary* bomb. Fallout is the least of its effects. The fire caused by an H-bomb will not only burn out everything within a radius of twenty to fifty miles or more, depending on the size of the bomb, but will cause fire storms which devour all the oxygen, so that even in a deep fireproof shelter you would smother. If not bake. In Hamburg, in the last war, with ordinary incendiary bombs, people were roasted alive in shelters. This is the brutal truth, and we might as well face it.

Hence if the bomb were to hit anywhere near here a fallout shelter would be useless. The higher in the air the bomb explodes, the wider the range of the fire. If the bomb explodes on the ground then there is more fallout. There is no reason for exploding the bomb on the ground around Louisville (though maybe at Fort Knox). If they wanted to hurt Louisville, they would just burn it out with one bomb exploded fairly high up.

An atomic scientist built himself a fallout shelter in California last summer, and what happened? An ordinary brush fire came through and destroyed his house, his garage, and his fallout shelter. Lots of shelters that have been built have caved in or filled with water, etc. I am not saying that a good shelter cannot be had but the question to be asked is, is this a reasonable expense? A lot of people I know, rather than build shelters, are taking the cost of a shelter and giving it to a fund to build houses for poor people in underdeveloped countries. And so it goes. My own feeling is that it is absolutely against religious poverty to risk money on a thing like that. If it were something everyone could easily have and which could be very effective, then I would say by all means build one. But since it is so risky and precarious and might be totally useless, as well as absurd, I think the best thing is to trust God and wait until we find something that makes a little more sense. This is my opinion, anyway. I have no intention taking shelter if anything happens. If I am still around after the bomb explodes, and am not blinded completely by it, I will try to help others. That, it seems to me, would be my serious obligation as a priest. Certainly if a nuclear attack takes place, there is going to be terrible confusion and suffering and though there is every reason for people to take effective steps to survive and try to build up the country afterwards, there is also every reason for those who don't give a hoot for survival to go about trying to help those who, like the majority, will be in need of some help in their last hours. This of course for a priest is not a matter of what he feels or thinks about survival, it is just his ordinary duty.

Another point in passing: the civil defense program has been fitted into a very dubious military policy, and is not only geared for the possibility of an attack on our country. A serious aspect of it is that it may also be fitted into a *plan for an attack on Russia made by us.* This is something worth considering also.

I just wanted to clarify what I think about this. I would say that everyone has a right and perhaps in some cases an obligation to take *effective* steps to preserve life and survive a nuclear attack. But no one is obliged to take a gamble of this magnitude, when there are serious reasons for thinking that it may be a pure waste of money and self-deception. Of course, there is nothing to say that one must not do this if he wants, but I think it is silly.

Anyway, God bless you all, and I hope that no such thing will ever be needed. If we pray and trust God, and if we do what we ought to do as Christians, there is every hope . . . But that is a big if, these days. It looks as though we are about to resume atmospheric testing, so watch your spinach.

43. To T.T. [Tashi Tshering], Seattle, Wash. [February-March 1962]

First of all I want to thank you for the wonderful gift of the *Life of Mila Repa* [*Tibet's Great Yogi Milarepa,* edited by W.Y. Evans-Wentz]. This is a splendid volume, and extremely interesting to me. I am absorbed in it, and it gives a wonderful idea of Tibetan Buddhism. It has a character of energy and power which is quite unique. Certainly the Western idea of Buddhism is terribly confused.

You mention the spirit of sacrifice in your letter, and the most notable thing about Mila Repa is the absolute totality of his sacrifice in order to attain to liberation. There was no price too high to pay. His will was indomitable. At the same time will alone is not sufficient. This is recognized, in Buddhism, by the idea of karma from a positive or good aspect, and in Christianity by the idea of grace. In any event it is clear that Mila Repa had received a special gift, a power to desire and to thirst for the light.

I believe that this gift is hidden in all of us, and that we should be aware of it, allowing it to awaken in our hearts. To me the Buddhist disciplines of meditation and asceticism are very interesting because of the very sure psychological realism they display. I believe that the wisdom of these techniques is not sufficiently appreciated. It is a pity that Christian scholars tend to approach Buddhism with many illusions, believing it to be in some sense a "rival religion." To think this is, in many ways, a complete misunderstanding. The very essence of Buddhism is that it is "non-competitive" because it does not set up barriers and divisions, but rather destroys them, seeking the deepest unity, beyond all oppositions, and seeking it on a philosophical and ascetic plane, rather than by means that would conflict with the Christian sacraments, necessarily. We are dealing with different levels and different ways of approaching ultimate unity.

In any case, Mila Repa is to me a very significant and fortunate discovery. I especially like his poems about the solitary life and am interested in learning more about the hermit tradition in Buddhism. I am very happy to hear about Prof. Deshong Tuku, there at the Tibetan Research Center. I am unfortunately not able to come out to Washington, but perhaps some day he may come this way, or we may meet somehow. I am very interested in keeping in touch with you and in hearing more about the research that goes on there. I am, you may be sure, a sympathetic friend to all that concerns Buddhism, and would like very much to strengthen the points of contact between Buddhist and Christian thought. I shall be sending you a couple of books, and shall also send something to Prof. Deshong Tuku.

Let us meanwhile work with ardent and disciplined hope for the light, and above all strike at the ignorance which fills our hearts with darkness, not only the ignorance that comes from lack of scientific knowledge, but also the deeper ignorance which comes from spiritual darkness and attachment to the external self. In a word, let us strive to unite science and wisdom in one!

44. To E.S. [Elbert R. Sisson], Maryland [February-March 1962]

Friends have been keeping me supplied with information, and as a result I have seen *Visible Witness*[34] and the King Hall pamphlet which I have not yet read but which is here. I liked the Young pamphlet very much. I will look into the book you mention, to which Jerome Weisner has contributed. It is good to know about him. If I had been aware of him before, I would have asked him for a contribution to a collection of essays I have been getting together, to be published in a paperback by New Directions [*Breakthrough to Peace*]. [Leo] Szilard I know, of course. What about this organization Szilard is running for peace?

I wonder if there ought not to be something done to get these various peace movements together in one solid bloc, so to speak.

Certainly it is very important that all the rational and clearheaded opinion which still exists in this country should become articulate and exert force. It would be a tragedy when so much good has been accomplished and when so much can really be done with the amazing power of science, if the whole thing were to run away with us and if the crazy people were to take over completely. Unfortunately the lack of balance between technology and spiritual life is so enormous that there is every chance of failure and of accident. Indeed it sometimes seems as if the wrong-headed ones are working inexorably for the worst possible issue. But we must not despair and we must really try to do all that we can.

I hope that you will keep in touch with me. I will send along a few more things of mine. Your wife's letter is a good one. God bless you and her and the children, and may He protect us all from the folly of our society, to which we have all made some small contribution, I do not doubt.

[34] In *Visible Witness: A Testimony of Radical Peace Action* (Pendle Hill Pamphlet #118, 1961), Wilmer J. Young writes of his experience of serving time in jail as a result of his peace action.

45. To A.R. [Ad Reinhardt], New York [February-March 1962]

Once, twice, often, repeatedly. I have reached out for your letter and for the typewriter. Choked with sobs, or rather more often carried away by the futilities of life, I have desisted. Dear relatives and classmates at tragedies. Ah yes, how true. As life goes on, as we descend more and more into the hebetude of middle age, as the brain coagulates, as the members lose their spring, as the spirit fades, as the mind dims, we come together face to face with one another and with our lamentable errors.

Our lamentable errors. My lamentable errors.

Truly immersed in the five *skandhas* and plunged in *avidya,* I have taken the shell for the nut and the nut for the nugget and the nugget for the essence and the essence for the suchness. Form is emptiness and emptiness is form.

You throw the centuries at me and you are right. Throw them all. Kneeling, I receive the centuries in a shower cascading all over my head. Weeping and penitent I receive upon the back of the head Jordan (8th cent.) Damascus (8th cent.) You do not mention Isphahan, or the place where the Blue Dome is and where some Imam whose name I forget is venerated (9th cent?). These are the centuries, indeed they are the centuries. And I, as I look at myself with increasing horror, I remark that I have become a boy of the twenty first century. Throw then your centuries at me, you are right, the centuries are right, and the twenty first century has very slim chances of ever existing.

Going further down I see you do mention Isphahan after all but you spell it with an F. Go on throw it, I deserve it with an F also.

I have embraced a bucket of shmaltz. I have accepted the mish mash of kitsch. I have been made public with a mitre of marshmallows upon my dumkopf. This is the price of folly and the wages of middle-aged perversity.

I thought my friends would never know.

Victor Hammer is coming today. He does not know. If he has come to know about this disgrace, I shall efface myself in a barn someplace and become a sheep. I shall weave rugs out of cornsilk, equivalent in substance to my artistic judgments which I eternally regret.

My artistic judgment has contracted the measles.

My love of kunst has become mumped.

My appreciation of the sacreds hath a great whoreson pox and is reproved by all with good tastings and holy lauds.

What would it be if he knew, the Imam? If he knew? Under his blue dome?

He would stir, he would stir.

You are pro-iconoclast and you are right. You are quietists and you are right. You are non objectivist and you are right. Down with object. Down with damn subject. Down with matter and form. Down with nanarupa. I mean namarupa. Sometimes get my terms wrong. Terms in general have the weasels.

Now the thing is, I am up to my neck. I am in the wash. I am under the mangle. I am publically identified with all the idols. I am the byword of critics and galleries. I am eaten alive by the art racket. I am threatened with publication of a great book of horrors which I have despised and do recant. Bring the bell book and candle and have me shriven. Lift the ban, dissolve the excommunication, release the golden doves from the high dome, let the bells ring and let me be reconciled with the Moslem Synagogue. Help, help, rescue your old fellow sachem from way back in 1937 or whenever there was sachems. Tell [Robert] Lax, help, help, help.

46. To S.E. [Steve Eisner], Detroit, Mich. [February-March 1962]

Forgive me for waiting so long to acknowledge the book. As a matter of fact I remember having some correspondence with Raymond Larsson several years ago and had kept track of him from a distance since then. I knew he was still writing, but I had no idea the poems he had done were so fine. It is a splendid book [*Book Like a Bow Curved*], and I congratulate you on it. And of course him also. I will have to get in touch with him, and send him something of my own.

Larsson has used traditional idioms with perfect integrity, and he is certainly a fine poet, underestimated and probably little known, for all I can tell. It is interesting that his sickness has given him a valid and a fruitful kind of distance, protecting him from movements and delusive fashions. More power to him. This is fine poetry, from a noble person.

Of course I knew Bro. Antoninus' [William Everson] book [*The Crooked Lines of God* (1959)] put out by your press [University of Detroit Press]. In fact I think the program of the press sounds very good, and can only encourage you with all my heart.

Of course, too, I thank you for writing. I am not one who believes that a man has to show his religious party card before one can speak to him. And I am well aware that there are plenty of people who shy away from religion and its institutional aspect precisely because of a certain abuse of this kind of thing. God asks of us, first of all, sincerity and truth. Conformity is not the first requisite, or the second, or the tenth. I do not know where it may stand on the list, or whether it is on the list at all, since God has not shown me His list. But since He has made us for the truth it stands to reason that we have to be true in order to know the truth.

Thanks again for Raymond Larsson's poem, and God bless you.

47. To J.G.L. [Justus George Lawler], Chicago, Ill. [February-March 1962]

Naturally your letter was very gratifying. I am sorry I have delayed in making a reply, but as you can imagine I get pretty busy at times and have been unusually so in the last few weeks.

There is no question in my mind that the articles you mention can form a nucleus for a book, and I am actively considering such a project. The point about letting the book appear under a Catholic imprint has weight, and there is no question at all that everything possible must be done to awaken the scandalous dormancy of the Catholic conscience in so many places, including high places.

I am certainly glad that you wrote, for several reasons. It is heartening to get such a good response on such an important issue, and the response has been good all along. Since the shelter panic last summer people seem to have been waking up, and I think the Jesuit Father [Fr. L. C. McHugh, S.J.] who commended the shotgun

in the shelter[35] has shocked Catholics, or some Catholics, into realizing how far we have descended. There is certainly a lot of more
or less articulate concern. But as you say, one wonders gravely
about the bishops and, I might add, the theologians.

It does not seem to me that the gravity of the situation is
sensed by the people who ought to sense it. They are hypnotized
by Communism, which is certainly a real menace, but by no
means the only menace. Nor is it perhaps the most urgent menace: on this I am perhaps not competent to judge. But the
descent into secularism and the drift into irresponsibility have
gone perhaps irreparably far. Do moralists realize to what
extent the gravest of decisions are now being made not only by
men who are frankly a-moral and opportunistic, but by
machines fed with their guesses and suppositions? Are the consciences of Christians in this crisis to be guided by the Church
and by the Holy Spirit, or turned over by Churchmen to the
blind guidance of computers? It is not a cheerful thought.

48. To W.H.F. [Wilbur H. Ferry], Santa Barbara, Calif. [March 6, 1962]

Thanks for your good letter from Mexico and the one sent on
returning, with its enclosures. I wonder why you chose a place
where you would be surrounded by squares in the first place.
There must be lots of other places. But as I understand it now,
the squares are all over and there is no island left where one can
escape them. Indeed they have come to specialize even in the
nicest islands.

That reminds me we have in the novitiate now a West
Indian Negro postulant from St. Lucia and he is refreshing
indeed. I am picking up from him bits of the charming French
patois they speak on the island. Its religious undertones are
warm and moving. It seems to be pretty much the same sort of
thing that is spoken in Haiti, as the Island was once French.

Time does not permit more of this pleasant kind of thing.

---

[35] See "The Shelter Ethic," *The Catholic Worker* (November 1961), for
Merton's response.

Criticism comes in about the *Commonweal* article ["Nuclear War and Christian Responsibility"] which perhaps you saw. It was doubtless oversimplified. The standard tactic of the defender of the status quo is to say that all moral criticism of the bomb is prompted by "fright" and is a manifestation of "emotionalism." The people who want to use the bomb are on the other hand qualified as objective and unemotional thinkers. True virtue is on their side. Etc., etc. It is the basic aberration of Cold War thinking, which I think Hallock Hoffman [fellow of the Center for the Study of Democratic Institutions] spots accurately. God knows I doubt there is much chance of it being so cheerfully repealed. Funny, the man who wrote *Commonweal* about the article, and whom I am answering, claims that nobody is really threatening to use the bomb at all. The question of a nuclear threat has not even been raised, he says, in the Berlin crisis. And anyway, there was so much indiscriminate destruction with conventional weapons in WW II that it is "nothing new," so what is there to get excited about, and so on.

Thanks also for Father H-'s letter. Here again I think the perspective is completely dominated by Cold War assumptions. He is of course more moderate and reasonable but in the end we always get back to the dominance of certain practical assumptions that are taken almost as absolute first principles. The first and greatest of all commandments is that America shall not and must not be beaten in the Cold War, and the second is like unto this, that if a hot war is necessary to prevent defeat in the Cold War, then a hot war must be fought even if civilization is to be destroyed. Once this is accepted, and of course it depends on how tight one hangs on to it, then other assumptions are not even considered, other possibilities are rejected as unreal and put aside without even a thought. The one great "reality" is the threat of Communism, and all else is illusion, fantasy, speculation, theory, or what you will. It is nice, but one is not even able to make the necessary effort of will to get one's mind focused on it. It amounts almost to an obsession and this is what really worries me most: so many good and intelligent and well-trained minds are held captive by this absolute principle which makes them unable to look at any else and take any other viewpoint than that of Cold War military practicality.

I admit that there is a tendency at the other end to go to the other extreme. But what we all have to do is get as free as possible from prejudgments in order to try to do the immense pioneering job of thinking that is demanded if we are going to come to grips with this problem at all. I suppose my contribution to this must consist in being a little less hortatory and a little better informed. The more subtle aspects of the question have to be brought out. All I have been attempting so far is to establish a basic moral principle with which no one can seriously disagree if he has any morality at all: and then prepare the ground to work from there, instead of from the more fluid and it seems to me opportunistic principle that conquest by Communism is the greatest evil. This is not in order to side-step the issue of Communism, but in order to face it more perfectly and more effectively. I may be fully certain of my moral principle. This may dispose me to favor unilateral disarmament. However that is an altogether different question, and an enormous amount of work has to be done in the practical order. I am innocent of political thought but it seems to me that one ought to discuss the validity of defending tooth and nail a viewpoint that is never likely to be shared by the people in power—unless one simply wants to protest and "witness" to the truth as he sees it.

Czeslaw Milosz wrote me some time ago and said my stand on peace was actually going to accomplish nothing but harden the right wing in its bellicosity.[36] This is to some extent true.

My conclusion is that once the moral principle has been established and accepted, and we see that for moral reasons we want to avoid an all-out nuclear war and eventually to make such a war impossible, then comes the long job of the ways and means for working for this. And do we have time for a long job, in the first place?

I am almost forced to fall back on the conclusion that our political action has to become in some sense dialectical. That is to say we are going to have to use proposals and plans dialectically, instead of simply formulating them and then sticking to

---

[36] For Milosz's critique of Thomas Merton's position see *Striving Towards Being: The Letters of Thomas Merton and Czeslaw Milosz,* edited by Robert Faggen (New York: Farrar, Straus and Giroux, 1997), 138-140 and *The Courage for Truth: Letters to Writers,* edited by Christine M. Bochen (New York: Farrar, Straus and Giroux, 1993), 79-80.

them in the teeth of all opposition. The strength of the Communists consists in their ability to stand back from the immediate issue and from commitment to their line, and see things more dispassionately, so that they are able momentarily to espouse the cause opposite to their own in order to use its potentialities in preparing the way for what they themselves want. But in the first place one must know what he wants, and want it along with a lot of other people who are equally clear about the whole thing . . . I am not the man to be talking about this sort of thing. I know nothing about politics.

By the way, what is that [Etienne] Gilson book H. Hoffman refers to?

I have to close now. Really it is vitally important that we now work at keeping the way wide open for thought, for discussion, for investigation, for meditation: and the thing that most blocks this is getting oneself permanently identified and so to speak classified as the holder of one or other set of opinion. And, by implication, as loyal or disloyal to our side in the Cold War. Even to question the primary importance of this kind of loyalty is itself regarded as disloyalty and immediately disqualifies all that one says from further consideration. We have got to keep thinking and asking questions. And the mere ability, once in a while, to raise the right question ought to be regarded as an achievement. May we learn to do this and keep at it. What did the Fathers of the Church say about Socrates being among the saints? And there are also the Prophets.

49. To the Editors, *The Commonweal* [March 1962][37]

Dear Sirs:

I admit that living in a monastery, as I have done for many years now, I am not in an ideal position to obtain up-to-the minute information about world events. But when your correspondent asserts that in the Berlin crisis "the use of nuclear

---

[37] Merton wrote this letter in response to Joseph G. Hill, who had written to *Commonweal* taking issue with Merton's article "Nuclear War and Christian Responsibility" (*Commonweal*, February 9, 1962). Hill's letter and Merton's response were published in *Commonweal* on April 20, 1962.

force has not come up for consideration," I find his statement barely credible. Is he serious? What are fallout shelters supposed to be for? In my utter innocence, I have been supposing all this time that they had something to do with the by-products of a thermonuclear explosion. True, I am told that one atomic scientist built one that was destroyed by a brush fire.

A moratorium on weapons? What is the budget expenditure for weapons and related items this year? Are we spending more on armaments or less?

I do not accept the argument that "massive and indiscriminate destruction of targets is nothing new," and the implication that since it was done in the last war a precedent has been established and we can now do anything we like. Pope Pius XII declared at the very beginning of World War II that such methods "cry out to Heaven for vengeance." According to him, even with conventional weapons, these destructive acts were criminal. What will they be with fifty-megaton bombs?

I do not claim to be a "lone voice" in this matter of irresponsibility. The Joint Letter of the U.S. Bishops in 1960 deplored the growing moral irresponsibility of our people, and it has never been more evident than now. I would like to ask whether the ever-increasing and ever-more decisive role of the computer in reaching crucial judgments in the question of war is not a threat to human and moral responsibility. It certainly places an enormous burden upon the expert who uses these instruments and thus guides the judgments of strategy planners. I am glad to hear that Los Alamos is full of conscientious men who are doing a lot of "clear unemotional thinking" because they are going to have to do a great deal more of it in the future. The rest of us are not going to be in a position to make a positive contribution one way or the other. And that is why I brought up that unpleasant hypothesis. We may be rendered physically helpless by the consequences of judgments made in high places over which we have no control. But that does not mean we can or should give up our moral freedom and our responsibility. President Eisenhower said that if governments do not soon make peace they will "have to get out of the way and let the people make it." I am not so sure that there is any likelihood of this happening, but the individual retains the right and the duty to refuse participation in collective crime. Of course it must be evident that what he refuses to participate in is immoral. My hypothesis clearly supposed a situation that was beyond control, criminal, and suicidal.

What basis do I have for contending that our foreign policy relies largely on deterrence? What is the ultimate sanction in our dealing with Russia if not the threat of nuclear destruction? What is Mr. Herman Kahn writing about all the time? What was the basis of the foreign policy of the late Mr. [John Foster] Dulles if not "brinkmanship" and the threat of "massive retaliation"? What is our policy shaping up to now if not to preemption? I do not say it has got that far, but can anyone assert that the idea of the preemptive first strike is not taken seriously in America today? Can anyone deny that such a strike might easily lead to a war of massively destructive proportions?

In an article on nuclear war an author is hardly expected to talk about the Marshall Plan and the Peace Corps. My thesis was not political but ethical. I wanted to make clear a point which cannot seriously be controverted, at least by a Christian: that *uncontrolled destruction* of entire populations and regions with nuclear weapons whose lethal effect may extend to neutrals and even affect future generations, is morally inadmissible. Whatever may be said about the feasibility of limited nuclear war, Pope John XXIII clearly told us in his Christmas message that heads of nations must do all in their power to avoid acts that might lead to disastrous consequences. What are the chances of our wars indefinitely staying "limited"?

Meditations on a dangerous book, the Bible, have convinced me that when the human race gets itself into a major crisis, it shows a strong tendency to abdicate moral responsibility and to commit sin on an enormous scale. That is the kind of situation we face now. Unless we realize the moral and spiritual roots of the problem, our best efforts to solve it in a positive and human way are bound to be meaningless. In my article I showed a mistrust of man's capacity to control nuclear power once it was unleashed in war. Your correspondent infers, quite gratuitously, that I am against nuclear energy as such. Where does he get that idea? Is he by any chance thinking emotionally?

To leave the plane of ethics and to draw a political conclusion: certainly I am in favor of every sane policy that can promote peace while preserving the spiritual, cultural, and social heritage of Christian civilization. I do not defend the thesis of peace at any price. But I do not believe that any policy in which individual nations can, on their own judgment, resort to nuclear force on a massive scale, is to be considered either reasonable or efficacious. I see no good results whatever coming from any such policy. I believe we are going to have to prepare ourselves for the difficult and patient task of outgrowing rigid and intransigent nationalism, and work slowly toward a world federation of peaceful nations. How will this be possible? Don't ask me. I don't know. But unless we develop a moral, spiritual and political wisdom that is proportionate to our technological skill, our skill may end us.

The first edition of the "Cold War Letters" ended with letter 49. Merton circulated mimeographed copies in late April or early May 1962.

50. To W.D. [unidentified], Oyster Bay, N.Y. [March 1962]

I will at this time, say at least the following: I agree with much which you have sent, but I cannot agree with all of it, and if I write on these subjects I think I will take a position which diverges from that which some of these books adopt. But there is a certain variety in the works you have sent, and some come closer to my viewpoint than others. Here is what I think, in a few succinct points.

There is absolutely no question of the utter gravity and seriousness of the Communist menace. We must resist this movement which is explicitly and formally dedicated to the destruction of the kind of society and culture which we know, and in particular its religious and ethical code, its whole spirit, and all that it values. We know that Communism is out to destroy us by fair means or foul. You of the so-called radical right are thoroughly convinced of the possible emphasis on the *foul* means. In many respects you are right, at least in principle. The Communists themselves have declared that there are no holds barred, this is a struggle to the death, truth and agreements mean nothing except in so far as they are politically advantageous to the cause of their revolution. They have demonstrated time and again that they mean exactly what they say in this, and this is their way of operating.

This being the case, it is also true that they work by infiltration, by espionage, by the clever manipulation of "front" organizations, and by the exploitation of well-meaning persons in free society who, often without being aware of it, take positions which are highly advantageous to Communism and prepare the way for further Communist successes. This is a real danger, and where the danger really exists it must be unmasked.

In these matters of principle, there seems to me to be no objection and no argument. But where it comes to putting these principles into practice I tend to question a lot of the conclusions and procedures that have been adopted by the extreme conservatives.

1. First of all I think that the zeal in ferreting out "Communists" tends to be very sweeping and confused. The difference between the Communist and the Liberal seems to be dangerously and systematically obliterated, and the term Communist comes to be applied to anyone and everyone who is not on the extreme right. For instance President Eisenhower has been accused of being a "card carrying Communist." I am sure almost everyone can see that this is a bit exaggerated. But I don't think enough are aware that it is a bit unrealistic to call J.M. [John Maynard] Keynes a Communist. I say unrealistic. It harms your own cause, and it brings discredit upon the arguments advanced in favor of it. I see no reason why you should not be opposed to Keynesian economic theories if you want, but then I think they should be classified more accurately and their possible tendencies in a collectivist direction must be shown for tendencies and not as accomplished facts. Hence, it seems to me that too-sweeping condemnations of one and all as "Communists" have caused the right-wing conservative youth to be regarded with suspicion as not fully responsible in their judgments.

2. I know that the classic reply to this is that the rejection of such disclosures is unfair and is itself the result of a Communist conspiracy. But this is not realistic either. There may certainly

be cases where Communists under cover of liberalism work to discredit attacks made on them in this way. But you do yourselves a grave disservice if you get in the habit of automatically dismissing everything and everyone who does not agree with you on the grounds that he is a conspirator. In a word, I would say that the case of the extreme right needs to rest on a much more disciplined and objective use of available data, and on real proofs rather than on indistinct and general argumentation. Mark what I mean: the real proofs are there, but there is so much indiscriminate use of all kinds of material together that the true may be buried in a pile of much that is totally irrelevant. Much more work needs to be done in thinking really hard and clearly defining one's terms and goals, and stating exactly what one is trying to prove. I think some of the authors tend to take the shotgun approach, that is to say they spray pellets all around the target instead of aiming at the bull's eye, and they are satisfied if they hit New Dealers and Leftish Democrats, even Republicans, as long as they hit someone. And everyone who is hit becomes, by that very fact, a Communist.

3. My objection to this is based on several counts. First the injustice to the persons concerned, and second to the very American ideals which we all want to defend. But passing over these, I would like to stress the objection that this procedure is of great value to the Communists themselves. My chief fear of the methods of the radical right is that this is just the sort of thing that Communists can use to great advantage. Remember, the Communist proceeds by dialectical thinking. His favorite way of preparing and softening up certain kinds of situation is to favor the extreme right wing, the dictator type, the autocracy which tends to discredit itself by its own extremism. In making an over-emphatic case for one extreme we drive people to the other extreme, and prepare them to accept it.

It seems to me that in reaction against right-wing radicalism a lot of people are going, and will go, more to the left than they would otherwise do.

However, what I am saying here applies mostly to the material concerning the danger of Communism in this country. I repeat, the danger is there. The books on Communist operations and takeovers abroad are also solid and objective evidence of the thing we have to expect anywhere, even here. My fear is that an unwise, undisciplined, amateurish reaction, based on emotion more than on reason, is just the thing that will favor and prepare the way for Communism or some other form of totalitarianism in this country.

What is needed is moderation, rationality, objective thought, and above all a firm continued reliance on the very things which are our strength: constitutional processes of government, respect for the rights we want to defend, rational discussion, freedom of opinion, and a deep loyalty to our inherited ideals. This requires mental and spiritual discipline, and we all owe it to our country and to our faith to develop this kind of discipline, along with objectivity, fairness, respect for rights. The fact that Communists do the opposite does not entitle us to take over all their methods, and I am afraid there is a tendency to learn from them and apply some of their techniques.

The danger is serious, and I am with you all the way in wanting to keep our country free, preserving all our basic liberties, and all our ideals, which have been the highest ideals in Western civilization. But I think we have a long way to go in finding out ways and means of negotiating our critical situation, and we must take care not to rely on means which will eventually destroy the very things we are trying to protect and defend.

Do believe me sincerely grateful for your interest, and let me sum up my message as a plea for a more middle-of-the-road course and for attachment to our basic ideals of freedom and rationality of thought.

51. To S.M.M. [Sr. Mary Madeleva], Notre Dame, Ill. [March 1962]

The chief reason why Julian of Norwich and the other English Mystics are not in the notes I sent, is that I did not have time to treat them adequately, and in proportion to my love for them. I also left out the Cistercians, practically. But Julian is without doubt one of the most wonderful of all Christian voices. She gets greater and greater in my eyes as I grow older and whereas in the old days I used to be crazy about St. John of the

Cross, I would not exchange him now for Julian if you gave me the world and the Indies and all the Spanish mystics rolled up in one bundle. I think that Julian of Norwich is with Newman the greatest English theologian. She is really that. For she reasons from her experience of the substantial center of the great Christian mystery of Redemption. She gives her experience and her deductions, clearly, separating the two. And the experience is of course nothing merely subjective. It is the objective mystery of Christ as apprehended by her, with the mind and formation of a fourteenth-century English woman. And that fourteenth-century England is to me and always has been a world of light, for I have almost lived in it. So many villages and churches of the time are still there practically without change, or were thirty years ago. One can still breathe the same air as Julian, with the admixture of a little smog and fallout, of course . . .

It was necessary that I bear witness to my love for the Lady Julian, and that is why I have written. But now that I am speaking to you, I know you will help me along with your prayers. I don't pretend to be a lone crusader for peace or anything romantic like that, but I do feel there is a job to be done that is not being done and that there is an awful silence on the part of the hierarchy and the clergy, especially in America, on this subject, which is really crucial. If I can possibly get together a few articles and make a book out of them . . . Please pray. I am not having it very easy in any way whatever, and it is not likely to be easier as the project develops. I speak now of a book of my own essays. It has been relatively simple to get together a book of essays by others, and I hope this will appear soon.

52. To H.M. [Herbert Mason], Gorham, Maine [March 9, 1962]

I am going to become a worse and worse correspondent I am afraid. So you must be prepared to bear with me. Visitors and letters are both more frequent at the moment and they will have to be rationed, otherwise they will cut in on the most important things. And then also this is Lent.

But I owe you so many letters and notes I can hardly

remember them all. In all of them you give me perceptive comments on the articles and poems, etc., and for these comments I am very grateful. Fr. [Max] Metzger you will by now have seen in *Jubilee* [10 (March 1962)], and it ["Testament to Peace"] might make a good little leaflet. Have you by any chance got in touch with the F.O.R. [Fellowship of Reconciliation] at Nyack? Did I speak to you about them?

"Christian Action [in World Crisis" published in *Blackfriars*, June 1962] will certainly not be published as it stands. It is still in the hands of censors, since months. Target and City ["Target Equals City"]: I do not agree with your comment on this.[38] I think the case is quite clear and needs to be stated. It would seem that this is the kind of evidence that needs to be stressed and it is incontrovertible. It shows that the opportunism of military policy overrides everything and that therefore to pretend that conscience has much of a part in it is over-optimistic. On the contrary, Cold War thinking, in which Christians let their minds be shaped (and so easily) by the fantasies of an aggressive policy, purely and simply determines them beforehand to give moral rationalization to justify that policy, however inhuman and unjust. This needs to be clearly shown, as against the cliché of those who confuse passivity with obedience and say that the "leaders know best" and the "government is always right," etc. This is the great danger.

On the other hand I absolutely agree with you on the danger of non-violent and civil-disobedience movements that go ahead irresponsibly. There is a great danger of opportunism and improvisation here too, especially as a lot of them are young and lack perspective. There must be non-violence, and this is one of the only solutions. But precisely it must be real, mature, well prepared, disciplined non-violence. And for this we are by no means ready. There is every danger that resentment, immature rebelliousness, beatnik nonconformism, and so on may be taken automatically to be charismatic just because they are opposed to what is obviously stuffy and inert. And cruel.

---

[38] On February 27, 1962, Herbert Mason wrote: "Please be careful. Don't print something such as 'Target Equals City': only your enemies would publish that."

Unfortunately the opposition, the status quo, is very clever in finding the flaws and the untruths in a non-violence that is not true in depth and solid in charity and understanding. It requires a great deal of spiritual wisdom and formation to do this kind of thing. I am afraid that the little bud of non-violence that is beginning to show itself in this country may be killed by discredit, through the inexperience of its proponents. And through their obvious spiritual eclecticism, immaturity, instability, and so on. Yet, on the other hand, some of the kids from the Catholic Worker were down here and they are in general very solid. Or so I think. Especially Jim Forest seems to me to have considerable possibilities. He is in jail now, and perhaps ought not to be there. I mean he perhaps precipitated things in a way that should not have been done. Yet they have a refreshing hopefulness and energy. This seems to have been lost in the years after the war and is coming back at last, but perhaps too late.

The *Commonweal* article ["Nuclear War and Christian Responsibility," published on February 9, 1962] was well received, but met with a little opposition. I was perhaps too sweeping. However an atomic scientist wrote with injured innocence and demanded that I prove that anyone is planning to use nuclear weapons in war. Imagine that, all of a sudden. I would suppose that an atomic scientist would necessarily be literate, and would read the papers and perhaps even magazines, who knows?

53. To J.T.E. [Msgr. John Tracy Ellis], Washington, D.C. [March 10, 1962]

Clearly the issue is the practical one, the interpretation of strategy and of the implications of political action at the present moment. This is most serious and difficult. The main difference between my position and that taken by these theologians, as well as by most theologians in this country, it seems to me, is one of standpoint. It is a question of two radically different perspectives, and the perspectives depend on where you start out. They start out by accepting all kinds of assumptions which I do not accept. They accept, uncritically, it seems to me, all the viewpoints that are taken for granted by the mass media in the Cold War. In other words they start out to view a deeply disturbing and serious Christian problem with fundamentally secular presuppositions. They take as axiomatic the highly debatable questions of strategies and issues in the Cold War. And in so doing they seem to me to accept without question the rather pragmatic scale of values implied by the Cold War policies of our nation. This of course they are free to do, and there is no way of proving that they cannot start from such a position and end up with a position that is after all Christian. But it seems to me that this way of approaching the problem, while it may lead (with difficulty and danger) to an acceptable moral solution of the nuclear war problem as a *casus*, simply makes it impossible for the theologian to help others see their way *beyond* the Cold War impasse.

On the contrary, what this approach tends to do is to *dictate* as a "Christian solution" the one way out which the whole country is insensibly and irresponsibly coming to adopt all along with the mass media and the military-economic managers: that if we seem to be losing the Cold War, then the way out is a hot war, with perhaps a preemptive first strike on Russia.

It is my opinion that theologians who are in a position to influence the President's thinking and help him form his conscience on this most crucial of all questions today are going to be advising him that such a preemptive strike is not unacceptable to Christian morality. In point of fact that is precisely what one of your moralists says. Do please tell him to consider the necessity of taking a more detached view of this awful problem. I feel that it is our duty as priests and "theologians" (I put quotation marks insofar as I dare to include myself under that heading) to do much more than simply bless a pragmatic decision which may have frightful consequences, even though it may in some sense be technically "right." We must try as far as possible to open the way for a new and positive solution, something that will help us all work towards a peaceful and constructive issue from the nuclear dilemma. This means not an immediate answer on a case, but a whole preparatory job of rethinking the approach to the problems of our time in such a way that we can gradually prepare the way for a solid and lasting peace, meanwhile staving off the imminent danger of hot war. This danger is,

I believe, much more imminent than most people would like to think, and I do not believe that all the aggressiveness is on the Russian side, necessarily.

As you say, a permissive and even encouraging attitude on the part of moral theologians would be an abdication of responsibility in this crisis.

The apostolic constitution on Latin [*Veterum Sapientia*, promulgated on February 22, 1962] was read here. It is very very strong. The writers seem to find unusual zest with which to suppress all efforts at vernacularism. It is this more than the actual measures decreed which strikes me above all. The gusto with which they go about stamping out the flames of this small fire which bothers them. Can this be an encouraging sign before the Council? I mean the fact that something that is so ardently desired by so many and with understandable reasons should simply be put down with such total and uncompromising force? Certainly I can see the validity of the measures and of the reasons offered, and have no difficulty in continuing myself with this kind of policy in teaching, but once again, it is the "state of mind" reflected that is disturbing. And I think this "state of mind" is there and everywhere and it is going to have tremendous power in the Council.

You must by now have had a look at the new Hans Küng book, *The Council, Reform and Reunion.* If you have not, then do by all means get it as fast as ever you can. I think it is not out but I have a review copy. It will really gladden your heart. It is one of the most forthright, direct, and powerful statements of our actual condition and problem that I have ever seen. It is a most remarkable book and it will have terrific impact. What the results will be, no one can say, but it is in a lot of ways a portent.

54. To G.L. [Gerald Landry], Glen Garden, N.J. [mid-March 1962]

It has been a long time since you sent me your letter and the leaflet and later on your pamphlet. I am very moved by your story of your pacifism in Canada as a Catholic, during the last war, and of the support you received from the Bishop of Valleyfield [Joseph Alfred Langlois]. The story haunts one, it is so mysterious and so significant.

How sad it is that we have reached this strange present situation in the Church. I feel that we are in the presence of a very great mystery which leaves us almost helpless: not only helpless to understand God's designs in allowing His Church to become so completely implicated in the motives and ideals of the secular world, and in its obsessions, (some of which are pathological), but helpless to know what we should do about it ourselves. It is almost as if true conscience had been reduced to a level of total insignificance, as if what came from within man and presumably from the Holy Spirit were by that very fact automatically suspect, and as if external social controls were now at last the whole story, with no room left for anything else.

If it was hard to be a pacifist in the last war, and I was one too, to a modified extent, it will be harder in the present situation. It seems to me that the position of the Church, at least in this country, has become totally hardened and toughened, so that in spite of all the things that have been said by the Popes in favor of peace and disarmament, they are all now convinced that there is nothing for it but the "realist" policy based on testing, stockpiling, etc. And this inevitably leads to the hot war. I do not see how such a war can long be avoided in the condition in which we all are now, in spite of the good honest intentions of someone like President Kennedy. What can he do?

It is good to have your little leaflet and the booklet which I shall treasure as a valued possession. That too is a moving document, when one notices how articulate so many priests were in favor of peace in those days. And now, how few voices speak. I am meeting with very stern and resolute opposition, I can assure you, and I have no guarantee that I will be heard very much longer. But while I have a voice I will try to use it as best I can, with honesty and I hope objectivity. Meanwhile your booklet with its mine of material is an inspiration to me and will certainly prove useful. And it is a historic document in its own way.

We must try to make sense out of this senseless situation, with God's grace. Certainly we must never give up striving for Christian peace. The problems are almost infinitely complex and strange. There is so much that is totally new. May God protect and preserve us. Above all may He defend us from our own folly.

55. To J.T.E. [Msgr. John Tracy Ellis], Washington, D.C. [March 1962]

Many thanks for your kindness in sending me the editorial from *The Washington Standard.*[39] It was very important and helpful for me to see this editorial, from many standpoints. Naturally my writing from a place like this means that I suffer certain lacks of perspective, and being out of contact with opinion, and even to a great extent with events, is a most serious handicap.

For a while I toyed with an idea of writing to the editors of the *Standard,* but on reflection I realized that this might only confuse matters still further. In any case I do want to share my reactions with you, and I would appreciate your advice. Obviously I don't want to antagonize more people than I can avoid antagonizing, and since I tend to express my convictions with vehemence, naturally anyone who does not agree with them is liable to come back explosively. I recognize this to be largely my own fault.

I also recognize that my choice of words was careless and unfortunate when I sweepingly said "governments" were explicitly thinking of wars on an all-out scale and had practically said so. This could naturally be interpreted as a very unjust slam at President Kennedy. That was of course far from my intention. I fully recognize and appreciate the deep sincerity and obvious solicitude with which the President is trying to handle his most onerous responsibility. I do not envy him his position at all, and I regret very much indeed having given the impression that I was simply dismissing his administration off-hand as a bunch of potential war criminals.

At the same time, though I may be much mistaken or may

---

[39] Merton is referring to the *Catholic Standard,* the diocesan paper of Washington, D.C. The author of this editorial, published on March 19, 1962, was probably Auxiliary Bishop Philip Hanna.

be misled by my lack of contact with the outside world, it certainly seems to me quite clear from what I have read that there is no question that the military, in the U.S., have been building for many years a policy that involves the "massive" use of nuclear weapons, and that this has been made quite explicit. One quote occurs to my mind, doubtless not from one of the highest officials, but certainly representative enough: "We are not going to reduce our nuclear capability. Personally I have never believed in a nuclear limited war. I don't know how you could build a limit into it when you use any kind of a nuclear bang." This is ascribed to one Roswell Gilpatric who is Deputy Defense Secretary and is doubtless not a Catholic. The statement needs to be interpreted, and in any case it is an off-the-cuff personal opinion. But I repeat, it seems to me quite clear that this is the way the Pentagon thinks and probably indicative of much more strongly expressed values which do not get out in public. People who hold these views are, it seems to me, in a position to exert a decisive pressure on the President and in fact I believe they eventually will do so.

Understood in this light, I do not think my conclusions are altogether "gross," though I admit they were stated much too loosely in my article.

My quote from the U.S. Bishops was misunderstood. It was intended as a support to the statement that there was by and large a dangerous irresponsibility in public and private life in America. This of course was perfectly clear in the Bishops' statements of the years I referred to.

Finally, I think the writer of the editorial, in the heat of his indignation, misread my true thoughts about war. To begin with I am not an absolute pacifist and I am in no sense trying to claim that the Church has forbidden war as such, or even that the Church has formally denied that there can be a "just war" with the use of nuclear weapons, provided of course that use is limited. What I am contending, and I think this is abundantly clear from the documents of the Popes, is that the Church definitely frowns on and forbids an all-out use of nuclear weapons on a massive or indiscriminate scale, where civilians and cities are concerned. The rest is a question of the interpretation of scientific and political fact: can a total nuclear war be kept within the bounds of justice, and is it in fact the intention of the strategy makers to keep the war within such bounds? I recognize that there is a very respectable body of opinion which states that in practice we have to build our hopes and our policies on the optimistic estimate that if nuclear weapons are used at all they will be kept within limits. But to me this opinion rests on pious hopes and not on solid prospects of actual realization. To guide our moral thought on such unsteady lines seems to me to be folly.

I think, finally, that the writer of the editorial did me an injustice by stating that I was guilty of a "startling disregard of authoritative Catholic utterances," which almost seemed to imply a rebellious and independent attitude with regard to the Church. I think I appealed very frequently to authoritative Catholic utterances in my article, but they did not happen to be the ones which the writer of the editorial felt were important. I submit that I could claim that *he* did not quote the authoritative Catholic utterances which supported my side of the question but of course this would be childish. He evidently believed that when I said it was the mind of the Church to hope that all governments would work for the *abolition* of war I meant that the Church was formally condemning all war. This is certainly not the meaning of my words.

The fact remains that we live at a time when we are faced with a stark choice between disastrous all-out war, or the abolition of war. Both are essentially possible. I do not say that the abolition of war is easy or likely. I must confess that I do not have a plan to offer that will bring about this end. But I do feel that if we simply let ourselves be hypnotized by immediate military solutions to our problems we are never going to seriously consider other solutions. No one can deny that this is against the desire of the Church and of the Sovereign Pontiffs.

In short I feel that, largely though my own fault, perhaps, my article was misunderstood by the writer of the editorial. If you know who he is and are on friendly terms with him, perhaps you might see fit to communicate this letter to him, and I hope this will help to clear up a little of the misunderstanding.

Certainly I feel grieved that I have given the impression of being a rebel against the Church. But equally certainly I do not feel that my conscience seriously reproaches me in this regard, at least as far as my own personal subjective dispositions are concerned. I am always of course extremely grateful for advice, criticism, and enlightenment, especially from well-informed and authoritative sources.

56. To C.M. [Czeslaw Milosz], Berkeley, Calif. [March 1962]

There are few people whose advice I respect as much as I do yours, and whatever you say I take seriously. Hence I do not feel at all disturbed or unsettled by what you say concerning my articles about peace, because I can see the wisdom of your statements and I agree with them to a great extent.

This is one of those phases one goes through. I certainly do not consider myself permanently dedicated to a crusade for peace and I am beginning to see the uselessness and absurdity of getting too involved in a "peace movement." The chief reason why I have spoken out was that I felt I owed it to my conscience to do so. There are certain things that have to be clearly stated. I had in mind particularly the danger arising from the fact that some of the most belligerent people in this country are Christians, on the one hand fundamentalist Protestants and on the other certain Catholics. They both tend to appeal to the bomb to do a "holy" work of destruction in the name of Christ and Christian truth. This is completely intolerable and the truth has to be stated. I cannot in conscience remain indifferent. Perhaps this sounds priggish, and perhaps I am yielding to subtle temptations of self-righteousness. Perhaps too there is a great deal of bourgeois self-justification in all this. Perhaps I am just trying to make myself feel that I am still in continuous contact with the tradition of my fathers, in English history, fighting for rights and truth and so on. And so on. In other words there is a large element of myth in it all. And yet one cannot know everything and analyze everything. It seems that there may be some point in saying what I have said, and so I have said it.

You are right about the temptation to get lined up with rebels without a cause. There is something attractive and comforting about the young kids that are going off into non-violent resistance with the same kind of enthusiasm I used to have myself in the thirties for left wing action. But this too may be a great illusion. I trust your experience.

As far as I am concerned I have just about said what I have to say. I have written four or five articles, which are gradually getting published, hailed, attacked, and causing a small stir. I may revise them all and put them together into a small book [*Peace in the Post-Christian Era*]. One publisher [Macmillan] wants such a book badly and has made an enormous offer for it. Etc. I am not going to rush into this, however.

I think that I will have to remain available to speak up from time to time about the issue in moments of critical decision, or perhaps not.

In a word I have many doubts myself about all this. It seems to be largely self-deception. Yet to the best of my ability to judge, I feel that what I have done so far was necessary. Perhaps it was not done well. Perhaps it was naïve. Undoubtedly I have not said the last word, nor has all that I have said been perfectly objective and well balanced. The fact that some Catholics are now angry with me is the least of my worries. I think too one of the articles may even have disturbed the President, and I don't want to be unfair to him. I have never aimed anything I said directly at any one person or small group.

Apart from that, however, I do think that the way people are going in this country there is growing evidence that a nuclear war is inevitable. Unless something unforeseen comes in to alter the whole picture.

Meanwhile, I enjoy the spring rains (and there have been a lot of them) and am getting ready to do my usual planting of tree seedlings for reforestation.

Keep well, and thanks for all your advice and for your understanding. I repeat that I value both.

57. To T.L. [Thomas J. Liang], Oakland, Calif. [March 1962]

Your friendly letter has waited about a month for an answer, and I have been taking it very seriously. I do want to help you if I can, in any work involving Asian students. I feel that this is very important and as a matter of fact the Holy Spirit in the last year or so has been multiplying my Asian contacts in a rather striking way.

Your idea of the Christian Unity Corps sounds really fine, and I especially like the last part, about Catholic American families giving hospitality to Asian students. I believe that the Asian, South American, and African students are in a way the most important people in the world today. They have magnificent potentialities. They also face tremendous dangers.

So, as I say, I want to help out. Yet at the same time I am afraid I cannot tie myself down to produce a certain definite something at a certain definite time. What would probably be more to the point, if you wish to use such feeble talents as I possess, would be to leave me on a footloose and informal basis, free to bat out a short letter to your bulletin or an observation or something, on spiritual matters. And I could not necessarily guarantee to do it every month. I have too many other commitments. But as I say it would be wonderful to feel that I were part of the group and accepted as a brother and friend by all who belonged to it.

Let me say this: I do not know if I have anything to offer to Asians but I am convinced that I have an immense amount to learn from Asia. One of the things I would like to share with Asians is not only Christ but Asia itself. I am convinced that a rather superficial Christianity in European dress is not enough for Asia. We have lacked depth. We have lacked the breadth of view to grasp all the wonderful breadth and richness in the ancient Asian traditions, which were given to China, India, Japan, Korea, Burma, etc. as preparations for the coming of Christ. I feel that often those who finally brought Christ may have fallen short of the preparation that the Holy Spirit had provided and hence Our Lord was not seen in all His divine splendor.

Yet at the same time I fully realize the complexity of the problem today. The Asians have renounced Asia. They want to be Western, sometimes they are frantic about being Western. They want to go places. They feel that there have been centuries of inertia and stagnation, and there is a reaction against the humiliations and misunderstandings of colonialism, calling for a defeat of the West at its own technological game. All this is dangerous but inevitable. Christianity of course has a crucial part to play in saving all that is valuable in the East as well as in the West.

58. To F.S. [Frank J. Sheed], New York [March 1962]

I have been reading Gordon Zahn's book [*German Catholics and Hitler's War*] which you published. It is a most important and very well-done job of work. It deserves far more than the obvious platitudes which spring to mind about any good new book. To say that it raises a vitally important issue is so short of doing it justice that it is ridiculous. It raises an issue that most of us are frankly incapable of understanding or even thinking about intelligently. It goes terribly deep, and much too deep for the average Catholic, the average priest, the average bishop. Zahn is objective with scientific innocence. There is no guile in his approach. He just says what he says, and overstates nothing. Where the impact comes is in the delayed action after one has read a chapter or so. Then all of a sudden one comes to with a jolt and says to himself: "This really means that something very dreadful is happening and has been happening, and that the bottom is dropping out of what we have been accustomed to regard as a fully satisfactory and complete picture of Christianity, or Christian civilization. Perhaps it has already dropped . . ." That is a mixed metaphor no doubt. The bottom drops out of a bucket, not of a picture. But perhaps one tends to feel that the picture itself has just dropped out of a frame.

Then the Hans Küng book, *The Council, Reform and Reunion.* This too is splendid. One's reaction is more hopeful and more positive. But the sense of urgency remains the same. This Council has got to fulfill great hopes or be a disaster. It is absolutely no use reaffirming the disciplinary and juridical positions that have been affirmed one way or another for a thousand years. This is not reform, not renewal. That is what comes out of these two books, with great force. This is not the world of Gregory VII, or Innocent III, or Pius V, or even Pius X. To be a perfect Christian, even a saint according to their pattern, is no longer enough. On the contrary, it is apt to be terribly dangerous, even fatal.

59. To K.McD. [Kilian McDonnell], Trier, Germany [March 1962]

I certainly envy you going to study under [Hans] Kung at Tubingen. I am finishing his book [*The Council, Reform and Reunion*] now and it is really one of the most exciting books I have read in years, without exception of books intending to be exciting in the most obvious way. There is really a breath of new life about this book and about his outlook. It is awake and frank and not wild, but objectively Catholic in the finest sense—not the sense of the poor good people who have been paralyzed for ages by rigidities and conventions. A book like this makes one realize many many things. It enables one to judge and to accept many things that were felt heretofore in the conscience only as obscure and ambiguous gnawings. It is then quite true that we are right to feel so uncomfortable and so terribly beaten down by the old negative, falsely conservative, and authoritarian spirit that purely and simply clings to the status quo for its own sake. It is quite true that so many things that we have feared to call dead, are really dead after all. "Why do you seek the dead among the living?" There is after all something to the spiritual and Churchly sense which remains uneasy and crippled under the burden of what have to be frankly admitted as "dead works." And evasions and even dishonesties, not perhaps fully conscious ones.

Realizing this does not make one proud and rebellious. It is a chastening and humbling experience. One sees that so many people, in good faith, and with subjectively good reasons, are clinging blindly to ways of life and ways of seeing life which lead to spiritual blindness and which almost choke the life out of the faithful. The priestly mentality that comes out of so many seminaries. The beaten down bright subservience and cultivated stupidity of the Catholic layman. The official and managerial insolence and self-complacency of some in authority, so often. The diplomacies, the subterfuges, the wiles, the manipulations of the law to keep people "quiet and happy." And when one sees all this frankly, he realizes that he himself is likewise involved, likewise at fault. One does not have temptations to rise up and shatter it all with violent criticism, on the contrary. One feels the need to meditate and do penance interiorly and keep silent until such time as one or two quiet words may be indicated by grace. One wants to obey with a new seriousness and responsibility, seeing at the same time with clearer eyes what one is about, and seeing the limitations and deficiencies in which one is oneself involved. Obviously Christian humility is not purely the humility of the subject who is always wrong before the official who is always right, but something far deeper, nobler, and more human: the humility of the member of Christ who realizes that he and all the other members are so unworthy of their Head in so many ways, and yet that they can help one another by honesty and humility to be more worthy of the Spirit Who is given to them all.

Thanks for the material on Una Sancta and Fr. [Max] Metzger's prison letters. I have not plunged into these yet, it will take time. I want to write a bit more about him[40] and make him known: a great man, one of the seven who, out of so many thousands in the German peace movement, continued to stick to his principles after Hitler long enough and uncompromisingly enough to pay for them with his life.[41] That too is terribly significant, a strangely meaningful chapter in the history of the Church.

I will return the English life of Metzger when you come back here. There is talk of republishing it in the U.S.

60. To J.G.L. [Justus George Lawler], Chicago, Ill. [March 1962]

I appreciate what you mean about the series "Quaestiones Disputatae." The few articles I have on peace now add up to around forty thousand words [the ms. of *Peace in the Post-Christian Era*] and that would go well in the series. However I think I had better go along with Macmillan, who got in ahead of you with an equally enthusiastic suggestion. But I am grateful above all because I am in contact with you. I owe this to the

---

[40] See Thomas Merton, "Testament of Peace: Fr. Metzger's Thoughts about the Duty of the Christian," originally published in *Jubilee* (March 1962), and reprinted in *Passion for Peace: The Social Essays,* edited by William H. Shannon (New York: Crossroad, 1995), 53-55.

[41] Fr. Metzger was executed by the Nazis in 1944. His act of resistance was his work for peace.

nasty business of war. It has brought me in contact with wonderful people. A kind of closing of ranks among the *anawim,* I suppose. (I hope it is all right to call ourselves the "poor of the Lord.") What with you and Gordon Zahn and Dan Berrigan and others, I can see that there is a lot of life in the Church here, and this helps me in my own turn to wake up a little. We have been hibernating too long.

Your article on the Bishops is very timely and I appreciate it fully having just finished Küng's remarkable book on the Council [*The Council, Reform and Reunion*]. How right you are. I am so afraid that the concept of "renewal" will turn out to be nothing more than a tightening of the screws on the poor rank and file religious, clergy, and layman who has been hog-tied for so long. This Council is going to have to be a proof that we are not just a monolithic organization: because that is how such organizations renew themselves: by tightening their grip on the rank and file and re-asserting the perpetual rightness of the managers. If that happens this time, so help us, it will be one of the most horrible scandals that ever took place. It will be a disaster. That, principally, is the object of my prayers: that it will be a real renewal, or a step towards it. But honestly, I am scared. I ought to have more faith, one might say. It is not exactly that. I am scared because in a way I think we have deserved to come out in our true light. We have deserved the fate of efficiency for good and all. But God is merciful. He can save us from an endless succession of Good Joe Bishops whose greatest concern is to keep up a perpetual flow of innocent Irish drolleries about Pat and Mike and never say a serious word about anything except that so-and-so's marriage case is hopeless.

What you said about martyrdom struck me: it is what I am thinking and it is also what you are thinking, I see. It is to the point.

Now please tell me: the bishop who lost his see on p. 11: is it the one in Iowa in the last war, who got the axe for being a pacifist? Can you please give me the details of that story? One of my priest novices has been asking about it, and I don't have the information.

I am most grateful for the books. [Karl] Rahner's *Theology of Death* was the first thing I grabbed, and I finished it quickly. It is superb. Funnily enough my reaction would shock him, but besides clarifying my Christian faith it threw immense light on the real nature of Buddhism. He would be horrified. But that is precisely the Buddhist approach: that death can and should be an act of complete liberation, a going forth, an *act* by which one freely and completely leaves behind all that is not definitive, and the affirmation of the meaning hidden in all one's other acts. He of course tries to dismiss Buddhism as a spiritual sin, and he may be right of certain aspects of it. But I have been studying it a bit, and I think this is the real meaning of nirvana, and it has absolutely nothing whatever to do with a quietist ecstasy. The other books came yesterday and I shall enjoy them, bit by bit.

Now thanks for the reference to the various articles. We have *Thought* here. But I would definitely like the one on aggression from the *Journal of Existential Psych*[*ology*]. [Jacques] Barzun sent me an offprint of his article, haven't read it yet. [Jean] Danielou I can get. Stuff on peace, nuclear war, etc., I am interested in, of course. Also be sure to send me anything of yours and anything good on the Orient, or Latin America too (I am always wanting to translate Latin American poets. Have friends who are that. Did you say you saw the article in *Blackfriars* [February 1962] on the Giants ["A Letter to Pablo Antonio Cuadra concerning Giants"]? I think so).

In conclusion, I will send you some offprints and some mimeographed material you might be interested in. You may share them with anyone you please. Do please keep in touch. Anything I can do for you except write prefaces and blurbs, I will try to do.

61. To J.F. [James Forest], Hart's Island [prison], N.Y. [March 28, 1962]

Your note just arrived and put an end to my wondering about the sentence. I too had hoped it would be suspended. Since you have fifteen days at Hart's Island, then there is meaning in it. It is part of the plan and part of your training. It is an experience and a trial that you will need, and by which I pray that you will profit. You have been completely right in following your convictions, and I am sure that you have taken care to express them in a way that was true and direct, in order to make clear that you were defending a strictly moral issue that could not otherwise be made fully clear.

The CNVA [*Committee for Non-Violent Action*] *Bulletin* confirms me in all this. I think the observations by Bradford Lyttle were very intelligent and clear-sighted. I am glad he sees the problems in perspective. The Peace movement needs more than zeal. It certainly needs to be organized on a very clear basis, and it is necessary for the people who know what they are trying to do, to be formed into a coherent nucleus who can make things clear to others. It is not going to do any good for a lot of excited people to mill around without purpose and without definite means of making their protest clear and intelligible. Especially if a lot of them are not too clear themselves what they are protesting about. The movement is really only beginning and a lot of ground work has to be done. I admit that there may not be much time.

I have got a better idea of the Cuba project[42] and I see more clearly what it means. It strikes me however that this project is premature. I don't mean for Cuba or for peace, but for the people likely to be involved. It is too big and still too ambiguous. I wonder if it takes sufficient account of the political realities. That is important. There is further ambiguity provided by the fact that Castro is now apparently on the skids. He has evidently reached the last stage of the processing which he has lent himself to and which will end with his own discrediting and rejection. For CNVA to get involved even indirectly in that situation and perhaps be used also in it, would be a fatal mistake. But if you go there you are bound to do so on terms that will imply involvement. Of course I am not well enough informed to talk about all this, but this is just my impression. I liked the *Bulletin* a lot anyway.

---

[42] The Committee for Non-Violent Action was sending a boat to Cuba loaded with children's toys—one of many initiatives. In its historical records, CNVA is described as "one of the first American peace groups to focus on nonviolent direct action including civil disobedience. Its purpose of organizing imaginative and dramatic protest demonstrations on both land and sea attracted radical pacifists and called the attention of the American public to the atrocities of nuclear warfare." Among its actions were protests at missile test sites and "Walks for Peace," such as a 6,000 mile march from San Francisco to Moscow and from Quebec to Cuba.

What you say about the prisoners is important. At a time like this, a jail sentence can be very meaningful even to the person who undergoes it. At the same time you need inner strength. The deep good in these dopesters, etc., is also tangled up with deep misfortune and tragedy. And this can subtly affect you also. But I only mean by that that you need lots of grace, and need to realize your need, and if you make mistakes don't say they are not mistakes. One can go from defending the health in these people to defending the sickness also. You know what I mean. But on the other hand the clergy tend to be altogether too scared of trouble, and take refuge in meaningless gestures, not even of righteousness but just of legality. Pfui.

62. To T.McD. [Thomas McDonnell], Boston, Mass. [c. March 28, 1962]

I owe you once again, five or six letters. Thanks for the most recent one which did not strike me as "neverous." I was sorry to hear about [Yevgeny] Yevtushenko.[43] Yes, he was bound to get it eventually. It is too bad that such courageous people in the Iron Curtain countries are exploited sensationally by the press on our side, for political and propaganda motives, and then get the axe as a result. It is the ambiguous position that one gets in by protesting and trying to be honest. Whatever you do, you can be sued by one side or the other and in the end you are discredited by everybody and gain nothing: except the invisible and unknowable gain of having witnessed to what is incomprehensible and therefore useless.

Thanks above all for the [John Howard] Griffin book [*Black Like Me*].[44] I found it moving and important, and of course read it right through with unflagging interest. As someone has aptly said: what we have in the southern United States is not so much

---

[43] See footnote 6 above.

[44] Griffin's *Black Like Me* (Boston: Houghton Mifflin, 1961) recounted the author's experience of darkening his skin and traveling through the South as a "Negro." Griffin and Merton later became close friends. After Merton's death Griffin was named to write his authorized biography, a project left unfinished by his death in 1980.

a Negro problem as a White problem. There is no question that there the real problem lies, and it is more than the race question. The problem of peace is involved too in the belligerency and obtuseness of the same types.

What other fifty-nine things have I omitted to thank you for? I am grateful for all. Don't overdo it!

Oh by the way: I never got around to writing to Steve Allen and I don't think I can write to [John Howard] Griffin right now. I have to be realistic. There is a drawer full of unanswered letters here, and I am not in a position to go looking for more trouble than I have already. I will pray for them instead. It is more effective anyway.

No more for present. It rains like mad, probably fallout coming down in every drop.

63. To E.G. [Etta Gullick], Oxford [March 30, 1962]

Another idea about the selections from Benet [of Canfield (1562-1610)] came to me: perhaps I can interest some Quaker friends of mine in printing it. It would of course be a very small and insignificant kind of publication, but anyway it would reach quite a few people who would profit by it. I am still convinced that the best thing to do with Benet is to get pertinent passages to the attention of people who can use them but who might otherwise bog down in the rather elaborate structure of the whole *Rule* [*of Perfection*].

Did you ever get anywhere with Julian of Norwich? Though it might not seem so at first sight, I think there is much in her that is relevant to the Dark Night, at least theologically, if not exactly in the order of the classic experience. But certainly the great thing is passing with Christ through death out of this world to the Father, and one does not reduce this to a "classic experience." It must remain incomprehensible to a great extent.

I was very interested to hear of Prof. [David] Knowles' lecture on St. Gregory and St. Benedict. If it ever gets published, please let me know.

Where did I see, the other day, something about a new edition of the *Mirror of Simple Souls,* and definitely ascribed to

Marguerite Porete? Perhaps it was somewhere in the new Molinari book on Julian of Norwich,[45] which I have only begun and then had to set aside for more urgent matters. If there is a new one out, I will wait to get that instead of borrowing the Orchard Edition.[46] But I could also probably get an old copy of that from T. Burns Oates.

Thanks very much indeed for the splendid [Georges] Florovsky article in *Sobornost*. This is a treasure. I have the greatest respect for him. It seems to me that he of all men today has the sense of what theology really is supposed to be.

Am I unpopular because of the writing on peace? You ask this. The answer is yes and no. Unpopular with some bishops, yes. Probably get hit over the head. Yes. Certainly criticized vigorously and unfairly. I get the impression that people have not the time to really think about this issue. They have the wind up and are moved to vehement malevolence whenever someone suggests that the bomb might not be the solution to all their problems, and might not be a fully ethical solution to any problem. I cannot see problems of spiritual night otherwise than in the context of collective stupidity and crime in which we are all involved. I think a lot of the suffering and meaninglessness of the night comes from unconscious involvement in the general evil.

Now I must stop again. Forgive my delays but I am sure you understand them.

64. To T.McD. [Thomas McDonnell], Boston, Mass. [early April 1962]

Thanks for your good letter and the enclosures. And for the previous one which I do not think I have answered. I have always liked [Bertolt] Brecht a lot, the only thing I have wondered is how he managed to get along so long with the Communists. He is obviously not one of "theirs" any more than

---

[45] Paolo Molinari, *Julian of Norwich: The Teaching of a Fourteenth-Century English Mystic* (London: Longmans, Green, 1958).

[46] Julian of Norwich. *The Revelations of Divine Love of Julian of Norwich,* edited by James Walsh (London: Burns & Oates, 1961).

Picasso or Pablo Neruda, though Neruda manages to be a faithful and humble believer and as a result he turns out some awful trash.

Yes, I heard about the TV program: I am glad you approve of it, because I had my doubts about it. Thanks for reassuring me.

I am glad Bro. Antoninus [William Everson] has been with you all up in Boston, but very sorry to hear of his accident. He is greatly revered by the people down at the Catholic Worker, who sit around reading him aloud. I know because some of them were down here. When can we hope to have him in this part of the country?

I saw you reviewed the Julien Green book, and he sent me a copy.[47] He is a friend of Fr. [Jean] Danielou and has even expressed a desire to try translating some of my poems into French. I wish he would, but he is too modest about his own capacity to do so. The novel is curious, reads very well, but is much too intricate, I think. But he is absorbed in the problem of sin, and when it comes clear he does well. However some of the more sinister and stock figures tend to obscure the main issue. I suppose you could say he was doing a kind of medieval morality. His basic ideas on sin, or rather his basic haunting preoccupation with it, is interesting and real. Though within a kind of Calvinistic framework that makes it too "logical." Actually he struggles against the logic, wisely and rightly, but never fully succeeds in overcoming it.

The poem from *Encounter* is good. What have they done with the sanest of sane men, Eichmann?

65. To A.F. [Allan Forbes, Jr.], Philadelphia, Pa. [early April 1962]

Your good letters have been reaching me with their encouraging comments. I do indeed wish it were possible for the monks to come out on a walk for peace from here to Washington.

---

[47] Julien Green, *Chaque homme dans sa nuit* (1960) / *Each in His Darkness,* translated from the French by Anne Green (New York: Pantheon Books, 1961). See Merton's review essay, "To Each His Darkness: Notes on a Novel of Julien Green," in *Raids on the Unspeakable* (New York: New Directions, 1966).

Wouldn't that be something? But unfortunately though I might like this idea and a few others might join me, I am sure the majority would not understand it. That would be in part because they have just never heard of such things. And then I do not think most of them have a very good idea of the kind of situation we are in and are not able to evaluate it.

Yet as you say if there is anything of the prophetic spirit left in us, it can find something to do while we are here in silence. And I myself do not underestimate the power of silence either. I know that as a matter of fact I can do much more for peace here, in silence, than I can by coming out and showing my head above ground, so to speak.

This is just another way of saying that there are many, many unexplored aspects of resistance and of witness. But I have read Wilmer Young's pamphlet [*Visible Witness: A Testimony of Radical Peace*, Pendle Hill Pamphlet 3118, 1961] and found it deeply moving. I do hope we can all preserve the purity of heart and simplicity of spirit that must go into such a thing. It is certain that the Quakers and the Mennonites have retained an unassailable simplicity and sincerity in this dedication to peace and non-violence. There should be many many more Catholics in it with you.

66. To R. de G. [Roger De Ganck, O.C.S.O.], Belgium [early April 1962]

When Rev. Dom Edward was here I did indeed speak to him about my interest in the Beguines in the Low Countries and their relation both to the Cistercians on the one hand and to the Rhenish mystics on the other. He advised me to write to you but as I had little or no time to pursue the study further, I failed to do so.

But now it is a great pleasure to receive your letter, which came several weeks ago, I regret to say—I am behind with all my correspondence—and then the splendid book of Fr. [Alacantara] Mens on the Beguines. I have never tried reading a whole book in Flemish before and this will be a kind of challenge. But I am most grateful for your gift and deeply appreciate it. We have [Simone] Roisin here and though I have tried in vain to get [Ernest] McDonnell at a nearby library, yet I think it may be possible to trace a copy.

Certainly I will be very glad to send all the books that may be desired by the Sisters from Nazareth in their new foundation in California [Redwoods]. Please let me know when they arrive there and what their address will be. This foundation is very interesting, and I think it is fine that a foundation of Cistercian nuns should be made in America in the direct line of the great mystical communities of the Middle Ages in the Low Countries.

Will you be coming to this country with the Sisters? Perhaps I may have the joy of meeting and speaking with you here. In any case I assure you of my prayers for the success of the new foundation. From what I hear of the site, it is very well chosen and will be most inspiring.

67. To A.A. [Abdul Aziz], Pakistan [April 4, 1962]

Finally I must answer your letters, at least briefly. A brief answer will be better than none at all. If I wait until I can do you full justice I will wait too long. In December I sent you some articles and magazines. Herewith I am enclosing an offprint of the article on the English mystics ["The English Mystics" (*Jubilee*, September 1961)]. I was waiting for this offprint because it is a handy size to send in the mail.

I am glad you appreciated the Letter about the Giants ["A Letter to Pablo Antonio Cuadra concerning Giants"]. This has been published in England, Argentina, and Central America, perhaps also in Germany, and has been well received. I looked up in the Quran the references to Gog and Magog [Sura XVIII: 90 and Sura XXI: 95] and found them to be extremely significant.

The magazines containing the excellent essay on Sufi religious psychology reached me and I have read the essay with the greatest interest. It confirms me in my realization that there is much in common, on the level of experience, between Sufism and Christian mysticism. I see you refer in your letter to the book by Clark on Eckhart: I will finally get down to doing something about that, I am sorry to have let it go for so long.[48] I do not know if I sent you the notes of my Mystical Theology course, but will put an extra set in the mail as soon as I can. You will find there some references to Eckhart. I am interested in knowing whether you have gone further into St. John of the Cross.

St. Basil, whom you are probably reading by now, is an Ascetic who adapted Egyptian monastic practices to the Greek world. He stressed community life and manual labor, also humility and obedience. He had a strong influence on St. Benedict, who took many of St. Basil's ideas and adapted them to the Roman world, and thus founded the monastic Order to which I belong. St. Basil is very interesting but yet there are deficiencies in him. He was an active "organizer" rather than a contemplative and there is little or no mysticism in him. One feels a certain coldness and lack of deep inner spirit, though his faith was strong and his ascetic tendencies were virile and well ordered. In a word there is a bit of the formalist in him.

We are about the same age, perhaps almost exactly the same age. I am now 47. I was born in France, educated in France, England, and America. My outlook is not purely American and I feel sometimes disturbed by the lack of balance in the powerful civilization of this country. It is technologically very strong, spiritually superficial and weak. There is much good in the people, who are very simple and kind, but there is much potential evil in the irresponsibility of the society that leaves all to the interplay of human appetites, assuming that everything will adjust itself automatically for the good of all. This unfortunately is fatal and may lead to the explosion that will destroy half the world, of which there is serious danger. I entered the monastery twenty years ago, and am the novice master here. I believe my vocation is essentially that of a pilgrim and an exile in life, that I have no proper place in the world, but that for that reason I am in some sense to be the friend and brother of people everywhere, especially those who are exiles and pilgrims like myself. I cannot get along with formalists, I am alien to them and they to me. My life is in many ways simple, but it is

---

[48] James Midgely Clark, *Meister Eckhart: An Introduction to the Study of His Works with an Anthology of His Sermons* (Edinburgh: Thomas Nelson, 1957).

also a mystery which I do not attempt to really understand, as though I were led by the hand in a night where I see nothing, but can fully depend on the Love and Protection of Him Who guides me.

I am very pleased with the wonderful works of ['Ali b. 'Uthman] al Hujswiri [eleventh-century Sufi and saint of Islamic mysticism], a great contemplative spirit. I am still reading him slowly and meditatively.

I will keep you in mind as I come across other interesting points and articles. Do not forget me in your good prayers, as I remember you often, particularly at dawn. The whole world however is going into darkness and I think there are difficult times ahead. I want to write a book against Nuclear War [ms. of *Peace in the Post-Christian Era*] and am engaged in this now. I do not think this will make life any simpler for me, and may rouse enmity, but it must be done.

68. To L.S. [Leo Szilard], Washington, D.C. [April 12, 1962]

I have had the good fortune to receive and read a copy of the talk you gave in Washington last November. It was particularly welcome, since I am at the same time undergoing the disheartening experience of reading the book of Edward Teller [*The Legacy of Hiroshima*]. It was encouraging to hear the contrasting notes struck by a civilized voice, yours. Dr. Teller's book seems to me to be a systematic piece of amorality which will probably have serious and far-reaching effects. Hence my conviction that your proposals about a peace lobby are of the greatest importance. I wish to assure you of my desire to cooperate in any way possible with your plan.

One way which suggests itself to me is to devote a notable part of the royalties of a book I am currently writing, on peace [ms. of *Peace in the Post-Christian Era*], to your cause. Another part of the same royalties will go towards the formation of a Catholic Peace group which I am sponsoring. I do not have a regular income, being a member of a monastic Order. I think my Superiors will grant me permission to use these royalties in the way I have outlined.

It would seem that one of the most urgent problems is the prevalence of absurd, inhuman, and utterly distorted assumptions that have become the basis of the thinking and decisions of the majority, including the majority of those in power. The constant articulate resistance of an atomic scientist group has been the most effective corrective to this kind of thinking. But with people like Dr. Teller throwing the weight of their authority in the scales against the saner and more restrained views, the situation becomes serious. I need not add that the fact that many of the Catholic clergy and theologians have compounded the evils of the situation by mistakenly taking the so-called "realist" position. In my view the situation is now extremely grave, and if we go on in the direction we have now taken, in this country, the United States is liable to start a nuclear war out of sheer confusion, obsession, and misinterpretation of international realities.

Yet certainly there is plenty of clear thinking and sane analysis going on. I think we must do all we can to get these saner views more widely disseminated. It is a pity I did not know of your talk sooner or I would have asked to include it in a collection of essays on peace which I am editing [*Breakthrough to Peace*] and which should appear this fall. If you are making any further statements of this nature, or writing any articles, I hope I can get to know of them.

One encouraging thing, though it does not amount to much. A Senator [Frank] Kowalski [D. Connecticut] asked me to write a prayer for peace which he intends to read in the House of Representatives when testing is resumed.[49] At least a symbolic gesture. But what we need is a really strong organization of all the different peace groups, and above all some way of making clear that this is not a question of odd-ball pacifism or radicalism of some spurious kind. Yet it is extremely disquieting to see that serious and well considered discussions of the momentous issue of nuclear disarmament, such as Pugwash Conferences [on Science and World Affairs],[50] are automatically discredited and

---

[49] Merton's "Prayer for Peace" was read in the House of Representatives on April 12, 1962. Merton's "Prayer" is reprinted in *Passion for Peace: The Social Essays,* edited by William H. Shannon (New York: Crossroad, 1995).

[50] The first Pugwash Conference was held in 1957 in Pugwash, Nova Scotia. In 1995, The Pugwash Conferences and its originator, Joseph Roblat, received the Nobel Peace Prize.

set aside as somehow subversive. How can we possibly take the right steps toward peace if everything conspires to move us all towards violence?

69. To J.F. [James Forest], New York [April 29, 1962]

First of all I ought to have congratulated you and Jean long ago. The reason why I didn't was twofold. First I thought you would probably be in Nashville or on the walk, and waited to hear you were back in N.Y. Then also I have been trying to finish my book on peace [ms. of *Peace in the Post-Christian Era*], and have succeeded in time for the axe to fall. So congratulations. I hope you will be very happy. It seems everything is happening at once in your life. Jail, marriage, peace walk, eviction, and what else? Don't let it become an avalanche. You want to keep your footing and be able to look about you and see what you are doing. The trouble with movements is that they sweep you off your feet and carry you away with the tide of activism and then you become another kind of mass man. And in the long run it hardly matters which kind one becomes, it is the same in the end. So be careful.

Now here is the axe. The orders are, no more writing about peace. This is transparently arbitrary and uncomprehending, but doubtless I have to make the best of it. I am hoping to get the book through on the ground that it is already written. Of course the order does not apply to unpublished writing, but I have to be careful even with privately circulated stuff, like the mimeographed material. So for one thing, please do not under any circumstances publish anywhere anything I write to you on this subject or on non-violence, etc. It will only make it impossible to do whatever still remains possible. Besides the order is not yet absolutely beyond appeal and I can perhaps obtain some slight modification of it. But in substance I am being silenced on the subject of war and peace. This I know is not a very encouraging thing. It implies all sorts of very disheartening consequences as regards the whole cause of peace. It reflects an astounding incomprehension of the seriousness of the present crisis in its religious aspect. It reflects an insensitivity to

Christian and Ecclesiastical values, and to the real sense of the monastic vocation. The reason given is that this is not the right kind of work for a monk, and that it "falsifies the monastic message." Imagine that: the thought that a monk might be deeply enough concerned with the issue of nuclear war to voice a protest against the arms race, is supposed to bring the monastic life into *disrepute*. Man, I would think that it might just possibly salvage a last shred of repute for an institution that many consider to be dead on its feet. That is really the most absurd aspect of the whole situation, that these people insist on digging their own grave and erecting over it the most monumental kind of tombstone.

The problem, from the point of view of the Church and its mission, is of course this. The vitality of the Church depends precisely on spiritual renewal, uninterrupted, continuous, and deep. Obviously this renewal is to be expressed in the historical context, and will call for a real spiritual understanding of historical crises, an evaluation of them in terms of their inner significance and in terms of man's growth and the advancement of truth in man's world: in other words, the establishment of the "kingdom of God." The monk is the one supposedly attuned to the inner spiritual dimension of things. If he hears nothing, and says nothing, then the renewal as a whole will be in danger and may be completely sterilized. But these minds believe that the function of the monk is not to see or hear any new dimensions, simply to support the already existing viewpoints precisely insofar as and because they are defined for him by somebody else. Instead of being in the advance guard he is in the rear guard with the baggage, confirming all that has been done by the officials. The function of the monk, as far as renewal in the historical context goes, then becomes simply to affirm his total support of officialdom. He has no other function, then, except perhaps to pray for what he is told to pray for: namely, the purposes and objectives of an ecclesiastical bureaucracy. The monastery as dynamo concept goes back to this. The monk is there to generate spiritual power that will justify over and over again the already predecided rightness of the officials above him. He must in no event and under no circumstances assume a role that implies any form of spontaneity and originality. He must be an eye that sees nothing except what is carefully selected for him to see. An ear that hears nothing except what it is advantageous for the managers for him to hear. We know what Christ said about such ears and eyes.

Now you will ask me: how do I reconcile obedience, true obedience (which is synonymous with love) with a situation like this? Shouldn't I just blast the whole thing wide open, or walk out, or tell them to jump in the lake?

Let us suppose for the sake of argument that this was not completely excluded. Why would I do this? For the sake of the witness for peace? For the sake of witnessing to the truth of the Church, in its reality, as against a figment of the imagination? Simply for the sake of blasting off and getting rid of the tensions and frustrations in my own spirit, and feeling honest about it?

In my own particular case, every one of these would backfire and be fruitless. It would be taken as a witness *against* the peace movement and would confirm these people in all the depth of their prejudices and their self complacency. It would reassure them in every possible way that they are incontrovertibly right and make it even more impossible for them ever to see any kind of new light on the subject. And in any case I am not looking merely for opportunities to blast off, I can get along without it.

I am where I am. I have freely chosen this state, and have freely chosen to stay in it when the question of a possible change arose. If I am a disturbing element, that is all right. I am not making a point of being that, but simply of saying what my conscience dictates and doing so without seeking my own interest. This means accepting such limitations as may be placed on me by authority, not merely because it is placed on me by authority, and not because I may or may not agree with the ostensible reasons why the limitations are imposed, but out of love for God who is using these things to attain ends which I myself cannot at the moment see or comprehend. I know He can and will in His own time take good care of the ones who impose limitations unjustly or unwisely. That is His affair and not mine. In this dimension I find no contradiction between love and obedience, and as a matter of fact it is the only sure way of transcending the limits and arbitrariness of ill-advised commands.

70. To J.G.L. [Justus George Lawler], Chicago, Ill. [end of April or early May 1962]

Thanks for your good letter of last month and for the article. I liked the latter a lot and thought for a moment of making a last minute effort to get a place for it in "my" anthology [*Breakthrough to Peace*] that is now more or less going to press. But as we are already pushing and pulling to get an article by a Protestant theologian into it, no more can possibly be done. I do hope it will be a good book and know you will be interested.

I am in trouble also with my own book about peace [ms. of *Peace in the Post-Christian Era*]. It appears that the Higher Superiors have suddenly decided that my writing about peace "falsifies the monastic message." Can you imagine that? I have appealed the case though, and am hoping that they will at least relent enough to permit this book to be censored, though even then they may decide that it is scandalous, subversive, dissipated, and worldly. Offensive, in a word, to pious ears, which are of course first of all monastic ears. Let our ears not be contaminated with any news of what is happening. Let us go up in radioactive dust still blissfully imagining it is the twelfth century and that St. Bernard is roving up and down the highways and byways of old France preaching the crusade to troubadours and occasional jolly goliards, but not too jolly, it would falsify a message.

Monks must preach to the birds, for the birds, and only for the birds.

The excerpt on capital punishment was hair-raising, dreadful. I still haven't read [Jacques] Barzun. I have seen the PR symposium, have seen nothing from the *Commentary* but the [Erich] Fromm-[Michael] Macoby thing on civil defense ["The Question of Civil Defense: A Reply to Herman Kahn"] which I am using in the anthology [*Breakthrough to Peace*]. I have a friend who occasionally sends something from *The Nation*.

I close with no more to add now except to say this prayer was asked for and read in Congress by Frank Kowalski[51] who is having a tough time getting reelected in Connecticut. The Democrats are mad at him for being too forthright and are

---

[51] See footnote 49 above.

smearing him, and trying to prevent his getting back on the ballot. He was a military governor in Japan and helped rebuild Hiroshima. You may know more about him than I do. If you do, please let me know.

71. To V.H. [Victor Hammer], Lexington, Ky. [May 1962]

More and more I see that it is not the moral principles which are at stake, but more radically, the whole outlook of modern man, at least in America, and the basic assumptions which tend to guide his thought, if it can be called thought. We are living in an absurd dream, and a very bad one. And it is the fruit of all sorts of things we ought not to have done. But the whole world is in turmoil, spiritually, morally, socially. We are sitting on a thin crust above an immense lake of molten lava that is stirring and getting ready to erupt. Nothing will stop this eruption. But at least we can refrain from setting off bombs that will start it in some far worse way than it normally would.

72. To A.F. [Allan Forbes, Jr.], Cambridge, Mass. [May 1962]

It was a bit of a jolt to see that your letter was dated February 5th. I cannot remember answering it, and so apologies are in order.

By now you know that the anthology is coming along with your essay in it, or rather the part on the arms race itself ["An Essay on the Arms Race"], with I believe a short summary of your proposals. I am very glad to have it in the book [*Breakthrough to Peace*] and I think it will be a very good little collection. There have been quite a few such anthologies lately but I am optimistic enough about this project to think that this is one of the best so far.

Your paragraph about the possibility of a preemptive strike being seriously considered has been substantiated, I think, by developments. I am not able to keep track of everything here, but in any case I heard of the interview Kennedy gave to some writer in the *Saturday Evening Post* saying "we may have to take the initiative." That might mean anything. Of course the initiative, he said, would be "limited."

On one level one sees that it is impossible and even a bit absurd for the common man (whatever that is) to make a moral judgment in this situation. Nobody knows enough to make any serious judgment, I suppose. And everything is kept hidden in a jungle of doubletalk from beginning to end, so that one wonders if the people who think they are running things understand what they are trying to do themselves.

But on another level everything is plain as day in the obvious nonsense and ambiguities of the double talk itself. One has only to put one cliché up against the next and see how they react on one another. "We will take the initiative but the initiative will be limited." That tells us all we need to know.

73. To R.C. [Roger Caillois], Buenos Aires [May 1962]

I wonder if there is anyone in the world of Western culture today who does not know Victoria Ocampo,[52] and who has not come within the sphere of her radiance. She is one of those wonderful people, alas rapidly becoming less and less numerous, who includes in herself all the grace and wisdom of a universal culture at a given time. I advisedly refrain from using the word cosmopolitan, which in an age of tourism has been reduced to meaninglessness and vulgarity. In a sense she is a model for all of us in the breadth of her interests, her sympathies, and her capacity for sensitive understanding. She is in our age of miraculous communications, miraculously a person who has something to communicate. The rest of us, perhaps, use our fantastic instruments merely to echo one another's noise. And communication must always fulfill one essential condition if it is to exist at all: it must be human, it must have resonances that are deeper than formal statements, declarations, and manifestoes. And

---

[52] Victoria Ocampo (1890-1979) was an Argentine publisher, writer, and critic. She was particularly influential as the founder of *Sur*, in its time the most important literary journal in South America.

yet at the same time one of the great things about Dona Victoria is that if an intelligent manifesto is still possible, somewhere, somehow, one is likely to see her name on it. I do not make this as a statement of accurate fact, as I am in no position to follow all the manifestoes and declarations that are made: but simply as a kind of poetic truth about Dona Victoria. She is a symbol of the bright and articulate judgment of a cultured person. To me she symbolizes America in the broad sense, the only sense, in which I am proud to be numbered among Americans. I am honored and delighted to join all those who, in proclaiming their admiration and love for her, are thereby taking what may perhaps be one of the final opportunities left to men to declare themselves civilized.

74. To V.D. [Valerie Delacorte], New York [late May 1962]

Your letter was wonderful. It is a pity I have so little time to write decent letters promptly, this war business has brought me in touch with so many wonderful people. It is a grace, in that sense. I think the Lord is waking us all up to the real futility and absurdity of our society that thinks purely in terms of quantity.

I had heard a little about the Women Strike for Peace. It is good to hear from one of you directly, and to be able to tell you how deeply I share your conviction of the rightness and importance of your action. I do believe there is a deep, hidden spiritual meaning in woman's part in our crisis.

The crisis of the world is, for one thing, a crisis of falsity. The enormous lies by which we live have reached a point of such obvious contradiction with the truth that everything is contradiction and absurdity. But I think it can be said, at least I feel that this is worth saying: woman has been "used" shamelessly in our commercial society, and in this "misuse" has been deeply involved in falsity. Think for instance of advertising, in which woman is constantly used as bait. And along with that, the mentality that is created for woman, and forced on her complacently, by the commercial world. She becomes herself a commodity. In a way the symbol of all commodities. In the false image of woman, life itself is turned into a commodity in its very source. Woman too has been used to create a kind of spiritual smokescreen behind which the "reality" of the power struggle evolves. Give the soldiers enough pin up girls and they will go gladly into battle.

I won't philosophize longer. But the first and most basic affirmation of all, that you must all make, is to refuse any longer to be part of the image of woman that is created by the commercial world. I leave you to meditate on the implications of that. Your refusal to remain passive in the fantastic nonsense of the big campaign to sell shelters has been providential. You have reacted against one of the more ultimate commercial perversions of the sacred reality of the family (commercialism exploits the family all down the line, and in doing so undermines the proper formation of the child's mentality, etc.). These are realities of great seriousness, and if it is granted us to have time we must try to think about them. But the springs of thought have been poisoned. Thank you for trying to help purify them.

Yes, I am working on a book [ms. of *Peace in the Post-Christian Era*]. I hope I can get it done and then get it into print. The obstacles are real and grave. There is much official opposition. I do hope you will pray earnestly that I may get this thing said. It is a book about nuclear war, practically finished in the first draft, and one publisher is already most eager for it. But there is always the question of permission.

75. To R.McD. [Robert M. MacGregor], New York [late May 1962]

As to the Tibetan monks, if you have any influence with them please urge them from me (and I have plenty of experience and am well qualified to advise) that it is most important for them to protect themselves against all forms of indiscrete press and other publicity, and that they protect themselves against visitors. They must have a cloister or enclosure or something which outsiders absolutely are forbidden to enter except with the superior or someone else in charge. They must protect themselves against noise and inquisitiveness and against everything. I agree that it is of the very greatest importance for them to be extremely careful of the influence this country can have on them, even with the best of intentions. They have to stay apart, and above all be very faithful to their life of meditation.

What is important is that they learn however to distinguish between what is simply a difference between their culture and ours, and what is a deeper spiritual matter. On merely cultural differences they may perhaps find less danger in meeting us half way, though this is also questionable. But God forbid that they adopt any of the prevailing philosophy of life. Do please make sure that these thoughts get through to them. If there is anyone concerned there that I could or should write to, please urge them to consult me if they have any questions at all or if they need anything.

I am really very anxious to see them some time if it is at all possible. It would be wonderful if they could ever come down here, or if three of them could, the rimpoches for instance. I do hope we can look forward to a time in the future when they would make a visit here to study our monasticism, such as it is. It would of course be to our mutual advantage and liking if this were done without any publicity whatever and in the greatest quiet and simplicity.

I enjoyed the excerpt from *The Guardian*. Very true. Here is a thing of mine you may not have seen.

Please give my very kind regards to the Reverend Monks from Tibet and assure them of my deep respect and fellowship and my readiness to serve them in anything I possibly can. And may we share in a common desire for truth and enlightenment, and may this be blessed with success. Such is my prayer for them and I hope their's for me.

76. To Nuns [Sisters of Loretto (making final vows), Kentucky, May 29, 1962]

The day has come for you to give yourselves completely to Christ Our Lord. You will never appreciate, in this life, what it means to surrender yourself totally to Him. This must, from now on, be part of the mystery of faith in which you live. You will not *know* that you belong to Him: you must *believe* it. And this will require more faith than you have had up to this time. But He will give you the faith to believe it.

In the beginning, perhaps, this faith will not be too difficult. Later on, under trial, it may become hard at times. A faith that is not tested is not worth much. Your faith must grow always, without ceasing. That is why trial is necessary.

The faith of a first communicant is not enough for a postulant in religion. The faith of a postulant is not enough for a novice. The faith of a novice is not enough for a professed, and the faith of a newly professed is not enough for one who has been years in religion.

Sometimes we think that the purity of our faith is all in the past and that what we have to do is "recover" the fervor of our first communion, or of our days in the novitiate. On the contrary, we must go forward, not back. And going forward may at times be grim, because later on, when we go forward, we realize that we are getting to the end. However, at that time whatever was valuable in the beginning will be brought back to us in a new form by the Holy Spirit. It is not for us to be anxious about arranging our lives, even our spiritual lives.

If we belong to Christ, we must also believe that He belongs to us. And that is much more important. That is why we do not have to run our lives, for He is our life. We must not imagine that we can dictate to Him. Our gift of ourselves to Him is a surrender in joy, so that we henceforth allow Him to have His way with us.

Wherever you may go from here, remember me and pray for me. I will also remember you and keep you in my Masses and prayers. For since Our Lord has made us neighbors and friends on earth, I presume that He wants us to be neighbors and friends in heaven also. But first we must accomplish our assigned tasks on this earth, whatever they may be. Let us keep praying for one another that we may do this well, and with confidence and joy, without anxiety, trusting in Him to whom we belong.

I shall remember you in a very special way at Mass this Thursday, and if it turns out that I have a Mass intention to dispose of, I shall offer it for you, together with my own novices. I do not yet know if I will be able to do this.

77. To W.F. [Wilbur H. Ferry], Santa Barbara, Calif. [June 4, 1962]

Have been going back to Origen and Tertullian, where I belong. What do I find? Preaching non-violence. Christians never kill with the sword, these characters say. They haven't heard that this is a bad image. Father of the Church, bad father image. But well, we all know what everybody thinks of Origen and Tertullian (if they have heard of them). Augustine came along and fixed up the image ok. The war of the merciful fought for love, he says. Nice image. Non mutant resistant. You can pour anything you want on that image and it won't change, it is official.

So let the merciful non-resistant mutants resist and travel. Let them pack up our troubles in their old feedback and kick off for anyplace. Our mutants will come home to roost.

The anthology (it has had a couple of sporadic title changes since I last wrote but it is a non-mutant and it keeps coming up as "Breakthrough for Peace") [published as *Breakthrough to Peace*] this is going through. At least it is going through the press. So that is that. I think it will be good, anyway. And certainly the essay ["Peace: A Religious Responsibility"] in it is long enough and full enough to say what I have to say.

78. To R.L. [Robert Lax], New York [June 4, 1962]

Here is an answer to your riposte of the nth. Since that time my dear agent we have been in contact with chiefs and sub chiefs, hostages and proto hostages, crypto chiefs and proto communists, proto pentecosts and crypto baptists, out and out card carrying propter hocs, and pseudo sub rosa investigating pinks. I have momentarily lost my crypto card and I am at a loss for words, plans, programs, hostages, protos and cryptos. But I have seen the man with the portrait under his arm. It is a picture of a crypto you know. It is a photo of a card carrying vestige. It is an image of a void. It is a most impressive card of identity, and all must whip out at a given moment the cards of identity.

Propter hoc ostendat unusquisque faciem suam et judicabitur.

In this amazing liturgy of chiefs I too have exchange the hostage, the ham, the hambone, the smoked trout, the vino rosso. Best hostages you ever saw. We sat in the grass and talked over the plans.

The plans are very simple. Take over the Pentecost.

Wipe out the identity cards and start over with the Holy Coast.

There's gold in them thar. Which? Them. Them.

Now here is a secret poem about my agent in Jodhpurs.

I have been silence. I have been nacht und nebel for my war book. I have been put in the calabozo. I have been shut up in a tin can. I have been shrewdly suppressed at the right moment. I have been stood in the corner I have been made to wear the cap. I have been tried and tested in the holy virtue of humility. I have been found wanting and tested some more. I have been told to shut up about the wars, wars is not for Christians except to support.

Hence my dear charlot the laments in the current Jubilee ["Religion and the Bomb," *Jubilee,* May 1962] is my finale.

It comes a little agent with too big an overcoat and false glasses with a copy of the contraband war book in about six weeks. Nobody to print, nobody to show. Just read the damn war book.

They have develop a newe bug. He flies to Moscowa and flies back. No ddt can kill the new bug. He cause all the disease. Science has progress and it will all go out not with a bang but a whimper. You'll see. Feel a cough coming in? Well, that's it.

Your Pennsylvania Chum

79. To C.H. [Catherine de Hueck (Doherty)], Ontario [June 4, 1962]

Your long, wonderful letter has gone for nearly three months without an answer. But you can guess all the reasons. And now perhaps if I answer it is because the voice which was shouting, momentarily, about peace, has been told to shut up. And I have a little time to return to other things such as writing letters.

I knew I didn't have much time to get said what I felt ought to be said. So I got it all out as best I could, in a jumble of words and articles, and even finished a book. The book is on stencils, and when the last stencil was typed the order came in not to print or publish anything more on topics "not befitting a contemplative monk." Apparently the most crucial problems, and the struggle with the demon, these are out of the range of a contemplative monk. I was told it would be all right if I prayed over these matters, however.

You ask me if I am weary? Sure. Perhaps not as weary as you are, but weary in the same way, weary of the same things. It is complicated by the fact that one is tempted to feel he has no right to be weary of the actions and pronouncements of a lot of very good, sincere people who are themselves weary of something or other. We are like a bunch of drunken men at the last end of a long stupid party falling over the furniture in the twilight of dawn. I hope it is dawn. Probably not, though. But the thing that eats one up is the anguish over the Church. This of course leaves me inarticulate because I know that anyone can show where and how and why I am not a good Catholic, a good Christian, a faithful member of Christ. And yet there is this conviction that the Church is full of a terrible spiritual sickness, even though there is always that inexpressible life, but Christians themselves are taking arms against their own life and fighting it down and preventing it from thriving in the Church. It is as if we were all desperately determined to finish the whole thing off by being false Christians. I wonder sometimes if we are not all half crazy.

It is at such a time as this that one has to have faith in the Church, and the fact that we suffer from the things that make us suffer, the fact that we cannot find any way out of the suffering, is perhaps a sign of hope. I do not pretend to understand the situation or to analyze anything. Your answer is correct. What is wanted is love. But love has been buried under words, noise, plans, projects, systems, and apostolic gimmicks. And when we open our mouths to do something about it we add more words, noise, plans, etc. We are afflicted with the disease of constant talking with almost nothing to say. From that point of view I suppose it is just as well that I am saying nothing more about the war business. Saying things does not help. Yet what is there to do? You're right again, that what one must do is meet the needs that He brings before us, when and as He does so. We will not see anything clear, but we must do His will. We have to be heroic in our obedience to God. And that may mean cutting through a whole forest of empty talk and clichés and nonsense just to begin to find some glimmer of His will. To obey always and not know for sure if we are really obeying. That is not fun at all, and people like to get around the responsibility by entering into a routine of trivialities in which everything seems clear and noble and defined: but when you look at it honestly it falls apart, for it is riddled with absurdity from top to bottom.

I have to finish this now. I do not know if I will be able to get something to you to print in the paper. You can always quote anything from a letter, and I will try to write you more letters. Meanwhile, let us pray for one another. Do please pray for me, I need it badly. I think I am perhaps finished soon. Or maybe that is just self pity (or a funny kind of optimism). Maybe we are all finished. But what matters is His Kingdom, and that is coming.

80. To R.L. [Ray Livingston], Minneapolis, Minn. [early June 1962]

On looking at your letter again I see you are really asking me whether I would like to see your book, rather than saying that it is being sent. I thought it was on the way and was eagerly awaiting it. Now that I see you may be in danger of giving me up as a lost cause, I hasten to urge you to send it. I have long admired [Ananda K.] Coomaraswamy, have been in correspondence with his wife [Dona Luisa Coomaraswamy], and even planned a little book of selections from his works which may or may not get published some day. So I am naturally very eager to see your work.

Also I am very anxious to see the article on "Measures of Fire" that you mention in your letter, and if it is still possible to have a copy made, I would be grateful to you.

As to the Patristic sources you ask for: I can only give you some leads, not precise references. But the point you mention, about the harmony of the universe being intimately connected with man's spiritual condition, is tied up with the recapitulation theory of Irenaeus and with the apocatastasis of Origen and the Greek Fathers, but not in the heretical sense of the restoration of all after the last judgment. The Classical Scriptural text would be Romans 8:18-27 with commentaries on it. Also see Colossians and Ephesians. By the way, returning to Origen above, I see what I wrote could be misleading. There is an orthodox sense in which Origen speaks of the restoration of all things in Christ, and a heretical one in which he carries it to the point of emptying hell: though this is held by the Russians and Greeks to some extent. It is an interesting point.

You might find interesting leads in [Louis] Bouyer's new book *The Seat of Wisdom* [New York: Pantheon Books, 1962]. And of course there is always [Nicholai] Berdyaev . . . his "Sense of Creation" (if that is the English title, I read it in French) is full of wild ideas, but a few good ones also. Have you by the way read [Thomas] Traherne's *Centuries of Meditations,* published recently by Harpers? He has delightful insights on this subject. As to the Scholastics, I would say try St. Bonaventure's *Collationes in Hexaemeron.* (In general all the Patristic treatises on the work of the six days would offer interesting material.) I am on and off reading Clement of Alexandria and will try to keep you in mind if I run across more material. Then there is Gregory of Nyssa . . . A new collection of texts by [Jean] Danielou and [Herbert] Musurillo[53] should offer a few possibilities.

I will send a mimeograph of a little thing that is remotely connected with this point. It is a piece of mine that is being privately printed.

81. To W.M. [William Robert Miller], Baltimore, Md. [early June 1962]

Thank you for your kind letter and for the copy of the *United Church Herald* containing your article. I read it eagerly and I agree with you that the evidence of charity in the Japanese

---

[53] *From Glory to Glory: Texts from Gregory of Nyssa's Mystical Writings,* edited by Jean Danielou and Herbert Musurillo (New York: Charles Scribner's Sons, 1961).

death camp on the River Kwai is, like so many other unexpected things in our time, clear evidence of the divine realities which we have so long neglected. We have taken Christianity for granted for hundreds of years and now all of a sudden I think some of us are beginning to wake up to the fact that we have almost forgotten what it means, and that our ideas of God and His ways are far from corresponding to the actuality. I am giving some talks on the prophets to my novices here and this brings the truth home very forcefully.

We live in prophetic and eschatological times, and by and large everyone is asleep. We realize it dimly, like sleepers who have turned off the alarm clock without quite waking up. It is a time of awful struggle and awful torpor. And we need faith. Moreover we need to realize how true it is that faith is purely a gift. And that the Holy Spirit is the Giver who, in giving all other gifts, is Himself given by the Father and the Son.

It happens that, as I had rather expected, my writing about peace is now being limited, in fact it has for all practical purposes stopped. I foresaw this and wanted to try to say as much as I could before I would have to stop. I am glad I was able to appear a couple of times in the pages of *Fellowship*.

82. To J.W. [John C. H. Wu], Newark, N.J. [June 7, 1962]

I had better get this letter written before any more time flows under the bridge (what bridge? what time? this is our illusion). But in any case time has something to do with the fact that I am going to say Mass for your intentions on June 15th, a week from tomorrow, which will be Friday in Whitsun week, and I shall be praying that you obtain not only that gift of the Holy Ghost which is assigned by St. Andrew's Missal for that day (whatever ideas the St. Andrew's Missal may have on the subject, and I don't especially care), but for you to receive all the gifts in all abundance and all the fruits and beatitudes and the Holy Spirit Himself in incomprehensible fullness. This Mass is being said for you at the request of Mrs. O'Brian and I promised her a long time ago I would let you know. We don't have, or seem not to have, those little Mass cards around here, so I am sending you a letter. In fact it finally occurs to me that in this matter of saying Masses and getting notices out to people about it I am at the topmost peak of inefficiency and I do not know how I survive in the American Church with such slapdash methods: I just say Mass for people when I get a chance. Primitive, almost heretical.

But it will be a joy to stand in the presence of the Heavenly Father, in Christ, and speak of you and all whom you love and of China.

Paul Sih has obtained for me a wonderful reprint of the [James] Legge translation of the Chinese Classics, and has also sent the Wang Yang Ming. I am awed and delighted with the great volumes of the Classics. I do not intend to read them lightly however, and they are waiting until other things can be cleared away. But I must admit I have done absolutely no work at all on Chinese, because I find that I simply waste too much time fumbling around in the dictionary and so little is done that it does not make sense to continue until some time in the future when I can get some instruction. So it will all have to wait a bit. I am working on the Latin Fathers, with whom I can make enough headway to know what is happening. Perhaps I shall do a translation of an excerpt from Cassiodorus. I think you would like him. He is very much the Confucian scholar, Latin style. A great librarian and student and copyist of books but also a polished writer and an engaging thinker, besides a man of prayer. His monastery of Vivarium is most attractive: it was a monastery of scholars.

And now to turn suddenly from scholarship to less pleasant subjects. I hesitate to send you the enclosed angry and bitter poem ["A Picture of Lee Ying"]. It is savage, and its savagery hits everything in sight, so that it is not kind to anyone, even to the poor sad desperate Chinese girl whose picture broke my heart and suggested the poem. I wish I could have said something full of mercy and love that would have been worthy of the situation, but I have only used her plight to attack the hypocrisy of those who find no room for the Chinese refugees, and who always have a very good reason. And the sad plight of a whole society which nods approval, while pronouncing a few formulas of regret. I suppose I should not get angry, and that it represents a weakness in myself to get excited still about the awful tragedies that are everywhere in the world. They are too awful for human protest to be meaningful, so people seem to think. I protest anyway, I am still primitive enough, I have not caught up with this century.

83. To J.H. [John Harris], England [June 8, 1962]

I suppose it was really rather foolish of me to send you the CW letters [the first edition of mimeographed letters completed in April 1962] as a present on your entry into the Church, instead of the letter which I ought to have written, and in which I could have said things a little more to the point. But I do now want to tell you how happy I am that it is finally settled. I was in fact mumbling to myself about getting some sort of action going, as if I could. But I thought it was about time someone built a fire under those people in Rome. I suppose I am the last man to do that. Rome does not want distant monks telling them what to do. Distant monks should neither be seen nor heard.

What can I tell you about the Church? You have been very patient with her human deficiencies, and that patience is also her gift. Your letter reflects the extraordinary serenity with which the new convert accepts *everything*. And one has to. In a sense it is true that one only comes in with blinders on, blinders one has put on and kept on. One has to refuse to be disturbed by so many things. And you are right in the refusal. These are temporal and absurd things which, in the eschatological perspectives, which are the true ones, must vanish forever along with many other things that are more precious and far from absurd in themselves.

The Church is not of this world, and she complacently reminds us of this when we try to budge her in any direction. But on the other hand we also are of the Church and we also have our duty to speak up and say the Church is not of this world when her refusal turns out, in effect, to be a refusal to budge from a solidly and immovable temporal position. And that is the trouble with this war business. The Church's voice is clear enough, but the people who are responsible for supplying Catholic principles to political action are acting in a way that is more secular than sacred. The current war ethic is pagan and less than pagan. There is very little of Christianity left in it anywhere. The truth and justice have been drained out of it. It is a lie and a blasphe-my, and this has to be said. Not by you. But certainly if I have felt obliged to say it, I have been left without alternative. The urgency with which I have shouted what I wanted to say is due to the fact that I knew I would not go on shouting for very long and indeed the shouting is already over. You may perhaps see an issue of *Blackfriars* ["Christian Action in World Crisis," June 1962] one of these days with the last echo of my outcry.

But to get back to you and Emy, I am so happy for you. You will have grace to see through all that is inconsequential and unfortunate in the Church. She is still the Church, the Body of Christ, and nobody can change that, not even some of those who imagine themselves to represent her perfectly when they have simply twisted her teaching to suit their own secularism. Be true to the Spirit of God and to Christ. Read your prophets sometimes, and go through the Gospels and St. Paul and see what is said there: that is your life. You are called to a totally new, risen, transformed life in the Spirit of Christ. A life of simplicity and truth and joy that is not of this world. May you be blessed always in it, you and the children. I send you all my love and blessings.

84. To F.E. [Fr. J. Whitney Evans], Duluth, Minn. [June 13, 1962]

The idea is a fine one and I think your draft is very promis-ing. By all means go on with it, a lot of good will be done by it. I have already mentioned it, or will mention it, to Justus G. Lawler, editor of Herder and Herder ... Why not send him a copy to give him an idea of it. He will surely be very interested.

I think it could be somewhat expanded, to include perhaps some more material that has recently appeared, especially some of the work by Gordon Zahn [*German Catholics and Hitler's War*] on the way the German Catholics went along with Hitler in a manifestly unjust war, and the problem involved by this.

Most important however is I think inclusion of material by Leo Szilard, who helped Einstein get the first bomb project started, and who later protested against the use of the bomb at Hiroshima. He has evolved a plan, published in the *Bulletin of the Atomic Scientists,* April 1962, which comes as close as anything I have seen to fitting in with Catholic moral teaching and with the pronouncements of the Popes. It still permits the use of tactical nuclear weapons, but in a clearly and strictly defensive manner. I think Szilard's proposals are very sound and practical and he has implemented them in a way that might conceivably get somewhere. In a word I think that his proposals are about the most effective yet made and may even stand a chance to prevent a nuclear war if people get behind him.

Szilard can be contacted at the Hotel Dupont Plaza in Washington and can send information about his plan. I think Catholic support would be of great value. He knows I am behind him, for what that is worth.

We have to face the fact that peace or war may in the long run depend decisively on the decision of American Catholics. I do not think many Catholics realize the momentous seriousness of our position. It is tremendously important for Catholics to get the proper perspective, and not just go around in a state of confused belligerency. We have got to use our heads and our faith, and follow the lines pointed out by the Popes without distorting the perspective to suit short-term policies which appear to have pragmatic value. This requires long-term thinking, without distortions and falsifications, straight Catholic moral teaching and not too much probabilism either. This is not one of the cases where probabilism is permitted, it seems to me.

One more comment on your manuscript. I think the beginning (about putting their picture there) is arresting, but I think it puts too much stress on the idea of personal survival. The issue is not personal survival but moral truth, though of course the morality depends entirely on the destructive havoc wreaked by nuclear war. I think we ought to make clear it is a question of crime. Why not start out instead with the execution of the Nuremberg war criminals, and then suggest that those who start an all-out nuclear war might well be in the same position, and those who encourage and support them would be equally responsible? Anyway, God bless your zeal and your project. Can I have a few more copies? I would greatly appreciate some.

Keep me posted. All best wishes.

85. To W.W. [Will Watkins], San Francisco, Calif [c. June 15, 1962]

Your gift of the Eatherly-Anders book[54] arrived today and I am most happy to have it. It is something I had heard about and was anxious to obtain. So you have sent it, and I deeply appreciate your kindness. I will read it with the deepest interest and concern. Eatherly is a rare symbol in the history of war-making, and a very significant one. We are a country of strange ambiguities, and there is good in them after all, I think. But unfortunately the less ambiguous and the less conscience-stricken are the ones who are the best armed and the most convinced.

I had heard about *Everyman* [CNVA boat that sailed into the atomic testing area in the Pacific], I even got a letter from Hal Stallings, and I am following the case with interest. It is indeed a beautiful little boat, but I wonder if it would have been able to make it down there to the test area, if there were any storms.

Thank you again for your kindness. We have to be true to our conscience in everything, and true to humanity, for man is the image of God. This image cannot be defaced or destroyed. It must not. To defend it is to defend that which is most dear to God Himself.

86. To D.D. [Dorothy Day], New York [June 16, 1962]

It is true that I am not theoretically a pacifist. That only means that I do not hold that a Christian *may not* fight, and that a war *cannot* be just. I hold that there is such a thing as a just war, even today there can be such a thing, and I think the Church holds it. But on the other hand I think that is pure theory and that in practice all the wars that are going around, whether with conventional weapons, or guerilla wars, or the Cold War itself, are shot through and through with evil, falsity, injustice, and sin so much so that one can only with difficulty

---

[54] Claude Eatherly, *Burning Conscience: The Case of the Hiroshima Pilot, Claude Eatherly, Told in His Letters to Gunther Anders* (New York: Monthly Review Press, 1962).

extricate the truths that may be found here and there in the "causes" for which the fighting is going on. So in practice I am with you, except in so far, only, as a policy of totally uncompromising pacifism may tend in effect to defeat itself and yield to one of the other forms of injustice. And I think that your position has an immense importance as a symbolic statement that is irreplaceable and utterly necessary. I also think it is a scandal that most Christians are not solidly lined up with you. I certainly am.

I am glad you sent the article, rather the letter, on to Father H—. In reality the matter is one of terminology and theological outlook, rather than one of essence. I have always felt that Fr. H—'s "natural-supernatural" division suffered from being over-simplified and too much based on the scholasticism against which he instinctively reacts, so that it seems to me that he cannot say all he would like to say, and cannot say it fully effectively. I think the whole question needs a lot of study, and do not pretend that I have any answers that are startlingly new. I just approach the question from the viewpoint of the Fathers and the Bible, regarding nature as God meant it to be and not in its fallen state, still less in its abstract state.

I am so happy you are going to Brazil. Amoroso Lima is the translator of one of my books, and I met him some years ago. Is Aimee his wife? If so I met her also, and she is charming, as also were their children, then quite young. I saw one of his sons recently with his wife. They are a lovely family and wonderful people of whom I am very fond, but he has an altogether exaggerated idea of my powers as a writer, I am afraid. Do be sure to give them my most cordial messages. In fact before you go, please let me know and I will send you a couple of things to take to them. I have an awful time trying to get things through to Brazil by mail.

I will be sending you a copy of the Cold War Letters [the first edition of mimeographed letters completed in April 1962], too.

Since I am not writing anything about war anymore, I have gone back to the Fathers, to Cassiodorus, Cyprian, Tertullian etc. I will try to type out bits of things they say that could be used in a box here and there by the CW [*Catholic Worker*] and will send them along. I will probably do a few translations, and maybe write some prayers. I have to do a book on Cassian[55] some time, and thanks again for the translation you sent. We always use it.

It is no use speculating too much about the world situation, but it is certainly a very risky one. The whole world is under judgment, and one feels it keenly. Without saying what I think something is going to happen, I think I can say reasonably that there is just no reason in the world for it *not* to happen. I think the evil in us all has reached the point of overflowing. May the Holy Spirit give us compunction and inner truth and humility and love, that we may be a leaven in this world. And that we may help and bring light to those who need it most: and the Lord alone knows who they are, for the need of all is desperate.

87. To C.K. [Carl Kline], Wisconsin [June 1962]

I want to thank you warmly for your appreciative letter. It means a lot to receive such reactions because it shows that for all the confusion and self-contradictions in our society, conscience is not asleep.

The situation is, however, terrible. It is quite impossible for us to see it as it really is. That would require the charismatic gifts of a Jeremiah. We are too close to it, too involved in it, whether we like it or not. For better or for worse, we are not ants. We have intelligence, and intelligence is a terribly destructive power when it is no longer held in check by the power of the spirit, focused on the meaningful symbol and the sacrament.

The secularization of religion is of course one of the great tragedies of our time, but religion is secularized because everything else is too. Whether we can survive this illness is the great question. I mean as a society. For as individuals we have to have the courage and the effrontery to cling to spiritual meanings and direct our lives by them in spite of everyone.

---

[55] Merton's Novitiate Conferences on Cassian have been published as the first volume in a series of Novitiate Conferences. See Thomas Merton, *Cassian and the Fathers: Initiation into the Monastic Tradition,* edited by Patrick F. O'Connell with a Foreword by Patrick Hart, O.C.S.O. (Kalamazoo, MI: Cistercian Publications, 2005).

I think I have about said all I will be able to say in print on the subject of war. I have a book finished, on the subject, which is not likely to be printed right now [ms. of *Peace in the Post-Christian Era*]. But since you have expressed interest I am sending you a mimeograph of the text, which contains a few mistakes but is on the whole intelligible.

88. To G.M. [Gwen Myers], Watertown, Maine [June 1962]

Thank you for writing to me. I feel very close indeed to the Friends and I always have, so you must not feel embarrassed about the difference in our religious affiliations. Besides, you have read many books that are very much in line with the kind of contemplative life we have here. Dom [John] Chapman [OSB] is especially good. [Jean Pierre de] Caussade is of course a master.

Naturally the idea of a "Church" supposes that we all have an ingrained need for one another and that we all aspire by a kind of basic instinct of grace to a community in which the Spirit of Christ will speak to us and guide us. However there are groups and groups, and community life is now more and now less transparent a medium for the action of the Holy Spirit. You must not be surprised or sad if in your prayer group your own aspirations are not understood, nor is it possible or easy to find understanding when you travel a rather lonely way.

We can always say that the way of the contemplative should not be unusual or lonely, and that for him to think of it as unusual is certainly dangerous. But the facts are there and so is the experience.

It remains for you to trust God, not to make you infallible but to protect you from serious error and to make good the smaller mistakes. And thus with confidence in His guidance, even though you may not always interpret it correctly, you can advance peacefully. I am sure He will guide you safely in everything if you take care to keep your heart quiet and pure, as best you can, and listen to His voice in simplicity, trying to avoid the more obvious illusions, and keeping as close as possible to the solid bedrock of faith. With that, He will do all the rest. And He will put books into your hands that will tell you what your friends cannot.

I am a bad correspondent, but if you ever need me, please write.

89. To J.W.S. [John Whitman Sears], San Mateo, Calif. [June 23, 1962]

Thanks for your paper on "The Arms Race as a Chain Reaction." I think it has a lot of very good things in it and completely agree. I think you have hit the nail on the head, as also [Erich] Fromm and others have. It is a question of insanity.

We are just not big enough to handle all the ironies and contradictions we have brought upon ourselves, (innocently enough, I suppose) by developing too fast. Yet looking at it on another level as a spiritual problem, it really becomes apocalyptic. I know men are seriously asking themselves now whether this sort of thing has happened somewhere before, and whether on other planets somewhere there have been races which have reached a point of development where they ended by destroying themselves.

Reading as I do the obscure writings of the fourth-, fifth-, sixth-century Church Fathers I find that in the light of all this the doctrine of original sin is not as absurd as it sometimes sounds in a blatantly puritanical context. It has subtleties which even a Zen man appreciates, and so I send you an offprint of a dialogue with D.T. Suzuki ["Wisdom in Emptiness, A Dialogue: D.T. Suzuki and Thomas Merton" (*New Directions* 17, 1961)] on this subject. I think you may be interested.

Do keep me on your list for any other mimeographed pieces you are sending out.

90. To B.N. [Rev. D. Brendan Nagle], Malibu, Calif. [late June or early July 1962]

You are quite right, of course, I do not claim to have kept up with all the latest technical terms in the Cold War and the arms race. This would not be fully possible where I am. Also, as I too am rather pressed for time, I cannot give this subject the fully leisurely development that a real answer to your letter would demand. However I hope that I can clarify my position regarding the main points you raise.

Merkelbach [traditional Catholic moralist] may have a probable opinion when he says that an offensive war may be just, but it is certainly not incorrect to say that the more common statement of Catholic tradition on this point, as represented in Pius XII's numerous statements and especially his Christmas messages, is that the just war is a defensive war. It is certainly not "the common doctrine of the Fathers" that an offensive war is a just war. St. Augustine, who is the father of the just war theory as far as I can see, evolved his doctrine in the light of the barbarian attacks on the Roman Empire and was at pains to show that the previously common doctrine of Christians, who avoided participation in any war, usually, was not a *prohibition* of all military activity on the part of Christians. Historically the Crusades present as much of a problem as a proof that a just war is also aggressive. However, as you say, this is secondary, a matter of speculation. Let's get down to business.

We can agree that your "minimum deterrent posture" which implies the willingness and readiness to wipe out enemy cities on a large scale if he attacks us, is immoral by Christian standards. It is a way of holding millions of civilians as hostages and destroying them if the need arises. Also I would add that this policy would not seem practical in any way, as our cities would also be destroyed to a great extent in such a war.

First counterforce strike. I will agree that this can be acceptable *in theory* in the light of the teaching of the moral theologians, and that a Catholic could hold this, but I would lay down certain very stringent conditions (and I would not hold this opinion myself in any case). Here are the conditions I would lay down:

a) I would say that first counterforce strike could be permissible in theory if there were reasonable certainty that fallout or other side effects would not do serious damage to neutrals and friends, or even to our own future generations.

b) I would say that for a counterforce first strike to be permissible at all there would have to be *real imminent certainty* that the enemy himself was planning such a first strike on our own installations or on our cities.

To make a first strike, even counterforce, simply because we felt the enemy was menacing us politically, or even because the enemy was about to effect a political takeover of an allied country like Austria, would not seem to me to fit the conditions for a just war according to Christian ethics. I would not think the counter-force first strike idea would be legitimate under any circumstances except in the extreme case when *it was the only possible way to prevent our own annihilation,* by Nuclear, Chemical, or Bacteriological weapons let us say. Or at least by nuclear weapons.

In this case I think one could legitimately appeal to the *ratio defensionis necessariae.* However, even then I think this is not a sound or practical policy and that as free men in a Christian society we ought to be able to come up with better ways of solving our problems.

Let us get down to this question of what is and what is not realistic. This is the question. Your friends, who I assume favor this counterforce first strike capacity, probably do so because they imagine it is realistic. And as a correlative to that view they use the current cliché which classifies nuclear pacifism as "hysterical."

Father, let's face it: there are all kinds of clichés and accusations flying around on this subject, and I have seen it stated with what seems to me a high degree of probability, that the kind of thinking that claims to be "nuclear realism" is basically paranoid. I only mention this to show that psychiatric clichés come rather cheap and one can use them without much effort of thought. I prefer the diagnosis that sees traces of paranoia in the "hard" position, because this statement has been made by people of sound judgment and high professional standing—who have of course been attacked by others of high standing (though not in the same field!). Besides, the people I have met who are most apt to be breathing fire and smoke on this war question have seemed to me to be not quite balanced mentally, certainly they have profound emotional problems. However, this may be due to a chance sampling of specimens who have come my way.

Do you really think it is realistic to suppose that we can attain to "maximum superiority in the number of weapons, maximum invulnerability of one's own delivery system, maximum intelligence about the enemy's"? Obviously such a "maximum" must be relative and fluid, and, to pass over all the other points that might be questioned in such a policy, it is just absurd to think that stability and secure peace can be built on such a system. Obviously the "enemy" will strain every nerve to attain "maximum superiority," etc. and this will mean an arms race without foreseeable limit.

Father, one does not have to be a pacifist to state with full assurance, as Leo Szilard and others have stated, that the continuance of such an arms race means full-scale nuclear war by within ten years. And even the most sober analysts who favor the reasonable practicality of nuclear war, [Herman] Kahn, etc. assure us that there is almost no chance at all of the democratic society we now know surviving even a victorious all-out nuclear war. At best it might be "rebuilt" after a long period. I just cannot see that such a war is "realistic."

Now let's look at some of the facts which these "realists" apparently ignore. What we want is to defend Christian civilization and our religious freedom, right? And we want to defend it against the immense and world-wide aggressivity of Communism.

What, I ask, is the cornerstone of the Communist world revolution? It is purely and simply this: that capitalism will and must inevitably destroy itself by war. That capitalism is so committed to an economic structure that adds up to bigger and bigger wars that it has no choice. The capitalist nations will, then, says the theory, blow each other to pieces and the Communists will be left to take over.

OK. Now let's be Chinese. As Chinamen in Peking, Chinese Communists, we look out at the world, and we see, with grim satisfaction, the capitalist west totally committed to the arms race and to an increasingly aggressive war policy. And we also look at Russia, which we secretly despise as a "state capitalism" which has betrayed the "pure Marxist tradition," and we see that it is inevitably being involved in the danger of war with the West, though preaching "coexistence." So what do we do? We look forward to the day when the two will blow each other off the map.

One man out of every four in the world today is Chinese. And we seriously, realistically, are evolving a policy which will lead to the kind of war that will leave our nation, even in Kahn's "optimistic" description, a helpless shambles. The Chinese could take us over with chopsticks after such a war. Father, this is not realism and it is not sanity.

However, I am really beside the point. The question, as I see it, is not one merely of political practicality. Nor is it (still less indeed) a matter of bodily survival. I would not give a hoot, personally, if this whole monastery and everybody in it were blown sky high this afternoon. I hope that my brothers and I are ready for heaven, or at least for a relatively short purgatory!! By God's grace, not by our merits. I also am sure that God's mercy would take care of millions of innocent or confused people who might perish in a nuclear war. Survival is a purely secondary question.

We are Christians, and we are going to be judged by Christ, according to the standard of His Law.

We have just witnessed the execution of Adolf Eichmann. In Nazi Germany, you may or may not remember, honest people, including perhaps many Catholics, more or less seriously accepted the view that the purity of the German race, the power of the German nation, was gravely menaced by "international Jewry." The policy of genocide (which has since been explicitly condemned by the Church, though no such explicit condemnation is needed, since the natural law condemns it) was accepted, or at least put through without significant protest, even from Catholics (there were of course exceptions). It seems that Catholics just looked the other way, if they did not actively approve and cooperate (the commandant of Auschwitz was a baptized Catholic, but I don't know if he continued to practice his religion.)

The Eichmann trial has shown that these people were "sane" and "normal." That they did their job like any other job. It was mostly a matter of paperwork at this top level, of course. But they knew very well what they were doing. They simply went by the fact that everyone in their society accepted this as "normal" and "right" and they shrugged off responsibility by saying it was their "duty" and that the needs of the state demanded this unusual procedure.

You and I can see Eichmann in a different perspective and we can agree that this was a horrible crime.

My main point is this: we are Catholic priests. Catholic means universal. We have a duty not only to our people—and your people, you say, are almost 75% employed in defense industries—but also to the entire human race. We have got to have universal perspectives. We have got to enter into the hearts and minds of "the others." This is demanded by the exigencies of the "whole Christ."

In this present world crisis, our duty is not merely to salve the consciences of our parishioners and enable them to go ahead in peace of heart with a job that may involve them in collective responsibility for what, in spite of Merkelbach, may well turn out to be a collective crime. I know this sounds mad, utterly extreme. Well, Father, we still have to face the possibility. We are going to be judged by the way we have reacted to this great moral and spiritual challenge of our time.

In all seriousness, in all humility, with all deference to, and with no personal reference intended, I must in conscience say that there is danger of us Catholics, myself and all the rest, tending to think in some way as the Eichmanns did in Germany. Not of course that we will, by God's grace, be so blind. But that kind of blindness is not beyond us, even though in a lesser degree. How? By being so utterly and totally convinced of the gravity of our danger that we forget the principle that the end does not justify the means.

I am not preaching disarmament. But I do think that there are ways of using nuclear weapons for defense that will quite adequately fit our needs, without promoting an extreme spiraling arms race, but, on the contrary, pointing to eventual stability and relative sanity on all sides. I will not outline the policies, but Leo Szilard, in the April *Bulletin of the Atomic Scientists,* seems to me to make proposals that exactly fit the principles laid down by the Popes.

Anyway, Father, this is my opinion. In all charity, let us at least continue to ask Our Lord to guide us through these difficult straits, and trust Him. I keep you and your people in my prayers. Pray for me too.

91. To S.E.M. [Sr. Elaine Michael Bane, O.S.F.], Allegany, N.Y. [July 4, 1962]

This is not an adequate letter, but I do want to get some kind of reply into the mail for you, as the project of the *"retiro"* [a Cloister] sounds most interesting. It is something that deserves every possible encouragement and I want to do my bit. I will try to remember to fill an envelope with materials that might be of use to you and get it off in the next couple of days. You can guess however that I have not much time for handling mail, and secretarial facilities are, well, rudimentary as I don't want to overburden the novices and that is the only "work pool" to which I have access. One or another of them do help out, though, and I am grateful.

[Dietrich Von Hildebrand's] *Transformation in Christ* [*On the Christian Attitude of Mind* (New York: Longmans, Green, 1948)] is a difficult book, and I let the novices read it, without however pushing them. On the other hand Von Hildebrand's *In Defense of Purity* [: *An Analysis of the Catholic Ideals of Purity and Virginity* (Baltimore, MD: Helicon, 1962)] is, it seems to me a superbly spiritual treatment of chastity. There is a lot about marriage in it, but I feel the novices ought to appreciate the married state which they are renouncing. What good to renounce it if they do not know its dignity? For a *retiro* however the needs might be different.

[Louis] Bouyer on *The Meaning of the Monastic Life* [New York: P.J. Kenedy & Sons, 1950] we regard as standard. In an older context, there is Dom [Columba] Marmion [O.S.B.], always safe and solid. Bouyer's new *Introduction to Spirituality* [New York: Désclée, 1961] is a bit advanced, but I should think you might be able to use it. A perfect biography of St. Therese which is very useful for all religious is *The Hidden Face* [: *A Study of Saint Therese of Lisieux* (New York: Pantheon, 1959)] by [Ida Friederike] Goerres. We always like [Romano] Guardini here. To my mind he is one of the most important and articulate Catholic authors of the moment. He has good things on prayer, faith, and so on. *Prayer in Practice* [New York: Pantheon, 1957] comes to mind as excellent. Fr. [Jean] Danielou is liked by the novices and I like him too.

These are just a few books that spring to mind as I write. I will try to dig up one of our novitiate reading lists and put it in the envelope I hope to send.

I remember St. Elizabeth's well, and you have a lovely place for a cloistered contemplative life—except perhaps for the trains, but who cares about a few trains once in a while? Are you right in the old convent, or are you somewhere apart?

Remember that in the enclosed and solitary life, your solitude itself will do an immense amount for you. The sisters need not strain and struggle and worry too much about "degrees" of prayer. The great thing is to be emptied out, to taste and see that the Lord is sweet, and to learn the way of abandonment and peace. Littleness is the chief characteristic of the solitary, or else he is not a genuine solitary. Silence is a rare luxury in the modern world, and not everyone can stand it: but it has inestimable value that cannot be purchased with any amount of money or power or intelligence. The gift to be silent and simple with the Lord is a treasure beyond counting and it almost takes care of everything else, at least in some souls.

I wish you all success and send you every blessing. Do remember me in prayer, please. I keep hoping to eventually get permission for a more solitary life, though I do have a fair amount of solitude now, thanks be to God.

92. To H.M. [Henry Miller], Paris [July 9, 1962]

It was good to hear from you. I have often thought of writing to you, and usually that is the first thing that comes into my mind when I am reading something of yours, like the earlier part of *Big Sur* [*and the Oranges of Hieronymus Bosch* (New York: New Directions, 1957)], for example, or parts of *The Colossus of Maroussi* [San Francisco: Colt Press, 1951] (which I think is a tremendous and important book). I have always refrained because it is foolish for me to write letters anyway, and then I know you have little time. I am sure you must get much the same kind of mail that I do, including the poets who send you their collected works in weekly installments, and the anonymous painter who, today, sent me a large abstraction. This is all fine, but where does one get the time to collect his thoughts and come up with some kind of an intelligent word, in the presence of so many manifestations? I detest writing letters about which I do not think, at least when thought is called for. It is perhaps fortunate that there are some letters one can write without thinking: business letters. They come out like sweat.

One of the things I have wanted to discuss with you is our

common admiration for [Jean] Giono. Something must be done to get a good selection of his stuff published in English: to get hold of some of his shorter prose pieces about Provence, and they are remarkable. His view of things is the sane one, the one that must be preserved as a basis for some kind of vestigial humanism, if humanism is to remain possible. I have not read his historical novels, and there are lots of his novels about Provence that I have never come across: as I say, I have read mostly essays. I think New Directions ought to do something with him.

I expect to find a lot of the same in the [Joseph] Delteil book which arrived the other day. I have not got far into it yet, but I think something ought to be done with it in this country, nor is there much difficulty in that. Does Delteil read English? He might like the banned book [ms. of *Peace in the Post-Christian Era*] I have just written (you are not the only one, you see!) about peace. My book is not satisfactory however, because I was fool enough to try to write one that censors would approve, and this led to compromise and stupidity. And in the end they did not approve anyway. Does he, do you, know of Fr. Hervé Chaigne, the Franciscan who is a Gandhian and involved in the non-violent movement in France?

Returning to Giono: I am thinking a lot of Provence because I am doing some work on the early monastic literature surrounding the Provencal monasteries of the 5th century, particularly Lerins. It was a great movement. That and Cassiodorus too, in Italy. One thing I envy you is your freedom to get around to such places.

93. To E.A.S. [Evora Arca De Sardinia], Miami, Fla. [August 2, 1962]

I deeply feel with you all the emotions that have shaken you, on meeting the prisoners returning from the Isle of Pines.[56] I want to try to help you weather the storm, but God alone can really do that. God and the Church.

---

[56] Cuban exiles captured during the failed Bay of Pigs Invasion in 1961 were imprisoned on the Isle of Pines.

One thing I have always felt increases the trouble and the sorrow which rack you is the fact that living and working among the Cuban émigrés in Miami, and surrounded by the noise of hate and propaganda, you are naturally under a great stress and in a sense you are "forced" against your will to take an aggressive and belligerent attitude which your conscience, in its depths, tells you is wrong. You react rightly against the pressure of hate, and you strive to "be a better Christian" and take more and more sacrifice upon yourself. In this you are following the right instinct but because of your position you are not able to follow it far enough, or in the right direction. I could wish you were able to get away from Miami for a while and restore your perspective, and calm down, and get some peace of heart that would enable the Holy Spirit to strengthen and teach you in silence.

The noise that surrounds you at Miami is necessarily misleading and in very great part it is false. The picture of the U.S. and Cuba that underlies all this pressure and hate is exaggerated and distorted. We have got to base our ideals and our action on a greater and more stable element of truth and justice. The evil that is taking place in Cuba is partly the fault of bad Cubans, but it is also partly the fault of the United States. When did the U.S. ever make any fuss about Batista? This aggravated situation is not at all simply due to Castro and Russia, though they have their part.

Whether you should raise money to ransom your husband, when he wants to stay on the Isle of Pines. Evora, it is a complex question.

1. He wants to stay with his fellow prisoners and suffer with them. This in a sense is a greater supernatural good for him. He will do more for Cuba there, *he is closer to the truth there,* than he could do in Miami. If you buy his way out, you may perhaps be diminishing his merit and his power to help Cuba spiritually.

2. On the other hand, his situation may also be spiritually dangerous, and it may constitute a temptation. If you think there is danger for him, spiritually, or if you believe that in some way it is a greater evil for him to stay in prison, in every sense of the word, then you should ransom him.

3. The principle to follow is charity. Your clear-sighted charity must seek what is his real good, his highest good, such as he

himself would want it, in his heart. You must not force on him a higher good he does not want, or cannot bear: but on the other hand you must not force on him a lesser good, which he more probably does not want. If he is willing to stay, honestly, I would not raise such a tremendous sum to ransom him.

4. Remember that by paying a hundred thousand to Castro you are working against what your group believes to be the true political interests of Cuba. I am in no position to judge in this matter.

You may ransom him if you wish, listening to your heart. But if you leave him there for reasons of the highest charity and depending on God to deliver him, you may be doing better. I do not impose either course on you, you are perfectly free, and either one is good. It is for you to decide and God will reward you in either case.

94. To E.S. [Elbert R. Sisson], Maryland [August 2, 1962]

I was very happy with your letter and above all with the pictures, especially the drawings of the children. I was so moved by Grace (pun) and by her house and her lovely little self that I wrote a poem which I enclose ["Grace's House"]. And as for Clare, even more than Grace, she has just stolen my heart completely and I don't know what to do or say. What a blessing it is to be surrounded with so many images of God and to live in the midst of the loves and sorrows and complications and simplicities that God has given you in them. May He preserve our world a little longer for the likes of such beautiful beings, whom He so loves.

About Cuba, there again I am inarticulate. I got a letter [Cold War Letter 93] the other day from a dear woman [Evora Arca De Sardinia] whose husband went over in the invasion and is now on the Isle of Pines, in prison. She asks me if she ought to raise a hundred thousand dollars to get him out, when he wants to stay. The whole thing makes me utterly furious. Here we, the richest nation that ever existed, make stupid and utterly dishonorable mistakes, out of greed, and out of unwillingness to let a poor and angry neighbor put anything over on us. And for this mistake who pays? The people we self-righteously claim to be "helping" and protecting. These poor good ordinary and even heroic people give their blood and then put themselves in hock for a hundred thousand just in order to enjoy a little freedom. Is this how we "free" our friends? When we have used them as cats paws to try out a fire we didn't know was quite so hot?

The next time I hear anything about the iniquity of Castro and the righteousness of the United States I am going to throw a bowl of soup at somebody. I guess I count as a security risk all right.

Keep turning on peace, as my beat friends say.

95. To H.M. [Henry Miller], Pacific Palisades, Calif. [August 7, 1962]

First of all I agree that it will be hard to translate [Joseph] Delteil, or to find a good translator. I am mightily tempted to try it myself, but I just cannot afford the time. I would enjoy the challenge of doing it, and I can think of what a living and riotous book it would make: a life of St. Francis such as there never yet was in English. But I have to resist the temptation to go overboard on translations these days, as I have to save energy for some strong statements that may be needed here and there, and I am supposed to be getting busy on another book. As for translations I am translating bits of Cesar Vallejo who is to me a most significant and meaningful voice, and moves me most deeply, probably because of his Indian resonances. He is the greatest of all the great South American poets we have had in this century, I think. There is another Central American, who has been out of his head for years but has written some fantastic poems: Alfonso Cortes. I am translating some of his stuff too. Beyond that I cannot go except into the Latin that I have to translate from time to time. More or less have to.

The Delteil book is frankly remarkable. It has an unusual zest and life. He works in big energetic poetic blocs of symbol. Each chapter is a carved-out symbol that runs and lives by itself and keeps affecting all the rest of the book with its own life. It is like the statues of the prophets of Aleijadinho, the Brazilian sculptor in Minas Gerais: only much more living, on the page.

The question of course comes up, what will the average

Catholic think about it? They will think that St. Francis belongs to them, and in thinking that they are perhaps so far wrong that they are out in the middle of outer space. But whenever the book comes out whoever brings it out will have to argue with those people, just as anyone who brings out a movie with some art to it will also have to argue with them.

I will write to Delteil, and I am glad you sent him the messages in the other letter.

Now to other things for a moment: I am in the middle of *The Wisdom of the Heart* [New York: New Directions, 1941] and it is you at your best. There is very fine material everywhere, one insight on top of another. The opening piece starting from Lawrence is full of arresting thought, most important for a writer to read. When you write as you do in the thing on Benno you are at your very best, this is marvelous. As I say I am going with you all the way with *The Wisdom of the Heart*. They sent me also *The Colossus [of Maroussi* (San Francisco: Colt Press, 1941)] which I already had but had lent to someone, and lent books never come back. And *The Time of the Assassins* [: *A Study of Rimbaud* (New York: New Directions, 1956)], which is going to mean much.

The English Carmelites sent me their review about those two late nineteenth-century people, but I thought all they had to say was very good indeed. How would it be if I sent them a poem? What do you think?

Scotland drove me nuts when I was there in childhood, but I have all kinds of dreams about getting on one of those outlying islands. Maybe this is the worst delusion. I wonder what you will think of it. The people as I remember them were absurd, and especially the place used to be full of Englishmen who wouldn't call a brook anything but a burn, and who stuffed their stupid faces with scones at all hours of the day and night while a character walked up and down playing the bagpipes to them. They deserved it.

I bet you are totally right about Ireland. The combination of faith and poverty has now become one of the things that cries out to heaven for vengeance, loud enough for the vengeance to be quite near.

In the whole question of religion today: all I can say, I wish I could really see what is there to see. Nobody can see the full dimension of the problem, which is more than a problem, it is one of those things you read about in the apocalypse. There are no problems in the apocalypse, just monsters. This one is a monster.

The religion of religious people tends at times to poke out a monster head just when you are beginning to calm down and get reassured. The religion of half-religious people doesn't tend: it bristles with heads. The horns, the horns with eyes on the end of them, the teeth, the teeth with eyes in them, the eyes as sharp as horns, the dull eyes, the ears that now listen to all the stars and decode their message into something about business upswing.

This is the greatest orgy of idolatry the world has ever known, and it is not generally thought by believers that idolatry is the greatest and fundamental sin. It is absolutely not thought, it is not credited, it cannot be accepted, and if you go around and speak of idolatry they will fall down and laugh and the heads of the monsters will roll and wag like the biggest carnival you ever saw. But precisely the greatest and most absurd difficulty of our time is keeping disentangled from the idols, because you cannot touch anything that isn't defiled with it: anything you buy, anything you sell, anything you give even. And of course the significance of it is absolutely lost. Anyone who sells out to even a small, inoffensive, bargain cheap idol has alienated himself and put himself into the statue and has to act like it, which is he has to be dead.

The religion of non-religious people tends to be clear of religious idols and is in many ways much less pseudo. But on the other hand, they often have no defense against the totalitarian kind, which end up by being bigger and worse.

I frankly don't have an answer. As a priest I ought, of course, to be able to give Christ's answer. But unfortunately . . . it is no longer a matter of answers. It is a time perhaps of great spiritual silence.

I must really read Emerson, I never have. Except little bits that I have liked a lot. Thoreau of course I admire tremendously. He is one of the only reasons why I felt justified in becoming an American citizen. He and Emily Dickenson, and some of my friends, and people like yourself. It is to me a great thing that you say I am like the transcendentalists. I will try to be worthy of that. This is not just something we can elect to try as a boyscout project: it is a serious duty for all of us, and woe to us if we do not take it for what it is.

The time is short, and all the idols are moving. They are so full of people that they are becoming at last apparently animated and when they get fully into action the result will be awful. It will be like the clashing of all the planets. Strange that the individual is the only power that is left. And though his power is zero, zero has great power when one understands it and knows where to place it.

96. To J.M. [Joost A. M. Meerloo], New York [August 1962]

I have been meaning to write to you about the offprint you sent a long time ago, and your letter with it. "Responsibility" is a very fine essay. I find that you pack a great deal into every sentence. That is why it was not too hard to "edit" the section of your book that I took over for the anthology ["Can War Be Cured?" in *Breakthrough to Peace*]. Your statements all tend to stand on their own feet, as aphorisms almost. I find the present essay very rich, and of course profited by it. I do hope you will keep me on your list for anything like that.

The book ought to be out by now, and for all I know it may be. Generally things take a fair amount of time to penetrate the walls and the community and finally come through to me. I hope the book will do some good, but I find it hard to be optimistic about the present situation. I must confess however that things look better in a way than they did this time last year: at least in the sense that there has been a reaction and that a significant element of the population has thrown off its passivity. On the other hand I cannot be totally happy about every aspect of the peace movement. It is in many respects a sick movement, and some of the people involved glory in the sick side of it. They make a virtue out of being sick, as if in that way they could somehow be revenged for the frustrations they feel they owe to the society they live in. Their feeling may in part be justified, but then are they themselves *not* part of the society they resent? I think they are very much part of it, and bear a good share of its karma. Not only that but they add plenty, for all of us to carry.

The impression I get is precisely that of a society that is doing nothing to lighten and make more rational its huge ethical burdens, but only increasing their weight senselessly. This "weight" is increased by irresponsible and passive deeds, by "ignorant" responses, by semi-deliberate blindness. I find that as a monk I have a full-time job simply trying to be clear sighted for two minutes a day. I am oppressed by the darkness that is all around us and in us. This is very serious and dangerous, and the darkness is so thick that I think we are coming close to a hidden center of wrath that will explode terribly.

97. To A.F. [Allan Forbes, Jr.], Philadelphia, Pa. [August 1962]

Your letter of a month ago has been waiting for a brief answer: I have wanted to set things straight if possible, regarding the Peace book [ms. of *Peace in the Post-Christian Era*].

Of course I had no intention whatever of calling in question the value of Quaker and Mennonite peace activity. I really am not sure whether the side remark I may have made, mentioning the two groups, was properly interpreted: doubtless it is unclear. And in my own mind, I did not intend to lump you all indiscriminately together with all shades of "pacifists." But it is evident that the whole statement was misleading, so I will try to clarify what I really think now, as I owe you this.

1. You are perfectly right to interpret my praise of Dorothy Day as praise also of the Quaker peace witness, and the genuine spiritual non-violent witness for peace. There should be no question about this. It seems to me that the long-standing Quaker position on peace is one of the most reliable and stabilizing forces we have at the moment, and I think it is of very great spiritual importance. I think it also has political importance.

2. You note that I am making a distinction between "spiritual" and "political" action. The two should not really be separate, but in fact there is a distinction all right. What may have great value spiritually may have little value politically. I certainly think that the rather simplified unilateralism that has been

more or less accepted as a basic position by the peace movements is of doubtful political value. This is where my Romanism comes in, I am afraid. I think that if there is going to be political action it ought to have a chance of really working in the current situation. I think there is just no practicality at all, in the concrete situation, in a purely unilateralist position.

3. In terms of politics, I think that the issue is to get down to some real sincere and practical negotiation in regard to disarmament. And this means first of all a more general willingness on the part of responsible parties, especially in this country, to believe that negotiation can and will work. If they think that "negotiation" means "unilateral disarmament by the U.S." this gives them the scapegoat they need to resist and to avoid all negotiation. It enables them to be irrational with what they think is a good conscience. Rather than twit them with their inability to see unilateralism I would prefer to make them see their own solemn responsibility to take negotiation seriously on a less drastic level, at least to make a beginning of serious negotiation and not to make proposals and withdraw them as soon as they seem to offer a practical possibility of acceptance. In other words negotiation must be honest and not just a question of "deals" and "blackmail" and "propaganda value." I think that for a while there was a serious possibility that the Soviets would have negotiated fairly honestly if we had shown a little confidence in them and a little trust. Maybe that time is now past. Maybe I am all wrong in having even the slightest hope for conventional and traditional political action. But it is the only action that can really prevent a holocaust. For the rest, the spiritual witness is in another dimension.

I see that the spiritual witness which you and the other Friends so gloriously present, and I mean this, is most important as an expression of conscience, as a reminder of spiritual positions and obligations. It may by some miracle start a chain reaction in the moral order, and this we can always hope. But I do not think it will effect large-scale political consequences. Perhaps I am wrong in this. But in any event I do not intend this opinion to be interpreted as "disapproval," still less as a fundamental lack of sympathy. That is certainly not the case by any means. If anyone is worried about this point you can explain how I stand.

The situation does not seem to get any better, does it? This testing is a serious matter, and the renewal of Soviet testing on August 6th is a grave symbolic gesture. Let us trust in God and purify our hearts as best we can. This is a solemn moment and now above all we must be in a position to hear His voice and neglect no slightest indication of His will. It is most important that all who believe in His Name may open their hearts to His merciful light, because the fate of the world depends on this. And all must prepare themselves for any eventuality. The events of the next five years may fulfill all the worse expectations: or on the other hand there may be a merciful reprieve. Who can tell? We must be ready.

98. To the Hon. Shinzo Hamai
Mayor of Hiroshima, Japan [August 9, 1962]

Most Honorable Mayor:

In a solemn and grave hour for humanity I address this letter to you and to your people. I thank you for the sincerity and courage with which you are, at this time, giving witness for peace and sanity. I wish to join my own thoughts, efforts, and prayers to yours. There is no hope for mankind unless the truth prevails in us. We must purify our hearts and open them to the light of truth and mercy. You are giving us the example. May we follow.

I speak to you as a most humble and unworthy brother, as a monk of a contemplative Order of the Catholic Church. As such, I have learned to have a very great love for Japan and for its spiritual traditions. There are in Japan several convents and one monastery of my religious Order. The Japanese Trappistine nuns are the glory of our Order. The finest and most fervent of our convents are those in Japan. May their whole-hearted prayers for peace and for the spiritual and temporal prosperity of your nation be heard.

Men should use political instruments in behalf of truth, sanity, and international order. Unfortunately the blindness and madness of a society that is shaken to its very roots by the storms of passion and greed for power make the fully effective use of political negotiation impossible. Men want to negotiate for peace, and strive to do so, but their fear is greater than their good will. They do not dare to take serious and bold initiatives for peace. Fear of losing face, fear of the propaganda consequences of apparent "weakness," make it impossible for them to do what is really courageous: to take firm steps towards world peace. When they take one step forward they immediately tell the whole world about it and then take four steps backward. We are all walking backward towards a precipice. We know the precipice is there, but we assert that we are all the while going forward. This is because the world in its madness is guided by military men, who are the blindest of the blind.

It is my conviction that the people of Hiroshima stand today as a symbol of the hopes of humanity. It is good that such a symbol should exist. The events of August 6th 1945 give you the most solemn right to be heard and respected by the whole world. But the world only pretends to respect your witness. In reality it cannot face the truth which you represent. But I wish to say on my own behalf and on behalf of my fellow monks and those who are like-minded, that I never cease to face the truth which is symbolized in the names of Hiroshima, Nagasaki. Each day I pray humbly and with love for the victims of the atomic bombardments which took place there. All the holy spirits of those who lost their lives then, I regard as my dear and real friends. I express my fraternal and humble love for all the citizens of Hiroshima and Nagasaki.

99. To M.V.D. [Mark Van Doren], Connecticut [August 9, 1962]

Here, a poem ["Grace's House"]. That is all. I have no other pretext for writing, but glad to have this one. It is a poem about a drawing of a house by a five-year-old child. What a drawing, what a house, what suns and birds. It is true that we do not know where we are.

That there are circles within circles, and that if we choose we can let loose in the circle of paradise the very wrath of God: this is said by [Jacob] Boehme in his confessions. We are trying to bear him out, but children can, if they still will, give us the lie and show us our folly. But we are now more and more persistent in refusing to see any such thing. All we will see is the image, the image, the absurd image, the mask over our own emptiness. And we will beat on the box to make the voice come out. And it will speak numbers to us, oracular numbers, delphic billions this way and that way.

I have read a little of Thoreau and know enough to lament that such good sense died so long ago. But it could still be ours if only we wanted it. We do not, we want the image, the consuming image, the dead one into which we pour soft drinks. The smiles of the image. All the girls are laughing because the image has a soft drink. He will, with the power of the drink, explode a moon.

The book on peace [ms. of *Peace in the Post-Christian Era*], did I say it? Was finished and told to stop. Stop they said this book about peace. It must not. It is opposite to the image. It says the soft drink is an untruth, and that exploding moons is not the hopeful kind of sign we have pretended. Or claimed. But let the moons explode and the books be silent. Let the captains whirl in the sky, let the monkeys in the heavens move levers with hands and feet, and with their big toe explode cities, for a soft drink.

I know this is the wrong kind of image. I have rebelled against an image. This is not safe, is it? Well, alas, so I must reconcile myself to the unsafe, because the safe I can no longer stomach.

Let them beat on the box while the voice comes out in a stream of lighted numbers. I have resigned from all numbers.

100. To R.McC. [Robert J. McCracken], Iowa [August 1962]

Thank you for your letter about the article on nuclear war, and for the questions it contains. I think that you have oversimplified my position a little. I do not declare that *all* atomic war is by its very nature sinful. I think it might be possible to construct an argument in defense of a very limited use of atomic weapons in a clearly defensive situation which would not be immoral. But I do think that in the present crisis we are going clearly in the direction of an unjust, immoral, and massive use of nuclear weapons, as well as chemical and bacteriological weapons also.

It seems to me that the extreme positions are to be avoided, because they aggravate the problem. I would say that the Church wants Catholics to follow Christian prudence. This means that just means of defense should certainly be maintained. But they must really satisfy the demands of justice, and that excludes, it seems to me, the massive use of nuclear weapons indiscriminately on cities or even on missile installations near cities, especially in a first-strike aggressive war.

It seems to me that the *duty* of the Catholic, whatever may be his choice of a defense system that fits in with just standards, is to *work for peace* in a reasonable and prudent way, by the use of the normal political means. I would say this meant giving close attention to the danger involved in the unlimited arms race, it would mean not voting for belligerent politicians, it would mean supporting those who favor a moderate, reasonable and peaceful approach to international problems. It would mean favoring and supporting positive and peaceful measures in helping out undeveloped countries, such methods as the Peace Corps, for instance. In a word I think it is a pitiful mistake for Christians to get rattled and to deceive themselves with a kind of crusading spirit that thinks our problems can be solved by nuclear war.

You have no obligation to join a group which you consider eccentric. You ought certainly to write your congressman and urge him to pursue peaceful politics rather than rash and aggressive policies. In order to do this intelligibly you have the obligation to form your conscience by intelligent reading and even some study of the question. Reputable Catholic magazines like *America,* the *Commonweal,* and others give different shades of opinion on the war question, whereas some of the more popular Catholic papers tend to be a little off-center. That is my opinion.

Should you refuse to serve your country? If you are absolutely convinced that the means taken to defend the country, or to advance its interests, are really unjust then the question of refusing service would arise. I do not maintain that a Catholic must by the very fact be a pacifist. I would hold that in certain circumstances a pacifist stand by a Catholic would be legitimate. It is for you to form your conscience regarding the rightness and justice of our present policies. My opinion is that these policies tend to be dangerous morally insofar as they tend to an *unlimited* arms race, to a wasteful and artificial economy which may ruin the country all by itself, and ultimately to a disastrous massive nuclear war which would involve the destruction of what we are trying to defend.

My advice to you is: read the Christmas messages of the Popes for every year since 1948, and learn the principles they have laid down: judge current events in the light of those principles, and you will judge as a Catholic.

Trust in God and in His Holy Spirit. Have courage and follow your conscience. Seek the truth with deep humble sincerity. Love your country and your fellow man. You will be blessed by God and will see the right course if you earnestly seek to do those things.

101. To J.F. [James Forest], New York [August 27, 1962]

Thanks for all the letters, poems, etc. I will comment on the latter when I have more time. There have been people visiting and when that happens there is no time left for anything else, so I haven't been writing letters.

The parish sounds fine, I will send the books along. I think it is especially important for you to be working in and with the parish at the moment. The Church is after all a reality, and the central reality: though her members have failed shockingly in their Christian responsibility in many areas, and though there may be a great blindness and weakness pervading whole areas of her life, nevertheless she is indefectible because God lives and acts in her. And this faith must live in us and grow in us, especially when we are tempted against it as we are now. I think you will get a great deal out of this effort.

As for the peace movement I am happy that it is getting space in the magazines, and that it is taking space for itself in the papers. I wonder if the Sane [Committee for a Sane Nuclear Policy] ads are not too subtle and mysterious. I wouldn't know. But it is encouraging. Though we are reminded by another of your enclosures that the other guys are much more help to this kind of activity and can do a much more sinister, corny, and effective job of defacing moral truth than we can do in its defense.

I think the peace movement is a great potentiality, yet I think also that it remains terribly superficial. But then everything is superficial now. And I am in no position to prescribe means of deepening everything, least of all the peace movement. The fact that I am really unable to keep it in right perspective, in spite of all the help I get from friends sending things, is evidence of the fact that I am really out of the game and can't do much in the ordinary way.

All the best to you and Jean, and blessings always.

102. To L.S. [Lou Silberman], Nashville, Tenn. [September 19, 1962]

Thanks for your letter and for the interesting offprints. I am glad to see our concerns are so nearly alike: how can we afford to ignore at a time like this the "scandal of prophecy?" The only hope we have is in scandals. All that is secure is a deception. I think that things are getting much more dangerous than they have ever been, and everybody seems to think this. At such a time we are forced to a kind of faith we had never imagined. But we are going to have to be forced very much further, for we have not begun to yield: I do not mean just "us" but the obduracy of the whole world is enormous. What will happen?

I have come across a manuscript of meditations by a Father Delp, S.J., who was executed under Hitler. Most of it was written in prison, and in reading it one gets the impression that only people like this know what they are talking about. I am asked to write a preface to this, and I wonder what one can say, except that this is truth and what is not like this is untrue [*The Prison Meditations of Father Alfred Delp* with "Introduction" by Thomas Merton (New York: Herder and Herder, 1963)].[57]

103. To L.D. [Leslie Dewart], Toronto [September 1962]

Thanks for your letters and for the articles, which are excellent. First I read the one in *Liberation* which is very gentle and understanding, and I think it says a lot. It touches on a very cen-

---

[57] Reprinted as *Alfred Delp: Prison Writings,* with an Introduction by Thomas Merton (Maryknoll, NY: Orbis Books, 2004).

tral problem. The whole issue today depends, in great measure, in the last resort, on the American mentality. And that mentality is involved in deep illusions, most of all about itself. These illusions are nevertheless part and parcel of its goodness. It seems to be an immensely complex problem. The problem of Christian hopes, after centuries of frustration and deviation, suddenly finding an unexpected, secular fulfillment and a new seemingly secular direction. The illusion of America as the earthly paradise, in which everyone recovers original goodness: which becomes in fact a curious idea that prosperity itself justifies everything, is a sign of goodness, is a carte blanche to continue to be prosperous in any way feasible: and this leads to the horror that we now see: because we are prosperous, because we are successful, because we have all this amazing "know-how" (without real intelligence or moral wisdom, without even a really deep scientific spirit) we are entitled to defend ourselves by any means whatever, without any limitation, and all the more so because what we are defending is our illusion of innocence.

I do not know if this holds out much promise of a Catholic era. I would say of course that I am in deep agreement with you on the religious level. I cannot but share your Christian hope. Not as a pious velleity, I do certainly believe that there is a Christian consummation in store for the world. But in the political field? In the world as we know it? That is not sure: it is precisely the venture and the risk. It is *possible*. And the possibility is open to us, and now is the time when the possibility becomes a near thing. But at the same time the folly, the helplessness of man, and his perversity, his wickedness, have never been so apparent (for all that he is so "good" and vestigially Christian).

Yes, I think there are chances, within the Church, of such an awakening. I think it has certainly begun. We do indeed have a different view of the world from that of the Franciscans who came in with the Conquistadores, (and yet remember the view so many of them had, especially my favorite, Vasco de Quiroga). (Forget if he was a Franciscan, maybe a Dominican, maybe a secular.)

In a word I am perfectly agreed that there is an opportunity for the realization of a fully universal Christianity, just as at the end of the Roman world there was not only the opportunity but even in some sense a relatively universal realization of Catholicism, but how relative!

But what will come of this opportunity? Nobody can say. In the book [ms. of *Peace in the Post-Christian Era*] of course I was only being provocative. I did not really consider the whole idea of the Post-Christian world sufficiently deeply, and certainly did not develop it. I would not say that it is really essential to the book as a whole, and the book could be just what it is without the injecture of this particular impertinence. Yet in a way I don't let go of it altogether. Opportunity, yes. But in fact we are very much *post*-Christian. I think that in the main the world has got beyond being a Catholic sinner. I think in reality the world has entered a kind of zombie stage which is not crypto-Christian at all. This is perhaps not a realized fact, maybe only a hazard. Maybe we are looking at the same thing, from the bright and the dark sides.

In the end, I cannot help hoping you are right. My heart is with you, but my head is on my side, I am afraid. But I admit that I have not sufficient evidence for a really strong opinion in favor of my own pessimism, and therefore perhaps it is better not to cultivate it. I wish I could avoid doing so.

Have you read the issue of *The Nation* about the "Ultras"? What awful stupidity and what a perversion of "Christian" values. When such stupidity is so powerful, and so intent on destroying the enemy, which is also the enemy of its dearest illusions about itself, what are we going to see?

This adds up to a complete agreement with your *Commonweal* article. I think it is very fine, very clear, and accept completely as a most valid and welcome clarification and development of my own ideas.

We are running off some more [mimeographed] copies of "Peace in the PCE" and I will send a couple. I don't think I ever sent you the Cold War Letters. There will be a new enlarged edition[58] of that, too, and I will try to remember to send them to you. And of course the Basilians absolutely have no need to worry about token donations. What I would much rather know

---

[58] Merton completed the first "edition" of the "Cold War Letters," containing forty-nine letters, in April 1961. The second "edition," which Merton was anticipating here, ends with letter 111, written in October 1962.

is: do they have any interesting texts of the XII-century school of Chartres that are not available in [Jacques-Paul] Migne and other common sources? I am especially interested in William of Conches, and far rather than a donation would like to get a copy of something of his, anything, for we have nothing. Microfilm, photocopy, anything. As you see I have a medieval mentality.

I am returning your article and the letters of the bishops which are most gratifying. Archbishop [George Bernard] Flahiff [CSB] of course I know about, through Dan Walsh. Maybe I will send him a copy of the peace book, though now he will probably be completely tied up in the [Second Vatican] Council. That Council! Such hopes and such fears! But the Holy Spirit really is in command there, though He may not be at the Pentagon. So there I can dare to hope without limitations. And without necessarily expecting to see clearly the object of my hopes realized.

All blessings, and with every best wish. Keep in touch, keep writing, as my beat friends say, keep turning on the peace.

104. To D.S. [Dan Shay], Detroit, Mich. [September 1962]

Your letter was very welcome. I think the idea is a good one, and I think you are very right to investigate reasonable ways of preparing yourself for the pilgrimage. This is quite important. With the help of grace I will try to think up a few ideas to contribute to your effort.

1. I would begin right away to think about people you ought to meet in Europe. First of all, the priests and intellectuals you may conceivably run into here and there will actually mean more, in many respects, than when you will meet in Rome: there you may meet practically nothing, or on the other hand it is possible you may get to see someone important. God alone knows. But in France you should try to get to men like Fr. [Pie-Raymond] Régamey [OP] and Fr. Hervé Chaigne, OFM. I don't know the latter, but the former can be reached through *La Vie Spirituelle* . . . [in] Paris. I don't know if he knows English. Do you know French? You ought to read some of his stuff. Both

these have written on non-violence. Recently a piece on Gandhian non-violence by Chaigne was in *Cross Currents*.[59] They could tell you at *Cross Currents* how to contact him, no doubt. Later I can give you info about more non-violent activists in France. Fr. Régamey's book on non-violence has not been translated.[60] He has a good book on poverty [*Poverty: An Essential Element in the Christian Life* (New York: Sheed and Ward, 1950)] and another on the Cross, [*The Cross and the Christian* (St. Louis: B. Herder Book Co., 1954)] not directly about war but good spiritual material.

2. Of the Popes you should read and master all the important passages in the Christmas messages since 1948. Easter messages too, sometimes. It is in these Christmas messages above all that the statements about the immorality of total war come out clear.

3. The most important thing is to study carefully your purpose and your objective. Especially when making a statement of your intentions and desires to the Council itself. I wonder if this can have much value at the moment. Isn't it too late? I mean for anything official. You don't want to just send something in that will get put on the shelf or get a rubber-stamp answer from somebody if it is answered at all. About this aspect of the matter I can't be of much help as I don't know anything about the court of Rome and I want to keep out of anything concerning it. But don't just go getting yourself a big cosmic run around.

4. The more I think about it, the more I believe it is theologically as well as tactically inadequate to try to get the Council to condemn the bomb in some form or other. The bomb does not need to be condemned, since it is already in many ways condemned by its very nature, and in any case, even if the bishops would go out on a limb and formally condemn it (which they wouldn't) it would not have that much effect. People who don't

---

[59] Hervé Chaigne, "The Spirit and Techniques of Gandhian Non-violence," *Cross Currents* XI (Spring 1961): 117-136.

[60] Merton wrote the "Preface" to the English translation of Fr. Régamey's book, *Non-violence and the Christian Conscience* (New York: Herder and Herder, 1966). Merton's "Preface" was reprinted in *Faith and Violence* (Notre Dame, Indiana: University of Notre Dame Press, 1968), 30-39, under the title "Non-violence and the Christian Conscience."

want to pay attention to the Church today never do, including Catholics, and including Bishops.[61]

I am not in favor of the kind of pressure that strives to get Rome to approve this and condemn that. In the long run it tends to be glorified infantilism and it prolongs the infantile type of theological thought we are trying to get rid of. I think there would be more meaning in a less theological and more political approach, a concrete peace proposition of some sort, or a peace initiative that could be backed by the Church somehow.

The thing to realize is this: we are members of Christ, and we have a voice, whether as priests or as laity. If we as members of Christ protest against total war, then it is already in some sense a work of the Church. The protest in any case has already been clearly made by the Popes and I think the best thing for you to do is to reiterate in very clear terms what the Popes have already declared: that total war is a sin and that the psychology that strives to settle international differences by total war is murderous and criminal. The mentality that thinks *only* in terms of total victory, by any available means, is an expression of moral apostasy from Christ. The use of the Christian ethical doctrine that self-defense can be justified is not a right use, when it is taken to justify total war, that seeks total annihilation of the opponent's cities and economy as a means of beating him down. This is Catholic doctrine, and what is needed is a strong Catholic peace initiative based on this doctrine. I would concentrate if I were you on steps that will lead to the formation of such an international movement.

Write Dorothy Day and ask her about the Goss-Mayrs [Jean and Hildegard] who are coming to this country in the winter I believe. They are the best people to know in this regard. You can quote anything I have said in this letter. I am with you in prayer and in the love of Christ's truth. May God bless you always.

P.S. Today I received a really shocking letter from an unknown (to me) Catholic woman in France. This devout she-wolf,

---

[61] In fact the Council Fathers did include this condemnation on nuclear war in the final document of Vatican II, "Pastoral Constitution on the Church in the Modern World": "Every act of war directed to the indiscriminate destruction of whole cities or vast areas with their inhabitants is a crime against God and man, which merits firm and unequivocal condemnation" (*Gaudium et Spes*, 80).

with doubtless the best of intentions, and in all good faith, was asking that I enlist the prayers of our community that America might finally open up with a nuclear crusade against Russia and bring in all the nations of the "Christian" West with her for, as this devout soul says, "we have just had enough." This is certainly a fearful frame of mind, and so many Christians are in it.

While the next two letters were reversed in the typing process, the carbon copies of the letters label the letter to C.T., London as 105 and the letter to E.E., Linz as 106—the order in which they appear here.

105. To C.T. [Charles Thompson], London [September 27, 1962]

I may think up a more expanded message later for the Spode House meeting, but if I do not get a chance, here are a few words:

"I wish I could be there with you to hear the talks and to share in the discussion, to carry away the light and encouragement they will certainly give. But in any case I will be there spiritually and will offer a Mass for the success of the meetings, if I can obtain permission to do so.

"The great issues that face us are the defense of man, the defense of truth, the defense of justice. But the problems in which we are immersed spring from the fact that the majority of men have a totally inadequate and rudimentary idea of what can constitute an effective 'defense of man.' Hence the transparent absurdity of a situation in which mass societies soberly and seriously prepare to defend man by wiping him out. Our first task is to liberate ourselves from the assumptions and prejudices which vitiate our thinking on these fundamental points, and we must help other men to do the same. This involves not only clear thought, lucid speech, but very positive social action. And since we believe that the only really effective means are non-violent, we must learn non-violence and practice it. This involves in its turn a deep spiritual purification. May we all receive from God the grace and strength necessary to begin this task which He has willed for us. May we go forward in our poverty to accomplish this task insofar as may be given us by His Spirit."

I hope the American Pax will really develop more and become a force in the rather incoherent but active peace front in this country.

Peace News is coming and I am very grateful for it. It is perhaps better than the peace publications in this country.

I don't think the situation in the U.S. is any better. If anything it gets worse, gradually. The war party is quite strong and gets stronger. It is not an organized group, but a very coherent stratum of rich people, backed by massive support from the middle classes in the less sophisticated and wilder areas, and above all California which is getting richer and richer on the arms race. Catholics tend to be found in the belligerent pressure groups. There is a specious atmosphere of crusade in the popular Catholic press, with a lot of completely illogical and fanatical thinking that assumes any means is legitimate to wipe out the devil of Communism. No apparent capacity to evaluate the disastrous consequences for *everybody*.

106. To E.E. [Elsa Engländer], Linz, Austria [September 30, 1962]

I hope you are patient with my defects as a correspondent. I was glad to get your letter, sorry you did not meet Gordon Zahn. I understand how you feel about his book [*German Catholics and Hitler's War*]. That is the impression it will create upon most German readers. But perhaps the book was not really addressed to German readers. Naturally, when an author undertakes to make such an analysis, he must expect to be read and judged by those whom he analyzes. But nevertheless, speaking of his thought, it seems to me that he had in mind the American public of 1962 and not the Germans of 1945, or even of 1962. You are all very far from the days he describes, you have gone far beyond that, you have meditated in a long and anguished silence, and with open discussion and frank self-examination, upon the events of twenty years ago. There is no question that this is primarily an affair of the German nation, and once they have examined themselves and come to their conclusion, we cannot lightly revise their decision and come to some other conclusion. I do not think that Zahn intended to do that in any respect. But I do think he was treating the German question in an *abstract scientific* form with a view to the concrete present needs of America. Without this perspective, I do not think his book can be rightly understood.

There can be no question that what the German Catholics did under Hitler was humanly understandable and in view of the fact that in such a crisis there are hundreds of extenuating circumstances, hundreds of varied reasons for people not coming to an abstractly perfect conclusion, it is actually what almost anyone would have done in the same situation. Hence it cannot be said in any way that Zahn is singling out the German Catholics for special censure. On the contrary, I think his real point is his preoccupation with the sobering thought that this is the way we all act, and we are not likely, even now, to rise above this standard. In particular, there is every indication that the American Catholic not only *will* make much the same kind of compromise, but is in fact already doing so.

Now this is a more serious affair. For German Catholics under most violent pressure and with imminent threat to their life to have come to conclusions that were still justifiable and approved by their pastors is one thing: but for the American Catholic today to accept almost without question the necessity of an aggressive weapon of total war which has been strongly criticized by the Popes, to simply push aside the evidence of Papal pronouncements, and to base their judgment on a few phrases which remind us that "self-defense is always licit," which they then twist out of shape and apply without logic to a totally different situation . . . this is another matter. Zahn's message then is aimed at these people, and so far I do not think it is widely accepted. This I think constitutes a serious problem. In a way it is much more serious than the one he discussed in his book, because here there is no coercion, except the occult pressure of the mass media. There is no threat of violence, though it is true that those who defend peace tend to be very unpopular and are not without being threatened in certain important ways (e.g., in regard to their jobs, etc.).

The tactic at present is to insist that anyone who is not in favor of an all-out war effort is a communist sympathizer, therefore a poor security risk, therefore ought not to be employed in schools, government departments, or even self-respecting businesses.

With this and the race troubles in the South one can see the beginnings and perhaps more than the beginnings of a Nazi mentality in the United States. There is in fact a Nazi party here, of little consequence at the moment because it is obviously part of a lunatic fringe. But much more serious is the presence of a very powerful and influential alliance of business and military men, backing certain politicians and leaders of anti-Communist movements, who are not content with opposing Communism as it really is, but who consider everyone who disagrees with them a Communist, a traitor, and a spy. These people could quite easily get the country into a total nuclear war, and it would not be difficult for them, given the right political situation, to take over the country and establish a totalitarian dictatorship, a police state. This is not imminent, but things move fast and it is altogether possible. The atmosphere is not unlike what I remember from the Germany of 1932.

Well, I will not go on with this. I have just finished writing a preface to the English translation of Fr. Delp's meditations in prison [*The Prison Meditations of Father Alfred Delp* with "Introduction by Thomas Merton" (New York: Herder and Herder, 1963)]. I found them most powerful and deeply moving. I think this is one of the great spiritual books of the age, and there was certainly someone who opposed Hitler frankly and vocally, without hesitation or compromise. It is a noble and great document of German Catholicism in World War II. I do not have a great deal of biographical material on Fr. Delp. It would be good to write a biographical note. Can you send me anything?

Thank you for the very interesting material about the convent in Jerusalem and the beautiful, touching little book on the Jewish children. These too are evidence of the warm Christian love and faith of the German Catholics. I may add that we are looking with great hope to the German and Dutch bishops in the Council. Germany may have been through some terrible times, but there is no question that German Catholicism is perhaps the most advanced and most living force in the Church today, together perhaps with the Catholicism of some of the African bishops, who knows?

It is wonderful to be united in Christ, and to live at such a time, terrible though it is. Let us thank Him for having called us into His world and His Church in a day when the struggle is crucial, and pray Him to enlighten us and give us courage to open ourselves entirely to the Spirit given us by the Victorious Savior.

Thank you for all your charity and generosity. I will send other papers and articles when I have them. I keep you in my prayers and thoughts, before the Lord.

107. To D.S. [Dallas Smythe], Urbana Ill. [October 22, 1962]

You must expect letters from me to be delayed: I have long since despaired of meeting my obligations in a reasonable and normal way, when it comes to correspondence. But I do want to thank you for sending me your very incisive conference on *Religion and the Mass Media*. I have read and re-read it, and agree all down the line. It is very clear, and is right on the target. I think you will probably be interested in the review I wrote of the new J.F. Powers book [*"Morte D'Urban*: Two Celebrations" in *The Literary Essays of Thomas Merton* (New York: New Directions, 1981)] which treats some of the same ideas indirectly.

Did your text come out in book form? I hope no cuts were made. I do not know much about Straus Hupe, but I have heard of him and know where to place him. I must say the mentality of Christians in this country is very disturbing. Except for a few minority groups like the FOR [Fellowship of Reconciliation], regarded as crazy by the others. Disturbing from a religious point of view above all, because it seems that there has been a real surrender, as your conference makes clear, to the values of what has always traditionally been called "the world," in the bad sense in which this term appears in the New Testament. What else is consumership but a systematization of one of the most essential elements in "worldliness." What has happened is, as you say, a complete secularization of religion in which the minister of God runs about frantically getting himself accepted as a member of the affluent society. The chief concern of Christians here seems to be to make sure they will never under any circumstances get excommunicated from the society of people who read *Time* and *Life*. If that is the case, then we can count on something pretty drastic within five or six years.

On the other hand I have been extremely heartened by the opening speech of John XXIII at the [Second] Vatican Council. I doubt if the resonances would be apparent to those who do not listen closely to this kind of thing, but there are really deep and insistent notes of change and renewal. I am sure that if he gets any cooperation at all, the Council will certainly do good and even great things. Not everyone has been feeling that way, in the Church. There has been a lot of pessimism on the theory that the Curia would be able to do what they wanted with the Pope. Not so, I think. Pope John seems to know what he wants and to be determined to go after it. Also his talk the day after the opening, to diplomats in the Sistine, was powerful and significant: a great blow for peace. Trouble is that statements like that appear on page two and are forgotten the next morning.

108. To E.G. [Etta Gullick], Oxford [October 29, 1962]

I really appreciate the letters and cards from France. Thank you so much. I did not envy you so much this year. The Dordogne is much more haunting, and I can imagine the coast crowded with Germans. The card of Arles was good, and I liked the one of St. Michel de Cuza, of course. It was pinned up with due pomp on the novitiate notice board with an awestruck sign, "Our Father Master was born at the foot of this mountain." Now I have gone and said the wrong name; I meant of course St. Martin du Canigou.

Banyuls I don't remember, Collioure I do. And I was always fascinated a bit by Narbonne, for no reason. It must be a dull place, nearly as dull as Perpignan. I am sorry I never got over the border into Spain. You ought to see Monserrate and Poblet. I think you would be impressed with the former and everyone says it has a lot of good scholars in it, besides clinging to the side of a cliff. An unusual combination.

Thanks so much for *The Mirror of Simple Souls* [by Marguerite Porete]. I am really enjoying it though I find that I have a hard time getting anywhere for great lengths in such books. A little goes a long way. It is an admirable book, but one which one does not really "read." I hold it in my hand walking about in the woods, as if I were reading. But it is charming and bold and right. I am more and more convinced that if you are in dryness and such, these books only increase the problem (if it is a problem).

At the same time I think we make problems for ourselves where there really are none. There is too much conscious "spiritual life" floating around us, and we are too aware that we are supposed to get somewhere. Well, where? If you reflect, the answer turns out to be a word that is never very close to any kind of manageable reality. If that is the case, perhaps we are already in that where. In which case why do we torment ourselves looking around to verify a fact which we cannot see in any case? We should let go our hold upon our self and our will, and be in the Will in which we are. Contentment is very important, of course I mean what seems to be contentment with despair. And the worst thing of all is false optimism.

I thought the opening of the [Second Vatican] Council was tremendous. You know the Roman joke that is going around now? Question: Where are Cardinals [Alfredo] Ottaviani and [Ernesto] Ruffini these days? Answer: Oh, haven't you heard? They are on their way to the Council of Trent.

Apparently they are on the liturgy now. I don't know what will come, but the whole thing seems to be making sense. Probably it is bound to bog down a bit somewhere, but it is going better than expected.

I haven't heard much about the touchy situation in Cuba so I won't talk about it. Of course things being what they were, Kennedy hardly had any alternative. My objection is to things being as they are, through the stupidity and short-sightedness of politicians who have no politics.

109. To E.S. [Evora Arca De Sardinia], Miami, Fla. [October 29, 1962]

This is a troubled time, in which you are going to have to collect your forces and muster up even more spiritual discipline. I know how you feel, but you have no right to get so discouraged. There is a sort of self-indulgence in it, and you cannot afford that at the present time. None of us can. It is precisely what the Communists reproach us with: they think we live on sentiment and emotion. Do not prove them right. On the contrary, we ought to try to be disciplined and self-sacrificing as they are, for we are working and suffering for truth, while they are knocking themselves out for an illusion fed to them by a bunch of crooks. Yet remember that whenever we on our side allow ourselves to get emotional and indulge in self-pity we are putting spiritual weapons in *their* hands.

Certainly it is hard to see your world broken up around you. No man can take that without suffering and self-questioning. But God has sent these trials to deepen your faith, not to destroy it. If you feel that it is hard to believe, this is because God is no longer presenting to you the image and idea of Him you once had. He is different from what you think He is and what you want Him to be. If He does not do things the way we want Him to, and we cease to believe in Him, then that means we only want to believe in a God made in our own image. That is why we have to have our faith purified and conform to His inscrutable will. So courage, and keep in the fight.

Like all of us, you have got your faith identified with a certain way of life. But we have to keep our faith even if our way of life is changed or destroyed.

In any case you are much better off than most people. What a lovely family you have, and they are well taken care of, healthy, good. God has blessed you. You must not complain if He also asks you to suffer with the rest of the world.

110. To G.D. [George Harold Dunne, S.J.], Washington, D.C. [October 30, 1962]

It was kind of you to send me a copy of the speech you gave (since bombs did not fall) last Thursday evening. I should be interested to hear how it was received. For my part I think you did an exceptionally good job, and I do not see how any one can complain of your clear arguments on Christian grounds. At best they might heckle you most unreasonably on what they deem to be grounds of political urgency or expediency.

It does not seem to me, in the first place, that the Cuba crisis invalidated your thesis that the Communist push is political and not military. On the contrary, the fact that [Nikita] Khrushchev yielded when pressed shows that his first and main way of handling international problems is not military. The missiles are for him means of precipitating political action of one sort or another. He may of course get it in the neck, now, for being weak. But he may on the other hand reap a certain amount of benefit for his action "for peace," thus eating his cake and having it. I don't know, and it is not wise to make statements from behind such a wall as mine, when they may already have been contradicted by the event.

It is my opinion that the great danger is, as you say, on the political and economic front. Especially in Latin America, Africa, and Asia. Latin America is the one place where we might have (perhaps even might still) do something. But I am also much concerned about the economy of our own country: not that I know much about it. But one doesn't have to know the first thing about economics to know that this present war economy spells ruin. I am easily persuaded that Khrushchev is just waiting for us to collapse. He does not need missiles except to stimulate our frenzy to the point of self-destruction. But of course it is a risky game, because there are more and more who want to destroy him and Russia along with themselves. But I am speaking primarily of the economic collapse of a totally wasteful and destructive system. This statement does not apply to the system in its essence, but in its actual dementia.

I do not think I would have wanted to change or add anything to your speech. I go along with it the whole way.

May your work with the volunteers have great success. It is maddening to think that the work of the Corps is stripped down to a bare symbolic gesture, in comparison with the enormous war effort which is both symbolic and dreadfully real. It must be very frustrating to take part in something so largely symbolic, the symbolic character of which is less and less interesting to the ones who are pushing for the great power play.

111. To E.G. [Rabbi Everett Gendler], Princeton, N.J. [October 1962]

My first reaction to the Peace Hostage Exchange[62] was to try to think of some way in which I could possibly get involved in it. But I am afraid it is out of the question for me. The main value of the pledge is its symbolic quality. Like everything else in this business about peace, it is a beginning of a way to communicate ideas. Where all the ideas are ready made for everybody and disseminated by mass media, it is an illusion for individuals or small dissenting groups to imagine that they have some way of making themselves heard if they just join in the general cacophony by writing letters to *Time*. There have to be other ways of making oneself heard. The various devices of the peace movement, the non-violent movement, etc., are steps in this direction. I think this peace hostage pledge is certainly one of the best.

At the same time I am impressed with the fact that all these things are little more than symbols. Thank God they are at least symbols, and valid ones. But where are we going to turn for some really effective political action? As soon as one gets involved in the machinery of politics one gets involved in its demonic futilities and in the great current that sweeps everything toward no one knows what.

Every slightest effort at opening up new areas of thought, every attempt to perceive new aspects of truth, or just a little truth, is of inestimable value in preparing the way for the light we cannot yet see.

---

[62] Also see letter to Stephen D. James, dated November 30, 1962, in *Witness to Freedom,* edited by William H. Shannon (New York: Farrar, Straus and Giroux, 1994), 86-87. The idea of the Peace Hostage Exchange was for the U.S. and the U.S.S.R. to exchange hostages. Merton recognized the symbolic value of such a proposed action.

Recipients of the Cold War Letters

Thomas Merton's Cold War Letter correspondents numbered eighty-one. While some are well known in their own right, as well as in Merton circles, others are relatively unknown. These brief biographical notes highlight some aspects of the life and work of the correspondents that are especially pertinent to Merton's Cold War Letters. The notes also illustrate the diversity of Merton's correspondents and demonstrate the breadth and depth of Merton's interests. Even as he focused his attention on the urgent problem of war, he explored, with energy and enthusiasm, many other topics of mutual concern to him and his correspondents.

For additional biographical information on many of Merton's correspondents, see the five volumes of Merton's letters: The Hidden Ground of Love *(HGL),* The School of Charity *(SC),* The Road to Joy *(RJ),* The Courage for Truth *(CT), and* Witness to Freedom *(WF). Also view the web site for the Thomas Merton Center, Bellarmine University, Louisville, Ky. at http://www.merton.org/. Biographical statements, included in the volumes of letters and presented on the web site, were helpful in the preparation of these notes.*

Brazilian **Paolo Alceu Amoroso Lima (CWL 3)**, scholar, teacher and writer, wrote introductions to Portuguese translations of several of Merton's writings and translated others, including *Breakthrough to Peace* and *Seeds of Destruction,* which contained Merton's Cold War Letter to Amoroso Lima. (CT 164)

Edward Deming Andrews (CWL 12) was an authority on the Shakers. Among his publications are *The People Called Shakers* (1953) and *Religion in Wood* (1982) for which Merton wrote an Introduction. Merton's admiration for Andrews' work and appreciation for the Shakers is apparent in Merton's letters. "The Shakers," Merton wrote to Andrews, "remain as witnesses to the fact that only humility keeps man in communion with truth, and first of all with his own inner truth." Merton visited the site of the Shaker community at Pleasant Hill, Kentucky. (HGL 31)

Educated in the U.S., **Evora Arca De Sardinia (CWL 27, 93, 109)** returned to her native Cuba and then fled, with her family, when Castro took power in 1959. Her husband, Eugenio, participated in the invasion of Cuba at the Bay of Pigs on April 17, 1961 as one of the 1,200 anti-Castro forces who had been trained by the American CIA. He was among those taken prisoner. In his letters to Arca De Sardina, Merton both reflects on the Cuban situation and provides spiritual support and direction. (WF 76-77)

Abdul Aziz (CWL 67), a Sufi living in Pakistan, corresponded with Merton from 1960 to 1968. Theirs was an exchange between two men of faith—a Christian and a Muslim—each deeply rooted in his own religious tradition, each intent on learning from the other as a way of deepening his own faith commitment. (HGL 43)

Sr. Elaine Michael Bane, O.S.F. (CWL 91), a Franciscan Sister in the Allegany community, wrote to the Novice Master at Gethsemani, seeking advice for how to establish a *retiro* or cloister to nurture a more contemplative life for a group of sisters. Brother Patrick Hart, O.C.S.O., notes that, to Sr. Elaine Michael's "great surprise," the Novice Master turned out to be Thomas Merton. (SC 144)

Mary Childs Black (CWL 24a) was Director of the Abby Aldrich Rockefeller Folk Art Collection in Williamsburg, Virginia. In his Cold War Letter to Black, Merton expresses his admiration for the Shakers, whose spirit is "perhaps the most authentic expression of the primitive American 'mystery' or 'myth': the paradise myth."

Jeanne Burdick (CWL 15) wrote to Merton after reading *The Seven Storey Mountain,* asking Merton to say more about "the disinterested love of God." In his response, Merton observes that "God is none of our idols, none of our figments, nothing that we can imagine anyway, but that He is Love Itself." (HGL 108-109)

Roger Caillois (CWL 73) was a French intellectual and writer, who lived in Argentina during WWII. He wrote to Merton from Buenos Aires. In response, Merton offers a tribute to Victoria Ocampo, the Argentinian writer, who, in 1931, founded *Sur,* a literary review, and in 1933, a publishing house under the same name.

Msgr. Josiah G. Chatham (CWL 13), a priest from Jackson, Mississippi, first met Merton at Gethsemani in 1940. Like Merton, Msgr. Chatham was opposed to war and the proliferation of nuclear weapons.

Mother Angela Collins (Mother Angela of the Eucharist), O.C.D. (CWL 42) had been prioress of the Louisville Carmel which Merton visited when he was in Louisville and where he sometimes celebrated Mass with the community. In 1965, she founded a Carmel in Savannah, Georgia, and served as its prioress. In his letter to Mother Angela, Merton dispels the myth that people can defend themselves against nuclear attack by building fallout shelters. (SC 33)

W. D. (CWL 50), Oyster Bay, N.Y. remains the only unidentified recipient of a Cold War Letter.

Dorothy Day (CWL 11, 86), whose prophetic witness to nonviolence and pacifism disturbed many in the Catholic Church, challenged and inspired others, including Merton. With Peter Maurin, Day founded the Catholic Worker movement in 1933. Merton published some of his key statements on war and peace in *The Catholic Worker,* including "The Root of War Is Fear" in October 1961. (HGL 135-136)

Roger De Ganck, O.C.S.O. (CWL 66) was a Belgian monk of the Trappist Abbey of Westmalle. He came to the United States and served as chaplain to the nuns at Redwoods Monastery at Whitehorn, California, where Mother Myriam Dardenne, O.C.S.O., was the first abbess. (SC 388)

Catherine de Hueck (Doherty) (CWL 79) fled the Soviet Union with her husband the Barron Boris de Hueck and settled in Canada. There she established the first Friendship House in Toronto and then another in Harlem, where the young Merton spent a few weeks in 1941, after hearing her speak at St. Bonaventure University.

Valerie Delacorte (CWL 74) wrote to Merton from New York City about her involvement in the Women Strike for Peace, prompting Merton to remark that "there is a deep, hidden spiritual meaning in women's part in our crisis." Observing how women are "used" in advertising, Merton quips: "Give the soldiers enough pin-up girls and they will gladly go to battle."

Sr. Emmanuel de Souza y Silva, O.S.B. (CWL 22) entered the monastery of the Virgin Mary in Petrópolis, Brazil. Her correspondence with Merton, which began in 1955, was an important link in solidifying Merton's Latin and South American connections. Sr. Emmanuel translated many of Merton's writings into Portuguese. (HGL 181)

Leslie Dewart (CWL 103) taught philosophy and religion at St. Michael's College at the University of Toronto. Dewart was born in Spain and lived in Cuba before moving to Canada in 1942. He sent Merton the manuscript of *Christianity and Revolution: The Lesson of Cuba* (1963) and Merton discussed the book with Dewart. In his Cold War Letter to Dewart, Merton promises to send him a copy of "the new enlarged edition of the Cold War Letters." (WF 282)

George Harold Dunne, S.J. (CWL 110) of Georgetown University sent Merton a speech he had given on Thursday, October 25, 1962—the day after Soviet ships carrying weapons were turned back from Cuba—and Merton affirmed Fr. Dunne's position. Merton also wished him well in his work with the Peace Corps. Fr. Dunne was a strong critic of racial segregation.

Editors, *The Commonweal* (CWL 49) received Merton's letter, written in response to a letter to the editors of *Commonweal,* written by Joseph G. Hill, who took issue with Merton's article, "Nuclear War and Christian Responsibility," published on February 9, 1962. Merton's letter ended his first edition of the "Cold War Letters"—consisting of forty-nine letters.

Steve Eisner (CWL 46) wrote from Detroit, Michigan and sent Merton a book of poetry by Raymond Larsson. Merton commends Eisner for his work with University of Detroit Press.

Msgr. John Tracy Ellis (6, 29, 53, 55), renowned historian of American Catholicism, taught for decades at The Catholic University of America and., for a time, at the University of San Francisco. In his Cold War Letters to Msgr. Ellis, Merton was able to explore how the threat of nuclear war posed a challenge to Christians. (HGL 174)

Elsa Engländer (CWL 28, 106) wrote from Linz, Austria. She wrote *In sehr grosse Freude* (1958). In his second Cold War Letter to Engländer, Merton responds to her concerns about Gordon Zahn's book, *German Catholics and Hitler's War,* noting that "perhaps the book was not really addressed to German readers."

Fr. J. Whitney Evans (CWL 84), who taught in a Catholic high school in Duluth, Minnesota, sent Merton a manuscript, which he had written for use in his classes. Merton suggested that Fr. Evans read Gordon Zahn and Leo Szilard and offered some ideas for Fr. Evans' consideration. In the course of his remarks, Merton observes that "peace or war may in the long run depend decisively" on American Catholics.

Lawrence Ferlinghetti (CWL 7), American poet and leader in the beat movement of the fifties, published Merton's Auschwitz poem, "Chant to be Used in Processions around a Site with Furnaces," in the *Journal for the Protection of All Living Things,* which also featured contributions by Albert Camus, Allen Ginsberg, and Bertrand Russell. (CT 267)

Wilbur H. Ferry (CWL 26, 39, 48, 77) served as vice president of the

Center of Democratic Institutions in Santa Barbara, California (1954-1969). In September 1961, when he first wrote to Ping Ferry, Merton was just beginning to face "the question of conscience . . . the question of war and peace" (HGL 202). In the years that followed, Ferry was, for Merton, a source of information as well as encouragement. (HGL 201)

Allan Forbes, Jr. (CWL 65, 72, 97) was a member of the Society of Friends, writing to Merton from Philadelphia and Cambridge. Merton expressed his admiration for the peace witness—the spiritual witness—which Forbes and other Friends "so gloriously present." Merton included an essay by Forbes in *Breakthrough to Peace*.

John Cuthbert Ford, S.J. (CWL 23) earned a degree in law at Boston College Law School in 1941. He taught ethics and theology at Boston College and at several other universities. He authored numerous articles and books, founded the journal *Theological Studies* and with Gerald A. Kelly, instituted the genre of the notes that are a regular feature of *Theological Studies*.

James Forest (CWL 25, 31, 61, 69, 101) was a young activist, committed to peace and non-violence and a staff member of *The Catholic Worker*, when he began corresponding with Merton in August 1961. Forest was one of the founders of the Catholic Peace Fellowship, an affiliate of the Fellowship of Reconciliation. Forest kept Merton informed on the peace movement and Merton, in turn, offered Forest encouragement and spiritual perspective. (HGL 254-255)

Philosopher, psychoanalyst and professor at the National University at Cuernavaca, Mexico, **Erich Fromm (CWL 5)** exchanged letters with Merton over more than a decade (1954-1966). Their correspondence, informed by their reading of each other's writings, explored issues of religion and culture. In his Cold War Letter to Fromm, Merton observes that "people have wholly failed to take into account the objectively evil force." (HGL 308)

Everett Gendler (CWL 111) served congregations in Mexico, Brazil, and Princeton, New Jersey, before moving to Temple Emmanuel in Lowell, Massachusetts, in 1971. Rabbi Gendler was active in working for racial justice, peace and the preservation of the environment. Rabbi Gendler wrote to Merton about the Peace Hostage Program and Merton recognized the power of its "symbolic quality." Merton's letter to Rabbi Gendler is the last of the Cold War Letters.

Jean Goss-Mayr (CWL 19) and his wife, Hildegard, shared a commitment to peace and non-violence throughout the world. Leaders in the Fellowship of Reconciliation, the Goss-Mayrs brought the issue of modern war and Christian responsibility before theologians and bishops, preparing for the Second Vatican Council, and shared with them materials and proposals. (HGL 324-235)

Etta Gullick (CWL 1, 14, 63, 108) studied theology at Oxford and taught at St. Stephen's House, an Anglican Theological College at Oxford. While the first letters she exchanged with Merton focused on her work on Benet of Canfield (1562-1610), Merton soon shared with Gullick that the "urgent obligation" occupying him was "working with such means as I have at my disposal for the abolition of war." (HGL 340)

The Honorable Shinzo Hamai (CWL 98) was mayor of Hiroshima, Japan when Merton wrote to him on August 9, 1961 in remembrance of August 6, 1945, expressing the "conviction that the people of Hiroshima stand today as a symbol of the hopes of humanity." (HGL 380)

Victor Hammer (CWL 24b, 71) was an artist and professor of art the Academy of Fine Arts in Vienna; Wells College in Aurora, New York; and Transylvania College in Lexington, Kentucky. One of Hammer's pieces, a triptych, inspired Merton's prose poem "Hagia Sophia," which Hammer printed in a limited edition under the imprint Stamperia del Santuccio. Merton regarded Victor and his wife, Carolyn, as dear friends and visited them when he was able to get to Lexington. (WF 3-4)

John Harris (CWL 83) was a schoolteacher in Devonshire, England, when he read *Doctor Zhivago* and wrote to Boris Pasternak. Pasternak responded and asked Harris to get a message to Merton, who had written to the Russian writer some months earlier. Harris' communication with Merton initiated a correspondence between them. In his Cold War Letter to Harris, Merton mentions sending him a copy of the "Cold War Letters" (the "first" edition) on the occasion of Harris becoming a Catholic. (HGL 384)

John C. Heidbrink's (CWL 2, 38) involvement in the struggle for civil rights and peace dates back to the late fifties, when, as a Presbyterian chaplain at the University of Oklahoma, he participated in a student sit-in. In 1960, he joined the Fellowship of Reconciliation as secretary for Church relations. (HGL 401-402).

Ethel Kennedy (CWL 10), wife of Robert Kennedy and sister-in-law of President John F. Kennedy, was the daughter of George and Ann Skakel. The Skakels were benefactors of Gethsemani. In his CWL letter to Ethel Kennedy, Merton acknowledges the role of presidential leadership: "The President can certainly do more than any one man to counteract" the "dangerous forces" at play in the world. ((HGL 443)

Carl Kline, M.D. (CWL 87) was working as a physician in Wausau, Wisconsin, when he wrote to Merton to express his appreciation of what Merton had written on the subject of war.

Gerald Landry (CWL 54) wrote to Merton from Glen Garden, New Jersey, and sent him a leaflet and a pamphlet which told of his experience as a Catholic pacifist during WWII. Merton was very moved by Landry's story.

Justus George Lawler (CWL 47, 60, 70), an editor at Herder and Herder, expressed interest in publishing Merton's *Peace in the Post-Christian Era,* the manuscript Merton was forbidden to publish. Lawler edited the journal *Continuum.*

Robert Lax's (CWL 16, 40, 78) enduring friendship with Merton began at Columbia University, where they both worked on *The Columbia Jester.* A writer and poet, Robert Lax was instrumental in publishing Merton's writings on war and peace in *Pax* and *Jubilee.* Over the thirty years (1938-1968) that they exchanged letters, they developed a language of their own—witty, satirical and sometimes bawdy. (RJ 142)

Sr. Therese Lentfoehr, S.D.S. (CWL 20) was one of Merton's most enthusiastic supporters and a dear friend. During the twenty years that they corresponded, Merton sent her materials and manuscripts, including one of the three copies of the manuscript of *The Seven Storey Mountain,* and she developed what Robert E. Daggy characterized as "the biggest private collection of Mertonia." The Lentfoehr Collection is housed at Columbia University. (RJ 187)

Thomas J. Liang (CWL 57) came to the U.S. in 1951 as a refugee from China. He served at St. Leo's Parish in Oakland, California, and worked with Asian students. Liang wrote to Merton about the Christian Unity Corps which provided hospitality to international students. (RJ 321)

Ray Livingston (CWL 80) was chair of the English Department at Macalester College in St. Paul, Minnesota.

Clare Boothe Luce (CWL 17)—writer, correspondent, editor, playwright—was a convert to Roman Catholicism. Her husband, Henry R. Luce, was president of *Time* magazine. Thanking Luce for books she had sent him at Christmas, Merton tempers his sense of impending destruction with the Christian conviction "that the Light not only shall and will triumph over the darkness, but already has."

Sr. Mary Madeleva, C.S.C. (CWL 51), president of St. Mary's College in Notre Dame, Indiana, inaugurated the first advanced degree program in theology for women. In his letter to Sr. Madeleva, Merton attests to his love for Julian of Norwich, despite the fact that, as Sr. Madeleva observed, he did not include Julian in the notes on mystical theology which he had sent Sr. Madeleva. Merton also decries the silence of the American hierarchy and clergy on the subject of war.

Herbert Mason (CWL 52) is an author, translator and professor of history and religion at Boston University. Among his many publications are *Gilgamesh: A Verse Narrative* and *The Death of Al-Hallaj: A Dramatic Narrative*. His friendship with Louis Massignon inspired Mason's interest in Arabic and Islamic Studies. It was Mason who introduced Merton to Massignon, with whom Merton also corresponded. (WF 261)

Robert J. McCracken (CWL 100) wrote to Merton with questions about Merton's position on nuclear war. In response, Merton clarifies his position on atomic war, the use of nuclear weapons, and the duty to work for peace.

Kilian McDonnell, O.S.B. (CWL 59), a monk at St. John's Abbey in Collegeville, Minnesota, and founder of the Institute for Ecumenical and Cultural Research, studied under Hans Küng at Tübingen. McDonnell sent Merton material on Una Sancta, an ecumenical movement for Christian unity and on Fr. Max Metzger, one of its founders.

Thomas McDonnell (CWL 62, 64), a writer for *The Pilot*, a publication of the Boston Archdiocese, was a frequent reviewer of Merton's books. He edited the first anthology of Merton's writings published in English: *A Thomas Merton Reader*.

Robert M. MacGregor (CWL 75) was managing editor at *New Directions*. According to David D. Cooper, editor of *Thomas Merton and James Laughlin: Selected Letters*, he was "JL's valuable right hand." As such, he played an important role in New Directions' publication of Merton's books.

Psychoanalyst **Joost A. M. Meerloo (CWL 96)** studied mind control and brainwashing techniques. Among his publications are *Homo Militans: The Psychology of War and Peace in Man* and *Delusion and Mass Delusion*. Merton included one of Meerloo's essays in *Breakthrough to Peace*.

Henry Miller (CWL 92, 95), renowned writer and novelist, initiated an exchange of letters with Merton after reading *Original Child Bomb*. Merton responded with praise for Miller's *Big Sur and the Oranges of Hieronymus Bosch* and *Colossus of*

Maroussi. In one of his Cold War Letters to Miller, Merton discusses the sin of idolatry to which "religious people" are prone. (CT 274)

William Robert Miller (CWL 81) wrote for and was managing editor of *Fellowship,* a publication of the Fellowship of Reconciliation, and later served as editor of the *United Church Herald,* a publication of the United Church of Christ.

Czeslaw Milosz (CWL 56), poet, writer and a member of the nonviolent resistance in Poland during World War II, joined the faculty of the University of California at Berkeley in 1960. In *The Captive Mind,* the book which prompted Merton to write to him, Milosz addresses the plight of Polish intellectuals in a repressive regime. Among Merton's Cold War Letter correspondents, Milosz was the most critical of his position on war and peace, considering Merton's position naïve and unrealistic. (CT 53-54)

Gwen Myers (CWL 88) was a member of the Society of Friends. Merton offers her spiritual encouragement.

Rev. D. Brendan Nagle (CWL 90) was a priest at a Catholic church in Malibu, California, where three-quarters of the members of his congregation were employed in defense industries. Merton writes to clarify his position in the face of Nagle's objections.

James Roy Newman (CWL 36) is author of *The Rule of Folly,* with a Preface by Erich Fromm. Merton was especially impressed by Newman's "dissection" of Herman Kahn.

Merton wrote to **Nuns (Sisters of Loretto) (CWL 76)** who were making final vows. The Sisters of Loretto were founded in 1812 under the direction of Rev. Charles Nerinckx in St. Charles,

Kentucky, with the mission of educating poor children. Originally named Friends of Mary, the community was later renamed the Sisters of Loretto. Given the proximity of their motherhouse to the Abbey of Gethsemani, Merton had opportunities to interact with the Sisters and to develop friendships with them, the most notable of which was his friendship with Sr. Mary Luke Tobin, former Superior General of the Order and one of fifteen women appointed as auditors at the Second Vatican Council. (SC 227)

Ad Reinhardt (CWL 45) and Merton became friends at Columbia University. While they corresponded "sporadically," Robert E. Daggy noted that only three of Merton's letters to Reinhardt survive, including one Cold War Letter. (RJ 279)

Edward Rice (CWL 33) and Merton met at Columbia University and when, in 1938, Merton became a Catholic, Rice was his godfather. As editor of *Jubilee,* Rice published a number of Merton's articles on war. With the publication of *Man in the Sycamore Tree,* Rice became Merton's first biographer. (RJ 283)

Archbishop Thomas Roberts, S.J. (CWL 9), archbishop of Bombay, India, who resigned his see so that an Indian bishop could be chosed, wrote to Merton from London, England. Describing the situation in the U.S., Merton proclaims the silence of the Church and clergy "scandalous."

Rabbi Zalman Schachter (CWL 37) was born in Poland, raised in Vienna, studied in the United States and settled in Winnipeg, Canada, where he taught. In his letters to Rabbi Schachter, Merton reflects on the witness of Jews as the great eschatological sign and the challenge of Jewish-Christian relations. (HGL 533)

Bruno P. Schlesinger (CWL 8, 34),

a professor at St. Mary's College in Notre Dame, Indiana, was a founder of the Christian Culture Program at the college. Schlesinger's description of the program leads Merton to reflect on "the urgent need for Christian humanism."

Stephen Schwarzchild (CWL 41) was a rabbi serving Temple Beth El in Lynn, Massachusetts, when he wrote to Merton. Rabbi Zalman Schachter had sent Rabbi Schwarzchild some of Merton's writings on peace and, in turn, Rabbi Schwarzchild shared some of his writings with Merton. In the discussion that ensued, Merton admits that guerilla warfare may be legitimate in some circumstances.

John Whitman Sears (CWL 89), a psychiatrist and Universalist minister, was living in San Mateo, California, when he sent Merton a copy of his paper, "The Arms Race Is a Chain Reaction," with which Merton agreed.

Peace activist and conscientious objector **Dan Shay (CWL 104)** of St. Louis, Missouri, had written to tell Merton that he would be participating in a peace walk from St. Louis to the East Coast, from which the group would travel to Italy and walk to Rome. While Shay wanted the Catholic Church to condemn the bomb, Merton wrote that he was "not in favor of the kind of pressure that strives to get Rome to approve this and condemn that."

Frank J. Sheed (CWL 32, 58) and his wife Maisie Ward founded Sheed & Ward, a Catholic publishing house, in 1927. Sheed reported that some readers—presumably Sheed was one of these—found two of Merton's articles, published as a booklet (*Two Articles by Thomas Merton: The Root of War & Red or Dead: The Anatomy of a Cliché*) "upsetting." Merton defends his position as grounded in "traditional moral structures" and

the teachings of the Popes. He assures Sheed that he is "in no sense communistic or subversive."

Maynard Shelly (CWL 4) was editor of *The Mennonite* and wrote to Merton from Newton, Kansas. Merton expresses to Maynard his "respect and reverence" for "the Mennonite tradition of peaceful action and non-violence."

Lou Silberman (CWL 102) was Hillel Professor of Jewish Literature at Vanderbilt Divinity School. He visited Gethesmani with Rabbi Zalman Schachter in August 1962 where he talked about the Dead Sea Scrolls.

Elbert R. Sisson (CWL 44, 94) sent Merton a picture, drawn by his daughter Grace. The picture moved Merton deeply and inspired Merton to write a poem he entitled "Grace's House." Merton was particularly intrigued by the fact that "Alas, there is no road to Grace's house!" Five years later, Grace sent Merton another drawing which she had entitled "The Road to Joy."

Sociologist and anthropologist **Dallas Smythe (CWL 107)** was working at the Institute of Communications Research at the University of Illinois, Urbana-Champaign, when he wrote to Merton. Smythe's friend, Wilbur H. (Ping) Ferry, had sent him a copy of the first edition (the short version) of Merton's "Cold War Letters."

Walter Stein (CWL 18) wrote to Merton from Ilkley, England. He edited *Nuclear Weapons and Christian Conscience* (1961)—a book Merton found "very impressive." The "essays in your book and their judgements," Merton wrote, "seem to me to affirm clearly and sanely: the human and the Christian measure."

Freudian psychiatrist **Karl Stern (CWL 35)** wrote to Merton from Montreal, Quebec. Among his publications are *The Pillar of Fire* (1951), an autobiographical account of his conversion from Judaism to Catholicism; *The Third Revolution: A Study of Psychiatry and Religion* (1954); and *The Flight from Woman* (1965), an exploration of two modes of knowing, scientific or rational and poetic or intuitive. Merton was especially moved by the latter, especially the chapter on Descartes.

Hungarian-born physicist **Leo Szilard (CWL 68)** conducted the first controlled nuclear chain reaction in 1942 with Enrico Fermi. In 1943, Szilard joined the Manhattan Project, working with scientists such as Robert Oppenheimer and Edward Teller, but, in 1945, Szilard and other scientists expressed their opposition to the proposed use of bombs against Japanese cities. After the war, Szilard voiced his opposition to the development of the hydrogen bomb and joined the movement to prevent nuclear war.

Charles Thompson (CWL 105) was a member of the English Pax Society and edited its bulletin from 1956 to 1963. Merton sent him "Red or Dead: The Anatomy of a Cliché" for publication in the *Pax Bulletin*. In his letter to Thompson, Merton included a message to be shared at a conference at Spode House in London. Learning non-violence and practicing it involves "a deep spiritual purification." (HGL 571)

Tashi Tshering (CWL 43) was a Tibetan student at the University of Washington in Seattle when he wrote to Merton and sent him a copy of *The Life of Mila Repa*, the eleventh-century Tibetan yogi, whom Merton cites several times in *The Asian Journal*. Mila Repa, Merton writes, "had received a special gift, a power to desire and to thirst for the light." (RJ 320)

Scholar, teacher and poet **Mark Van Doren (CWL 99)** was Merton's professor at Columbia University and became his lifelong friend, confidant and supporter. Van Doren was instrumental in the publication of Merton's first book of poetry, *Thirty Poems,* published by New Directions. (RJ 3)

Will Watkins (CWL 85) of San Francisco, California, sent Merton a copy of Claude Eatherly's book, *Burning Conscience: The Case of the Hiroshima Pilot, Claude Eatherly, Told in His Letters to Gunther Anders*. In concluding his letter to Watkins, Merton wrote, "We have to be true to our conscience in everything, and true to humanity, for man is the image of God."

John C. H. Wu (CWL 82) had a varied career as scholar, author, diplomat, Chinese Ambassador to the Vatican, dean of the College of Chinese culture in Taiwan, and professor of Asian studies at Seton Hall University. Among his publications are his autobiography, *Beyond East and West* (1951) and *The Golden Age of Zen* (1967), for which Merton wrote an introduction, entitled "A Christian Looks at Zen." Wu assisted Merton in his rendering of the writings of Chuang Tzu by sending Merton translations, including one Wu had done himself (HGL 611).

Sociologist, pacifist and conscientious objector **Gordon C. Zahn (CWL 21)** taught at Loyola University of Chicago from 1953 to 1967 and then at the University of Massachusetts at Boston. In the late fifties, he received a Fulbright Grant to study in Germany. His research led to the publication of *German Catholics and Hitler's War* (1962) and to his account of the story of Franz Jägerstätter, *In Solitary Witness* (1964). Zahn edited the first collection of Merton's writings on war and peace: *Thomas Merton on Peace* (1971) and a revised edition, *The Nonviolent Alternative* (1980).

Index

Highlighted numbers indicated Cold War Letters

"Target Equals Ctiy," 82, 106